A Toe on the Ladder

MOLLY WEIR

A Toe on the Ladder

HUTCHINSON OF LONDON

HUTCHINSON & CO (*Publishers*) LTD
3 Fitzroy Square, London W1

London Melbourne Sydney Auckland
Wellington Johannesburg Cape Town
and agencies throughout the world

First published 1973
Second impression June 1974

*This book has been set in Fournier type, printed in Great Britain
by R. J. Acford Ltd., Industrial Estate, Chichester, Sussex.*

ISBN 0 09 117860 6

For Sandy
Ever faithful, ever ready to help me
Watchootfurrastanks

Earning recognition without getting it is better than getting it without earning it.

We Scots have learned the lesson of poverty, that nothing comes without effort, and that we value most what costs us most.

JOHN BUCHAN

I

MY mother told me I sang before I spoke, and I danced before I
walked, but in spite of such early signs that I might have a
talent for the theatre, nobody, least of all me, could have foreseen
that with my unlikely background my dreams of becoming an actress
could ever come true. But I had taken careful note of the story of the
ten talents in the bible, and I was determined that not a single talent
of mine was going to wither and die in the ground. I'd develop every
single one of them, as the good Lord God instructed, and see where
they led me.

The sheer excitement of pursuing all my ambitions was so heady,
that I felt drunk as I raced back and forth between my office job and
the college, for now I was taking evening classes again at the invitation of the college, to see just how fast my shorthand speeds could
reach. Fancy all this happening to me! Special classes of one, with the
assistant head doing the dictating, for only his tongue could get
round the sentences fast enough and still remain intelligible. It
felt a bit daft to be sitting there in a large classroom, all alone,
perched up on my feet as usual, for I still hadn't grown enough to
let my feet touch the ground if I sat on the seat properly like everybody else, with Mr. McLeod standing in front of me, stop-watch in
hand, breathing deeply as though in training for a racing sprint.

But it was exciting. I had practised shorthand so lovingly and
assiduously that I could have written the characters backward if
asked to do so, and there was nothing which came between hearing
the words and sending the pen skimming over the note-book. Not a
second had to be wasted in fumbling for an outline. Each one was
there with the speed of sound. We easily passed the 200 words per
minute mark, and grinned at each other with approval. Then 250

words. After that, it was struggle all the way to add each extra ten words per minute. There were no grins now. My hand perspired, and the pen shook with tension as my fingers gripped it like a vice. My heart thumped as I pressed against the desk, and I had to lean back and readjust my seat or the beating would have slowed my speeding hand. Each night I sped up Renfield Street after my day's work was finished, and perched myself like a jockey in the echoing classroom, determined that tonight, yes tonight, I'd go every bit as fast with my pen as that man could go with his voice. It never occurred to me to feel that all this could be thought of as dull hard work after a day's stint in an office, where I was also writing shorthand and typing all day. But my mother was utterly bewildered. 'Whit dae ye have to go tae that college every night fur?', she'd demand. 'And without a bite to eat either'. For of course there was no question of dining out either before or after such speed practices. Tearooms were for celebrations, not for ordinary eating. When I tried to explain that the college were trying to find out just how fast I could write, because they wanted me to demonstrate high-speed writing as a 'star' pupil, she shook her head disbelievingly. 'You've goat a medal a'ready', she said, 'Can they no' just show folk yer medal?'. 'Mother', I said, 'It's like doubting Thomas in the bible. Folk'll no' believe what high speeds are, just from looking at a medal. They have to SEE me actually writing, and hear the rate Mr. McLeod gabbles oot his words!' Although I was ladylike in speech in the office, it was comfortable and restful to revert to Springburn usage when I was arguing at home. With typical contrariness, my mother pounced on my speech. 'Aye, it's a good job Mr. McLeod disnae hear ye talking aboot him gabbling', she said primly, 'And him daein' his best to improve you every night'.

But although I could talk so glibly to my mother about people having to see me demonstrating high-speed writing, I was absolutely terrified at the thought of having to do it. I knew I had the speed in my fingers all right, but I also knew what tension and nerves could do, for we'd had a few trial runs with one or two of the teachers present, and I had shaken so badly that my speeds flew down by a good ten words each time. I knew I wasn't ready for the public and I felt sick at the thought.

But training was telling. After about a week when we stuck at 270 words per minute, and couldn't get a syllable faster, we had a marvellous session when everything went like clockwork. It had started badly, with Mr. McLeod struggling through a bad cold, and me using so much pressure on the pen that the ink splattered and the nib scratched the page.

Then we settled down. Mr. McLeod cleared his throat, nodded to me, pressed the stop watch and we were off! At the end of the fastest piece of dictation I'd ever heard, he pressed the watch again, and his cheeks were tinged with bright pink. Without a word, he nodded to me to read back my notes. His excitement was infectious, and my voice trembled as I read the dictated piece. Not a single mistake or omission. He took off his glasses and wiped them. 'Molly', he said solemnly, after clearing his voice once or twice, for cold or emotion seemed threatening to choke him, 'That was three hundred words a minute'. I stared at him, speechless. We had done it. We hadn't actually admitted that this was the speed we were after, but we both knew it. A tremendous exultation filled me. I had done it once, and I'd do it again. And again. And again! Oh how *marvellous!*

And then came the quenching thought that now I'd have no excuse. We'd have to do it in public. Before an audience.

But first I would have to celebrate in some way. I must mark this historic landmark in a fashion I would never forget. What would it be? Suddenly I remembered that that day I had held the earring of an office colleague against my ear, and had been filled with the daring idea that I might one day wear earrings myself. But not screw ones. Oh no. For if ever I became an actress, and had to dance, I didn't want my earrings to fly off and spoil my concentration, much less that of my public. Now that I could write 300 words a minute, there didn't seem any reason why I couldn't also reach my other goal and go on the stage some time. So, without a word to my mother, I went into a top-class jeweller in Buchanan Street on my way to the office next morning, and made an appointment to have my ears pierced that night. It was expensive. Seven and sixpence, which was a fortune, and which would have to be taken from my holiday fund at lunch-time. But I couldn't risk less than the best with my precious ears, for everybody knew quacks were notoriously unreliable for cleanliness. And I needed good healthy ears for shorthand demonstrating and for acting.

Every time I thought of the evening appointment while taking notes in the office during the day, my stomach turned over. It was almost as bad as going to the dentist. I hadn't realised I could be so nervous over such a little thing. Why, thousands of women wore earrings and they had all had their ears pierced if they wore expensive earrings. Everybody knew that screw ones were not to be trusted, because they were always at risk with their insecure fastenings.

Trembling, I climbed the stairs to the room above the shop. It was after closing time, and the place was hushed, like a surgery. There was a wash-hand basin, and a sparkling clean white towel, and a few little instruments lying on a small table. The elderly man in the black jacket and striped trousers looked at me enquiringly. 'Now you're sure your mother approves of your having your ears pierced?', he asked me. My mother knew nothing about it, so I felt I could truthfully inform him that my mother had always wanted to have her own ears pierced but had never had the courage. Which was true, if slightly evasive as far as his question was concerned. If he saw through this, he said nothing.

He showed me a little spring, with a gold needle fixed to the end of it, and told me he was going to put a cork on the other side of my ear, spring the little needle through, and catch it on the cork, and then immediately slip a little gold 'sleeper' through the pierced hole. I shut my eyes. In spite of his assurances that I would feel no pain, I yelped like a dog whose paw has been squashed by a large foot, when I felt a stab through my ear lobe. The tears rushed to my eyes. It wasn't so much agony, as pain in a place where one had never felt anything until now. Like somebody pinching the tip of your nose in sharp talons. How would I ever let him do the other ear, I thought wildly. I'd have to go through life with one earring, like a gypsy.

I gulped, preparing to tell him this, while he was extracting the little needle from the cork with a tiny pair of elegant pliers. Before I could open my mouth he said, 'Do you know, I've pierced thousands of ears and I've never felt a thing.' I felt there was something strange about this sentence, and said wonderingly, 'Have you not?', and while I was trying to work out what he meant, he'd shot the gold needle through my other ear, and the deed was done!

Oh! the cunning of the brute, I thought. Still, it was just as well I'd been so stupid about comprehending his words, or I'd never have managed to get both ears done. I was instructed to bathe my ears with boracic and warm water, and to turn the little 'sleepers' regularly to prevent the skin adhering to them, and in a week or two my lobes would sport smooth round holes, all ready to receive the fancy earrings of my choice. Blood dripping gently on to my coat, I left him for the walk home to Springburn, and my mother's wrath.

The minute I walked in the door, my mother said, 'What's that on the shoulder of your coat? Hoo did ye get ink away up there?', then her eyes travelled upwards and she gasped, 'It's no' ink, it's blood!'. She couldn't take her eyes off the wee gold sleepers, for in spite of her outrage that I could have done such a tremendous thing without a word to her, I could see there was a slight envy that I had found the courage to submit my ears to this torture, while she herself had got no further than talking about it. As she flitted about the kitchen making the tea, she muttered to herself and to the heavens, 'Seven-and-sixpence, nae less. Seven-and-sixpence off her holiday fund. And nut a word to onybody! And here's me has wanted to have ma ears pierced a' ma life, and never managed it.' But we both knew it wasn't the seven-and-sixpence, fortune though it was, which had stopped her. It was fear.

But in the weeks that followed, she had good cause for rejoicing that she had kept her ears intact, for in spite of that posh jeweller and his little wash-hand basin and his strippit trousers, my ears became infected, and festered, and it was agony to have to turn the gold sleepers, which I forced myself to do every day, for I was absolutely sure the flesh would grow on to them if I didn't follow the man's instructions to the letter. 'Don't *touch* them', my mother would implore, as my hands would steal up to wrench them round their sticky home, 'Leave them alone till the holes heal'. And she'd pour more warm water on to some boracic powder, and tear off a wee tuft of cotton wool, so that I could bathe them for the twentieth time since I came home from the office.

As if the infection wasn't scourge enough, I simply couldn't get used to having things impaled through my ears, and when I was running a comb through my hair I'd forget to be careful, and the teeth of the comb would catch in the sleeper and yank it out, and there would be howls of anguish as I threaded it back yet again through the once-more bleeding orifice.

'Aye, ye wid have yer ears pierced', my mother would say, with what sounded suspiciously like smugness, 'If you'd asked me first, I could have warned ye.' And I could see she'd already come to believe she hadn't been frightened at all to have holes put in her ears, it was simply that she'd had the foresight to know it was a mug's game, and not worth all the pain and misery which would follow.

I was so absorbed in the drama of my oozing ear-lobes that I quite forgot why I'd had them pierced in the first place. But Mr. McLeod and the college hadn't, and without a word to me they had arranged the date for the first demonstration of high-speed shorthand writing before a tolerant public. It was held in the prize-giving room of the college, and he and I sat up on a platform, me at a little single desk, with the audience seated all round us. He dictated at varying speeds, starting at 140 words per minute, and going forward in 20-word-per-minute leaps until we had reached 300. After each piece of dictation, I rose and read back my notes. For the first time since those wee gold nails had gone through them, I forgot my ears, and they became once more just a part of me without nerves or feeling. The rest of me quivered like a jelly. My face burned, my palms sweated, and when I stood up to read, my legs shook so much I had to press them against my chair to steady them. It never occurred to me that, as far as our audience was concerned, it could all have been a trick. I'm sure none of them cared a jot about shorthand, and nobody was concerned enough about the accuracy of speed to have attempted to check our boasts with a stop-watch. It was a night out. It was buckshee, and they were seeing inside a college, a place they'd never have had the nerve to put a foot inside at any other time. They seemed amused by my tiny build when I stood up, and by my husky voice when I read back from my notes, but it might as well have been Chinese, for what did they know or care of Directors' reports, and statements from Company Chairmen, which was what the dictation was all about. But they applauded generously, and happily accepted brochures for the coming term, and drifted out in search of fish and chips and a tramcar home.

And that was the start of our 'double-act' as I later called it to myself, for I was still very much in awe of Mr. McLeod, in spite of the fact that we travelled the country together, to the various cities and towns where the college or Pitmans had an interest. My mother was amazed at the amount of money they must have spent on train fares, and we neither of us stopped to consider that if the railways made a tidy profit out of it, we ourselves made nothing, for of course nobody dreamed of paying me for those exhibition bouts. I was only too delighted to get free travel. Fancy riding all those hundreds of miles on trains, and not having to fork out a curdy. And staying in hotels, and having a bedroom all to myself in such posh places, and ham and egg breakfasts if I wanted them. It was just like the pictures, with crusty, elderly gentlemen walking silently to the sideboard in the mornings, lifting the silver covers from tureens and helping themselves to kidneys, or kedgeree, and once actually to roast beef. At nine o'clock in the morning! I'd never realised before that anybody's stomach could be ready for dinner at breakfast time. And I'd never come across so many people eating in such a profound silence. Once, when we were joined at breakfast time by the wife of one of the college principals, I was so pleased to see another female that I chattered non-stop to her in the way I usually did at home.

Suddenly I was aware that all knives and forks were suspended, and every head was turned my way, as outraged as though I had started doing cart-wheels in church. The words died on my lips, and I bent my head over my toast. It was made very obvious that I'd done the unforgiveable thing. I'd broken the morning calm. I was no lady.

My mother was entranced to listen to all the details of the journeys and the hotels, and what sort of sheets and blankets they had on the beds, and whether I'd been warm enough. For of course I only had one outfit for such public appearances, and that was my navy reefer coat and good velour hat for the train, and my red knitted suit from Watt Brothers which she had bought for me to celebrate my college prizes. So whatever the temperatures, these clothes were my uniform, and I merely added or subtracted a semmit to raise or reduce my temperature.

If I am now legendary for keeping a firm track of all my possessions under all circumstances, this is entirely due to my observation of Mr. McLeod's methods during those exciting journeys. He was a man of very correct habits, and the moment we entered the train he counted each item as he removed it, and named it aloud. Thus, removing his Homburg, and placing it on the rack. 'One—a hat,' he would say. Then came his overcoat. 'Two—one overcoat', and this was placed alongside the hat. 'Three—one pair of gloves', and they were tucked inside his sleeve. 'Four—one umbrella', which took its place at the back of the rack. 'Five—one briefcase', which he tucked carefully behind him on the seat. 'Six—newspaper', which he laid on his lap, ready for his enjoyment the moment we had ceased discussing the itinerary for next day. 'Seven—Molly'. 'Eight—Molly's hat', 'Nine—Molly's coat', 'Ten—Molly's case', 'Eleven—Molly's book'. It was always a book with me, either more shorthand tests, or a French grammar, or a poem which I was learning or a play. We indulged in no general conversation; I sat opposite him, and as soon as we'd checked on time of arrival, hotel, time of demonstration, etc. we both buried ourselves in our book and newspaper and didn't utter a word until five minutes before we were due at our destination. The newspaper was folded, and with a nod to me to close my book, he counted all our impedimenta once more, and when he was satisfied the numbers checked, then, and only then, did we leave the train.

I was always extremely nervous before a demonstration, and I became gradually aware how important a part good health played in giving of one's best before an audience. A heavy cold fogged the brain, and made the reactions so sluggish that there were times when I stood up to read and had to bite my lip with vexation because not all the outlines had been captured at the challenging top speed of 300 words per minute. Oh how ashamed I felt. And what a waste of the college's money to have brought me all those miles only to falter at the last hurdle. Not that the audience minded a missed word. But I did. And I couldn't meet Mr. McLeod's eyes in case I would read in them the disappointment he must surely feel. I made no excuses for myself. I *ought* to have been perfect. I had practised often enough. I would simply have to have another 20 words per minute in hand to make up for the times when I had a cold, or that scourge of Western Scotland, catarrh. There were other times, too, when feminine tension screwed me into a trembling jelly, and my heart sank at the prospect of the testing time ahead. But my grannie's words echoed down the years and I could hear her say, 'The back was made for the burden', and I would shake my head to clear away the mist of fear, and remind myself that nothing that was worth doing was easy. Oh and what a marvellous preparation all this was to be for the much tougher life later in the theatre.

For I hadn't given up my dreams of the stage, and in a strange way those dreams were all intermingled with my shorthand. There was a tremendous challenge in plunging into all sorts of new activities, as well as keeping up with all my old ones, and there seemed aeons of time for all of them.

One of the girls in the office said to me one day, 'Here's an advert. from the Pantheon Club which sounds just up your street Molly. They want actors and actresses for their new season'. My heart jumped, and I eagerly read the little notice as I leaned over her shoulder, and jotted down the address in shorthand. All applicants were invited to go to their rehearsal room in a hall in the Charing Cross district the following Tuesday. That was the one night in the week which was free of nightschool, Guides, choir practice, and bible studies, and was usually devoted to going for a walk with my faithful 'steady', or clearing out my chest of drawers, or washing my hair, or learning my poems for my beloved Miss Mitchell, for I was still taking elocution lessons. So on this Tuesday my 'steady' fell into step with me as I trotted eagerly back to town after swallowing my tea, and tried to sound enthusiastic about my taking my first small step towards my never-far-out-of-mind goal, that of becoming an actress.

I had thought there would be some impossibly difficult entrance test piece. Not a bit of it. A selection committee took a casual glance over the hopeful applicants, and divided those who said they could sing from those who said they couldn't, I opted for being one of the non-singers. I hadn't forgotten that singing master at school who had made me stand up all by myself and sing solo for the whole class and I didn't fancy this happening among all those big men and women, so I was duly registered as a drama member. A drama member! How exciting the words sounded. My heart pounded as we were handed copies of a little play, and as I was by far the youngest and smallest of the group, I was assigned the part of the schoolgirl in 'Mrs. Watson's Window,' one of a group of one-act plays to be entered for the Drama Festival. It wasn't a very big part, but it was a good one, and to my secret joy I was rewarded by a few giggles when I read it, giggles which alas evaporated to yawning boredom as we rehearsed it over and over again in the weeks which elapsed before we played before an audience.

My 'steady' had grown so hungry waiting for me that he had indulged an irresistible desire for a Mars bar, and had kept a piece to share with me, and always for me the taste of that succulent sweet is intermingled with the excitement of my first drama part, the cool air of an October night as we walked up Parliamentary Road, and the heady feeling that everything was opening out before me. They hadn't turned a hair, those actor-folk, that I had wanted to be one of them. Nobody had said I was too wee, as those employers had said when I first looked for a job. Nobody had found my accent laughable. I hugged myself with delight. My feet scarcely touched the ground, and my steady gloomily decided he might as well enrol for the night-school at a Tuesday class, for he could see I was lost to him for the winter. He chose shorthand, to share another interest with me, and we had a rare time thereafter writing wee secret messages on our postcards to one another, and in our diaries, in our best shorthand. It was like a secret code, and greatly impressed, or infuriated, those who happened to catch sight of the mysterious characters we'd penned so lovingly.

To my surprise, as well as being in the drama section, I was roped into the musical section of the club. In my innocence, I had no idea that it was well-nigh impossible to get people to go through the monotonous chorus rehearsals for singing and dancing, without the final hope of playing a solo part in the limelight. I thought they had found such good theatre material in me, they just couldn't bear to waste the smallest portion of it.

I had always liked singing and dancing anyway, and once I was assured I would have the comfort of more than two dozen other voices to help drown mine, I was in seventh heaven. How light-hearted musicals seemed to me. There was freedom to move around, and do spontaneous little gestures, without disturbing the feeling of the story, and I positively revelled in being taught how to dance. My mother was a beautiful dancer, and indeed had won many prizes for old-fashioned ballroom dancing, and I think we all inherited her natural feeling for rhythm. It seemed simply wonderful to me that the Pantheon Club were prepared to teach me how to tap dance, and do what was called 'personality' dancing for nothing. I had grown so used to paying for my elocution lessons, that I was astounded not to have to save for fees for this splendid bonus of developing any dancing talent I might have. I was so excited on the first night of the dancing class that I wouldn't even have listened if anybody had tried to tell me I would be using new and untried muscles, and that I ought to take it gently. I was determined to master the splits (I never did!), and launched myself to the floor again and again, furious that I couldn't collapse gracefully and effortlessly like the others in the class who had studied ballet and who seemed to have limbs made from India rubber. I kicked my height, forwards and backwards, sneakingly bringing my head back to meet my toe, and I whirled and bent and twisted like a Dervish.

Next day I tried to get out of bed when my mother called through that it was time to get up. I thought I'd damaged myself for life. A lightning pain zig-zagged to the top of my leg and shot through to my hip. I tottered on to the cold linoleum, and groaned with agony as I bent to pull on my slipper. The teenager of the evening before had been changed into an arthritic old lady overnight. My mother laughed when she saw me. 'Aye, ye'll know a' aboot it noo', she said, 'Gi'e me the Wintergreen oot the chest of drawers and I'll rub some in for you'. 'I canny go into the office stinking of Wintergreen', I wailed, 'I'll just have to wait till tonight'. 'Pride knows no pain', she sang, as grannie used to do, and refused to believe I had broken anything. 'Ye'll soon get ower it', she said cheerfully, 'I tellt ye ye had done faur too much in one night. Once yer muscles get used to it, you'll no' feel a thing'.

I didn't believe her. I knew I had torn umpteen irreplaceable muscles and tendons and I'd never walk to the office again. But the thought of paying fares soon steadied me, and somehow I managed to crawl into the town, and as the day wore on, the pain abated slightly, and by the end of the week I hardly felt a thing. At the end of a month, I was dancing with enthusiasm and had learnt the traditional time-step, which my mother described, to my annoyance, as a 'rer clog-wallop'. The chorus rehearsed apart from the principals, and indeed I thought we were the whole show and when my mother asked who was our leading lady I said we didn't have one. We just had singers and dancers. She stared at me. 'Ye MUST hiv comics and leadings ladies', she said, 'Naebody would pey good money just to look at chorus girls and fellows'. She was right too. One night we were told that the whole show would come together for a full rehearsal the following week. And I found that not only did we have a leading lady and gentleman, we had a soubrette and a juvenile comedy lead, and we had solo singers and dancers, and we hard-working bunch of choristers were only the tiniest and least significant part of the whole show. It was a shattering moment.

But the show was the greatest fun. It was far better than the Rechabite kinderspiels, although in a way not unlike. Ah! But we were in a real theatre, with footlights, and an orchestra, and the price of the top seats was five whole shillings. Oh we would have to be good to justify charging such a fortune.

We had no sparkling frost on our hair, which for me had been the greatest magic of the kinderspiels, but we had real dressing rooms, and we had people to make up our faces with grease-paints, although some of the others who had been in the Club for a long time were trusted to make up their own faces. I determined to learn to do this as soon as possible, and watched carefully as No. 5 and No. 9 grease-sticks were blended into my skin, and a thin black stick dramatised my lightish eye-brows. Bright lipstick made my teeth very white by contrast, and little red dots in the corner of my eyes, and white ones on the outside corners, were said to be to give the eyes definition and sparkle. Sequin bodices topped blue fluffy skirts, and transformed a dozen wee Glasgow lassies into slinky houris, and we bounded on to the stage, sure that we were as good as anything to be seen in the pictures. 'Smile', hissed our director from the wings, and we discovered we were so intent on our feet that we had forgotten our faces, and were as grim-faced as though we were tramping blankets in the bath. Our lips burst into scarlet instant response, and there was a titter of laughter from the audience. What cheek! We weren't supposed to be funny. We finished at exactly the same moment as the orchestra, which was a minor triumph, for we'd never achieved this in rehearsal, and skipped off to a round of generous applause. We poured with perspiration, but we were delighted with ourselves as we raced upstairs to change our costumes for the next number. Oh it was great not to have to think of lines, but just to enjoy ourselves belting out choruses and dancing to lilting happy music.

That was my first and last year as a chorus girl. Willy-nilly I was roped into the musicals, but as a principal. I never saw the chorus line again, except when I was leading them in a comedy number. 'The Marriage Market', 'Belle of New York', 'Good News', 'Show Boat', and last but not least 'Desert Song' where I played Susan to Harry Welchman's Red Shadow. He was an old man by that time, but still had his own magic, and he it was who insisted that my right place was in London. I laughed at the very idea, thinking of my mother's reaction, but I didn't forget his words. And although it was all exciting and marvellous fun, the most annoying thing about those musicals was that everybody, without exception, found my singing voice had far more carrying power than my speaking one. And I'd spent *pounds* and *years* on elocution lessons, and hardly a sixpence on singing coaching. It wasn't fair.

2

A ND then, everything seemed to happen at once. There was to
be an Exhibition at Bellahouston Park in Glasgow, the biggest
show ever, with exhibits from all over the world it seemed, and our
college was renting a stand. I was to do my high-speed demonstrating before the interested (we hoped!) visitors to the Exhibition.

As well as appearing in my capacity as high-speed merchant, the
Pantheon were putting on a sort of historical pageant, and I found
myself cast as a moaning Italian peasant, writhing, starving, on the
ground while I clawed at the feet of some noble who, I was told to
imagine, might be able to give me food and money. I was never
really clear as to what it was all about, but I fairly enjoyed my rags
and I rent the air with my foreign wails of 'Madre de Dios', as I
clutched at a vaguely seen pair of trousered legs in the half-light.
I knew perfectly well that Madre de Dios was Spanish, for my
'steady' was taking Spanish lessons from the Consul at that time and
we each benefited from the other's studies, but this had a far more
dramatic ring to my ears than the Italian 'Madre Mia' which I ought
to have used as an Italian peasant. I thought it might give any Tally
ice-cream vendors in the auditorium a good laugh, but I was fairly
certain nobody else would turn a hair, or be at all surprised that a
starving Italian had the gift of tongues and could moan in Spanish!

For some reason the lighting was very dim, which was just as
well, for I had no time for a complete change of clothing. I used to
tear up from the shorthand demonstrations, throw my ragged goonie
over my jersey and skirt, trusting that nobody in all that gloom would
guess that I wasn't fully dressed in character below my rags, and with
an enjoyable agonised wail of 'Madre de Dios' I was into the play.

The best part of all this was that because I was appearing as an artist (how I loved that word), I had a free pass to enter the Exhibition grounds, and once my performances were over I was free to rush round the rest of the Exhibition and see everything that was to be seen without charge. All my office friends came to the demonstrations and to the play, and we met afterwards and ate hot doughnuts and visited the other stands and had a glorious time.

I felt slightly ashamed that the play made so little impact on my imagination, but pageants have never had much appeal for me, and my preference has always been for something with a good strong story. Still, it must have impressed at least one member of the audience, for the boy friend of an office colleague came up to me after the pageant one night and pressed something into my hand for my 'spirited performance as a foreign wumman'. When I examined it under the light at the exit door, I found it was a teaspoon with the head of Princess Elizabeth at the top. He'd pinched it from another stand, he confessed, and I was terrified we'd be searched on the way out and I would have stolen goods on my person. I was a great one for reading the news reports on crime, and knew all the jargon. However, John point blank refused to take the spoon back, for although his courage was equal to spoon-lifting after an unaccustomed pint of strong ale, it was not strong enough to face the ordeal of a public confession, and I have the spoon to this day, my first gift from a stage-door Johnny! And stolen at that!

It was small wonder that with all the late hours I was keeping, it became more and more difficult to reach the office in time to sign my name above the red line in the mornings. This line was drawn at ten past nine precisely, and the man who presided over the official book was as incorruptible as St. Peter at the pearly gates. No amount of coaxing could persuade him to allow you to squeeze your name above it, once drawn. Even if you fell in at the door, breathless, as he was poised to draw his pen under the lucky last name, the red ink flowed remorselessly and he showed no mercy. More than three times in a month below the red line meant a visit to the boss's office, and a severe reprimand. The boss spoke quietly, but you were left in no doubt that it was desirable that you mend your ways, get to bed at a proper hour, and arrive in good time to attend to your duties, and refrain from robbing the firm of all that precious time for which you were being paid.

We all hated being summoned to this austere man's room, and it was even worse for me, because I now worked for him, and had to face his frowning disappointment as he studied the attendance book and found my name there far too often these days. It made no difference that I could get through more work than most of the other girls, thanks to my speeds. Timekeeping was a discipline, and anyone who couldn't keep correct hours must have other unsuspected flaws which couldn't be tolerated.

Strangely enough, he wasn't nearly so critical of my late mornings after he'd come to see me acting in Show Boat. I had more singing and dancing in that musical than in any of the other big shows, and among the numbers was a hilarious cake-walk. My mother, always reliable as an expert source for any sort of dancing, taught me how to do a proper old-fashioned cake-walk, and I in turn taught it to Jack Laurie, my partner. It was tremendously hard work, for we took it at a very fast tempo, with our backs bent down almost to the floor as we covered the stage. It brought the house down at every performance, and although the applause carried right through the following dialogue, Jack and I were thankful no encores were allowed to interrupt the flow of the story at this point, for we had neither breath nor strength to have given the audience any more.

This cake-walk fairly impressed my boss. He gazed at me next day, as I sat with bent head, eyes cast modestly down as I waited for my notes, regarding me as though I were the original model for Jekyll and Hyde. 'Can this be the same person I watched last night doing that energetic dance?', he murmured, 'No wonder you need a few extra minutes in the mornings.' I was delighted by this tolerance, but a bit surprised, for I never enquired of myself as to whether or not I was doing too much.

I even found time to run a wee sweetie shop in the office because once more I was raising funds for the Girl Guides. It never crossed my mind to drop one interest to make way for another. I kept them all on. The only thing I had to forgo during all this hectic period was choir practice for the church, and I wrote a little note to the organist explaining that because practice night now clashed with rehearsals for the Pantheon, I must regretfully give up the choir. He was entranced by my courtesy, because apparently everyone else simply ceased attending and he never knew whether or not it was his teaching which was at fault. I was very impressed by this reaction, for it hadn't occurred to me that such a confident clever man could have any doubts about himself or his music, especially when he had the courage and originality to play 'Moonlight and Roses' and 'In a monastery garden' as voluntaries instead of the usual religious pieces in church. It was now borne upon me that even older people could feel just as uncertain as youngsters like myself. It was a disconcerting discovery, for I had been so looking forward to being absolutely sure of everything once I was fully grown up. It was shattering to discover that utter certainty would always be elusive.

My sweetie shop was a tremendous boon for everyone, for we didn't have canteens in those days, and people either brought a biscuit or an apple to eat during a furtive visit to the toilets during the forenoon, or starved till lunch-time. But my shop changed the habits of the entire office. I had thought I'd have to advertise my wares, albeit secretly, for we weren't allowed to waste time chatting or doing anything other than work during our employer's time. In a day, it seemed, the whole building was aware that Weir's sweetie shop had opened. Two office drawers had been emptied, and my chocolate bars ranged neatly inside, with an empty typing ribbon tin serving as my cash box. I'd scarcely sat down before the first customer drifted over, demanding sustenance to keep her going till lunch-time as she hadn't had time to eat any breakfast. I'd imagined I'd find business brisk around 10.30 to 11 in the forenoons, and around 3 o'clock in the afternoons. Not a bit of it. Those who had resisted temptation all morning, found the smell of chocolate irresistible each time they came to get some work done, and with lunch-time seeming more and more distant, they would succumb and start wolfing chocolate after 12 o'clock in the day, successfully destroying their appetite for their proper meal. It was the same in the afternoon. Long past normal nibbling time men would come in, stop dead in their tracks and sniff the air, decide they were starving and buy a bar of chocolate. Although I wanted to make a profit for the Guides, I was concerned that their wives would be furious if they couldn't eat their tea, but it was no good trying to dissuade them. I had created the need by supplying the goods. My boss must have wondered what was going on, especially when everybody could be seen leaving my desk chewing happily, but if he smelt the chocolate he said nothing. I think he had learned by this time that whatever extra activities I was indulging in, I'd still get through my work, and the memory of the cake-walk seemed to throw a haze over his judgment of me.

I did such a roaring trade with my hungry colleagues that I had to race over the High Road to the Guide Captain's house at lunch-time for replenishment of my stock, and stagger down to the office carrying whole boxes of chocolate bars which then had to be smuggled into my office drawers without the boss catching me. Tolerant he might be, but I couldn't tempt providence by carrying in the goods too openly. This commerce lasted for three months and I was glad when it came to an end, for the cloak and dagger subterfuge was wearing me down, not to mention the weight of those boxes. I think my arms grew a good three inches during this period! However, I was able to hand over £20 to the Captain, which went a long way towards extras for our summer holiday camp that year.

But summer camp was a long way off, and I was very busy with rehearsals for the one-act play with which the Pantheon was sure that this year would bring them triumph as winners of the Drama Festival. The play was 'The Pagans' and I had a lovely part as the wee servant girl. I was servant to two artists, one played by Alan McKill, who himself produced many excellent dramas for the club, and the other by a fine actor called David Baxter. I had almost no contact with them at all on a social level at that time, for I regarded them as towering above me in every sense—grown men, with no interest whatever in wee lassies like me. But I poured it all out to my 'steady' as we walked back and forth to rehearsals, and he shared all my hopes that this play would bring the top Festival prize to the Pantheon and that I'd share in the glory. Four one-act plays were done each evening, and adjudicated by a professional judge at the end of the evening's performances. This public assessment of the plays was the highlight for audience and actors alike. The audience wanted to see if their opinion coincided with that of the judge, and we actors rejoiced if praised, and groaned if adversely criticised. Our Pagans was well received by a packed house, and the adjudicator was loud in his praise of the play. Of my performance he was almost at a loss for words, he said. I held my breath. Did he mean good or bad? The audience was very still. Then he continued, 'If C. B. Cochran saw this girl, he would take her to London at once.' I was stunned. I was also puzzled by this reference to C. B. Cochran, for all I knew of him was that he employed dazzlingly tall young ladies, and I couldn't by any stretch of the imagination fall into that category. But the audience found no such confusion. They broke into enthusiastic agreement and applause, and the next day the *Daily Express* had banner headlines, 'Call for Cochran at Drama Festival'.

My office colleagues were as excited as though Garbo herself had landed in the export department, and everybody vowed to be present at the finals on the Saturday night. There had been such enthusiasm from press and public that everyone felt that it was a foregone conclusion that the Pantheon would walk away with the top prize. But it was a different adjudicator for the finals, and this man took a very cool view of 'The Pagans'. He picked faults in the construction line. He wasn't overkeen on the production. He thought the wee servant girl gave the best performance (I hid my face. I couldn't bear to think what the grown-up men actors were thinking), and in short he could not award us a place. Consternation! Pandemonium! And such a stushie, indeed, that Jack House, then a radio reporter as well as a newsman with the *Citizen*, rushed to Broadcasting House to announce to a largely indifferent Scotland that he had come hot-foot from the Festival where the shock of the evening had been the Pantheon's defeat with what everyone had judged to be the best play to be seen at any Festival for years. And he was kind enough to add that the only point of agreement the adjudicator could find with previous judgments had been over my performance.

This defeat in the face of general acclaim had one good result though. It was so manifestly unfair that that was the last Festival where the awards were left to the taste of one man. From then on, a panel sat in judgment. So 'The Pagans' made history in its own small way.

My 'steady' and I had intended having a special celebration feast in the Royal Restaurant, whose menus we often studied on our way to and from night classes, but whose prices were away beyond our normal egg and chip treats in Reids. Now there was nothing to celebrate, so we just walked home, and tried to forgive that black-hearted adjudicator who had not only robbed the Pantheon of victory, but had deprived us of our victory supper.

However, one night when we couldn't get into the pictures because it was too cold to stand in the endless queue which twined right round the side alley at the Regent, where a lethal East wind bit through the thickest coat, we decided we would enjoy our delayed celebration treat, and have a wee hot meal in the famous restaurant in St. Vincent Street. We smiled to give each other confidence as we tip-toed through the heavy doors, assuming an ease we were far from feeling, and the sound of our footsteps was swallowed up by the rich carpeting. It seemed palatial to us. And we didn't even have on our best clothes, for we hadn't prepared for this, and had just acted on impulse.

How quiet the restaurant seemed, and how posh, with its dark panelling, and with waiters who stood with eyes gazing towards the ceiling while we studied the menu. We looked for the cheapest item, for we could only afford something which cost the same price as the pictures would have done—1/6d. each. We could only see one item anywhere near that price, and that was roes on toast for 1/4d. With a threepenny cup of tea, that came to 1/7d. altogether. Just an extra penny apiece. That would do. So we gave our order to the waiter and sat back to watch with interest, tinged with great envy, the plates covered with rich mixed grills, the chops and chips, the large Dover soles.

'They'll be up a' night', we whispered to one another. We were too overawed to speak out loud in such surroundings. 'Fancy eatin' a tight'ner like that at 9 o'clock at night'. Privately I was making up my mind that if ever I had the luck to celebrate anything else in the future, I was going to have a mixed grill, and enjoy the opulence of eating three dinners in one, for that's what chop, sausage, kidney, bacon, tomato and chips meant to me.

When the bill came for our insipid roes on toast, whose only appeal had been its price, we were appalled to find that the total came to five shillings and not the 3/2d. we'd expected, including our two threepenny cups of tea. With beating heart we called the waiter over, and pointed out the price for roes on toast on the menu. With a lofty arrogance he explained that there was a minimum charge of half-a-crown per person, no matter what was ordered below that sum, in order to discourage people making use of the restaurant for mere cups of tea.

We were absolutely outraged. Why couldn't the rotter have *told* us that, when he'd seen us studying the menu so intently. He must have *known* we could have eaten a mixed grill, given half a chance, and that we'd only taken their miserable old roes on oast because that was all we could afford, and because there wasn't anything cheaper on the menu. I ground my teeth in rage when I saw all the things I could have had for half-a-crown. Fish and chips. Sausage, bacon and chips. 'Don't gi'e him a tip', I hissed in a stage whisper, which I fully intended should reach this supercilious waiter's ears. My timidity in the rich surroundings had given way to seething fury at having been done, and I gave him a baleful glare as he held the door open for us.

Standing outside on the pavement we read the menu framed in the window to attract passing trade. There, in tiny print, at the very bottom, we found the words we'd missed in our excitement at actually being inside such an establishment, 'Minimum charge 2/6d.' Ever after, when I heard people say, 'always read the small print', I thought of that menu, and our disappointment at not having chosen something to the full value of our bill, and I may say that nothing written in small print has escaped my attention since then. I learned my lesson well.

As we walked home, we spoke of the day when we'd walk in with a swagger, wearing our best Sunday clothes, and order a mixed grill in that restaurant, but it would have to be something really marvellous we'd be celebrating, to justify spending all that money—whole three-and-sixpence on the grill alone, without tea, or bread and butter, or anything.

The celebration came sooner than we could have dreamed.

My brother Tommy had always been tremendously keen on playing the drums. As described elsewhere,* he drove us all mad practising his 'para-diddles' in a fast tattoo on the dresser, and on the rubber pad he'd saved to buy when he was promoted to the side drum in the Boys' Brigade. He was always interested in music and, like me, always singing. The neighbours were very tolerant of our rhythmic choruses, unselfconsciously warbled as we kept time with our feet when we trudged up our two flights of stairs for our dinner when we were children. I rather fancied what I regarded as posh songs, like 'In my sweet little Alice blue gown', or 'She left her baby lying there', but Tommy would thunder out:

> Dae ye ken Elsie Marleyhoney,
> The wife that mak's the barley honey,
> THE WIFE, THE WIFE, THE WIFE that mak's the barley,

with a fine heavy thump to each 'THE WIFE' which shook the stair. But the one which made my mother laugh, for no good reason that we could fathom was when he used to chant with great vigour:

> Lordy, Lordy, Lordy *how* I *loved* her!
> The birds were singing in the wild wood,
> My happy childhood comes back once more.
> My heart is sore.

Probably the fact that he was about eight years old at the time may have had something to do with her mirth.

Now his singing had given way to drum-beats, and after he discovered the world of Nat Gonella, Red Nicholls and his Five Pennies, and Joe Venuti, he was afire to start a wee dance band of his own. The B.B. had given him the necessary training with the drum-sticks, and Glasgow, which has always been a dancing city, provided endless opportunity for anyone willing and able to play at local dances for a few shillings' reward. So the dance band was formed. Tommy was on the drums of course, Dougie on the fiddle and tenor saxophone, and Jimmy on accordian and piano. Jimmy was a versatile instrumentalist, and free-lanced with other bands on the

---

* BEST FOOT FORWARD.

string bass. My mother was a great help with the tunes dancers liked, for she always found the energy to go out dancing fairly regularly, however tiring her job might be. The Highlanders' Institute was greatly favoured, and the Lesser Public Hall, while the Guild dances in Angus Street were a regular source of pleasure. With her increasing deafness, other forms of entertainment were becoming more and more difficult for her, but the rhythm of the dance could be felt through her feet, and the note of a violin sang for her and penetrated the fog of her partial deafness. Her eyes would grow misty as she recalled the talents of one, The Great Tucker, who apparently was a wizard on the fiddle. And she was in no doubt at all as to the tunes the boys ought to play for old-time dances like Pride of Erin, Military Two-step, The Valeta, St. Bernard's Waltz and the Lancers. For the quicksteps, slow fox-trots and modern waltzes they stuck to the tunes of their gods, Red Nicholls and Joe Venuti, and they soon acquired a reputation as a 'rer wee dance band' whose tempo was really strict, and whose musical sense was first-class. Dougie was a hot favourite, with his accurate ear for the styles of the musical giants of the day. His fiddling was modelled on Venuti, his tenor sax on Benny Carter, and in his singing he was a dead ringer for the immensely popular Fats Waller.

When they started this venture, they earned the handsome sum of seven and sixpence each for an evening stint which could last from 7.30 till 1 a.m., and naturally they preferred halls within walking distance, to which they could hump their instruments without having to pay fares out of their profits. Such was their popularity locally that it didn't take too long before this figure had doubled to fifteen shillings a night, and they felt their fortunes were made. But the true accolade came when they became resident dance band at Morrin Street dancing establishment every Saturday night. Tommy was torn between triumph over this regular Saturday engagement, and dismay that his climbing week-end was to be disastrously shortened. He was now playing the drums several nights a week after his day's work at the Co-operative, playing each Saturday night at Morrin Street, and up at crack of dawn on Sunday mornings to enjoy a day on the hills he loved. The hills were as necessary to him as breathing, and he never dreamt of giving up this form of relaxation and refreshment, however tempting the bed might seem after the Saturday dance sessions. Not for nothing had grannie taught us to use to the full every minute of our lives, and to waste nothing.

In their initial enthusiasm, the boys threw themselves into the evening's work with scarcely a pause between the numbers to wipe the perspiration from their brows. Then, as they grew more experienced, and before exhaustion completely overtook them, they began to realise that a proper vocalist might be a good idea. It would give them a rest, would allow Dougie some welcome respite between his scat numbers, and would also add a sophisticated touch to their outfit. So a swooning crooner was found, but he very soon refused to continue with them unless he had a microphone. He hinted it was an insult to his status as a dance-band singer, and anyway soft murmurings into mikes were the latest thing and he was determined to follow the current trend. Already the boys had begun to appreciate the restfulness of the moments when this warbler was charming the dancers, so they made the big decision—they would invest in a microphone. And it was this acquisition which led my footsteps in a direction I could never have dreamed.

The night it arrived, they were having their band practice in our house. Sometimes they went to Dougie's and sometimes to ours, to divide the racket fairly between the neighbours of both families. The tenement walls, thick though they were, couldn't baffle all sound, and both mothers were terrified of being reported to the factor for the noise the 'jam sessions' caused. Actually nobody complained that we knew of, although the noise inside the kitchen itself was earsplitting at times. I didn't blame Jimmy's mother for dissociating herself completely from such sessions, and refusing to let the trio set foot inside the door.

I was trying to study through the arguments which accompanied the setting up of the mike, but at last it was accomplished, with much racing back and forth between the room and the kitchen, and great experimenting as one sang a few notes while the other two listened. Suddenly Tommy said to me, 'You go through to the room and test it, and we can all listen in the kitchen and decide if it's working properly.' I raised my head from my book of poems 'What will I do?', I asked, giggling with nervous pleasure at being asked to co-operate. 'Och some of thae wee daft poems you're aye reciting', Tommy replied. So I pretended I was at my elocution class and launched into a little item which involved the use of several accents, and which was a sure-fire winner at concerts, as well as being a real bit of showing-off of anyone's skill with other voices. 'Dae something else', came Tommy's voice commandingly from the kitchen. I grew bold, as they hadn't laughed my efforts away in jeering scorn. I was generally told to 'shut up, I'm trying to read' when I went about the house doing my impersonations. This was a great chance to do the lot before anybody could stop me.

I was passionately devoted to Garbo, and I did the little scene where Basil Rathbone's dog discovers her in a barn. Not a sound from the kitchen. I followed this with Gracie Fields singing 'Sally'. I listened intently for any reaction, waiting to be yanked away from the mike. Nothing. So Dietrich's 'Falling in love again' was purred into the mike, then a bit of Zazu Pitts, and finally, as a raucous curtain piece, a chunk of Tommy Morgan. There was complete silence while I waited to be told if they wanted any more, or if they were satisfied that the mike was to their liking. Then Tommy came through to me in the room and stood gazing with amazement in his eyes. He wasn't exactly eulogistic, but he *was* impressed I could see. 'Here, you sound just like thae folk through the mike', he said, and walked back to join his pals. I was elated. I was as complimented as though I'd just been awarded a Royal Command performance. This to be said to me by a brother who had, up till then, dismissed my impressions as so much noise. I went back to the study of my poems like the cat who'd swallowed the cream.

And then, the next week Carroll Levis came to Glasgow.

It was Tommy who saw the paragraph in the newspaper. 'Here', he said to me as I sat doing my homework after tea, 'There's a man asking folk to apply to the Savoy if they want an audition to be considered for the stage. He's looking for discoveries'.

I seized the paper from him. 'Och it's for variety turns', I said, 'I'm not a variety turn'. I was busy with my elocution lessons, and my Pantheon rehearsals, and was in training to become a real actress, not a 'turn'. But it was tempting all the same, if only I could do a 'turn'. 'Yon wee things you did for oor mike would make a turn', said Tommy. 'What did I say?', I asked, knitting my brows, for I'd just made it all up as I went along. So we all sat round the table, and when they came in Dougie and Jimmy joined us, and we each remembered what I'd said as Garbo, a sentence here, a word there, until I'd jotted the whole performance down in shorthand. Thus armed with an 'act', I sent in my application in my best hand-writing penned with one of the special pen-knibs hoarded from the ones given to me for exams by my friendly girl clerks in the Co-operative, and I waited for a reply, half filled with hope, half with dread as I thought of having actually to perform that made-up act before grown up people.

'There's a letter for you on the dresser', my mother said when I came in from the office, a good week after the application had been sent. 'Dear Miss Weir', it said, 'If you will present yourself at the New Savoy at 10.30 p.m. next Friday, at the close of the final performance, you will be given an audition to consider your suitability as an aspiring discovery in the Carroll Levis show.' Sick excitement and cold terror struggled within me as my mother echoed 'Haufpast-ten at night. My Goad, fancy expectin' folk tae start acting at that 'oor. There'll be naebody there.'

'Well there canny be many folk wanting to be discovered when they're asking me to come so late', I said, 'So I'll no' likely be very long'. I wasn't so worried about the time of night as I was at the thought of getting up on the stage of the New Savoy and saying lines I'd written by myself, and pretending this was good enough to be described as an 'act'. Everything else I'd ever done had been originated by somebody else, and I shivered at my own daring and cheek at attempting to say my own words, and in competition with other folk at that.

In my innocence I had expected about a dozen people to be there at such a late hour. I walked from home, as usual, but it felt very strange to be walking towards the town at what was normally nearly my bed-time. When I reached the Savoy, I thought there had been an accident, or the place was on fire. It was seething with HUNDREDS of would-be discoveries. Carroll Levis hadn't just replied to those who had written neat, well-penned letters. He had written to every single person who had applied, and it seemed that Glasgow teemed with embryo performers. I could hardly get inside, although I was early, and I was right at the back of the stalls. And then, as I gazed in dismay at the jostling throng, somebody climbed up on to the stage and said that in fairness to us all, we would be taken in alphabetical order. And my name was, as it is now, Weir. Practically the end of the alphabet.

I felt as though I were in a dream as I watched jugglers, acrobatic dancers, Highland dancers, impersonators, singers, duettists, ventriloquists, appear and perform, in a never-ending stream. My stomach grew emptier and emptier, and the sleep which had threatened to engulf me at one point, now disappeared and left instead an icy nervousness which induced a feeling of nightmare. I had nothing to do with any of this. What was I doing here at all?

Then suddenly, when I had decided it really *was* all a dream, I heard my name being called. It was 1.45 a.m. My legs jerked into action and I walked quickly down the side passage, up through the pass door, and on to the stage. It was the first time I'd heard the proper name for the little door which divided audience from backstage, and even in my extremity I noted it, and was stirred. There were about six people in the audience. Carroll Levis, the Savoy

32

manager, and one or two friends. Everyone else had gone home. In a husky voice I gave my name and my age. Levis laughed and said I looked about 12. They themselves must have been punch drunk by this time, having watched hundreds of acts, and I could see from their tired postures that they were lolling in their seats, not paying much attention. When I had impersonated the well-known film stars of my choice, I announced 'This could be any British film star', and I assumed the high-pitched starlet voice which we in Glasgow despised, and laced the dialogue with the upper-class blasphemies very popular in British films at that time. The figures in the stalls jerked to attention and there was a ripple of surprised laughter. 'Who suggested that item?', somebody called up to me. 'Nobody', I was roused to answer indignantly, 'I made it up myself.'

When I had finished, they checked my name and address, said I would hear from them if I was successful, and the next moment I was out in Hope Street, facing the long walk back to Springburn, wide awake now and hoping I could creep in without disturbing my mother. The minute I put the key in the door, she was up, 'My Goad, you've a sin tae answer fur', she said. 'I was sure you'd been murdered. How did ye get oan?'. She was reassured when she heard there had been hundreds there, and not just one wicked impresario, and she had to be told everything over a cup of tea. It was quite like New Year, sitting there drinking tea in the middle of the night, especially when the boys wakened up and had to be given some too.

3

I DIDN'T tell a soul outside the family, and my 'steady', that I'd gone along to that audition, partly because I wasn't really sure if I wanted to become a 'turn', but more strongly because I felt that anything I had made up couldn't possibly be considered as a real 'act'. When four days went by and no letter arrived, although the boys and my mother said nothing, I could see they felt I was out of the running. But on the Thursday morning, the first post brought an invitation to take part in the eliminating round on the following Tuesday evening at the New Savoy. I was to be there at 8 p.m., with my music if required (I had none), and I was informed that one winner would be chosen on each of the week nights, which meant that five finalists would be judged by public applause on the Saturday night, to decide who would be No. 1 discovery for Glasgow. There would be a second and third prize for the runners-up. And all three would be invited to take part in the National broadcast from London at the end of the country-wide contests. First prize carried a prize of three guineas, second of two guineas, and third of a guinea. All would be judged by volume of public response in the cinema, which would be measured by a special machine.

Between Thursday morning when that letter was delivered, and Tuesday evening when I walked into the Savoy, I suppose I must have gone through the motions of eating and sleeping and working, but I seemed to be moving on another plane of existence altogether. I could hear myself talking and laughing, and I could see myself walking down to the office, and taking notes, and typing them out, but it wasn't me at all. The real me was muttering those impersonations over and over again, and trying to project myself in time to the moment when I would walk on to the Savoy stage and stand out

34

there in front of hundreds of folk, and try to hypnotise them into believing I was a real talent awaiting discovery by them. I didn't even have a sheet of music to help me. Not even a roll of drums. Just me. And a microphone.

Everybody in the office knew by this time. I had blurted it out when somebody who had been reading about the Carroll Levis show asked why I hadn't entered for it. My stage aspirations were common knowledge, and many had already seen me with the Pantheon. I hadn't meant to tell them, for I didn't want to broadcast my disgrace if I failed, but the truth just leaped out when I was asked point blank why I wasn't among the contestants. To my amazement, they were all agog with interest, and even a few of the men decided to rush home for tea and get back in time for the Levis show that Tuesday night. I felt sicker than ever, but it never crossed my mind not to turn up. If anybody asked me to do anything in those days, I did it, and indeed I'm pretty much the same today. My mother couldn't face the prospect of my getting 'the bird', and decided to stay at home. The boys didn't come either. Tommy had a band engagement, and Willie was going out. So at least the family wouldn't have to share any public odium if I were a flop. I didn't even want my 'steady' to be there, but he went anyway.

I walked home from the office as usual, but beyond sipping a cup of tea could eat nothing. My innards had suddenly turned to jelly, and I leaped out and in the toilet (thankfully indoors and not on the stair in this good house), until I thought I'd never have the strength to get to the Savoy in time for the performance. When people remarked on my confidence at later public appearances, my mother would echo, to my dismay, 'Confidence! My Goad, naebody can get near the lavy, when she's to go oot daein' onything. Ma life's no worth a ha'penny, for she's juist a bundle o' nerves.'

She was right too. For the butterflies which attended that Levis performance took up permanent residence with me and have never left me since. But I wasn't to know that then, and I thought it was just because this was a special sort of competition, and all the office would be there.

There were no dressing rooms in the cinema, so we all huddled in the wings and at the back of the curtain. Levis was a jolly plump fair-haired man, with twinkling blue eyes, in immaculate dinner-suit, who bounded about back-stage like an India-rubber ball. My mother always said fat men made the lightest dancers, and certainly Carroll Levis amply demonstrated this as he leaped around, checking everything, and deciding the order in which we would appear. He and the manager had assorted the acts, which must have made it pretty difficult for the audience to decide between a man with a concertina and a tap dancer, but they were intent on providing balanced entertainment and in catering for all tastes. It wasn't an examination after all, but a gigantic variety show.

My five fellow-competitors consisted of a pianist, a girl singer, a tap dancer, a boy with a melodeon, and a crooner. Everybody had music but me. Which, in my eyes, made them real variety turns. I was to be last. The discoveries came on at the end of the big picture, and for this special week there was only one main feature instead of the usual two, to keep within the regulation cinema hours. And to let people get home to their beds at a reasonable hour. They couldn't risk the audience deciding against losing their sleep over a bunch of amateurs and walking out if the show went on too long.

Even as it was, it would be 10 o'clock before I would go on, and I doubted I would survive until that hour, for now my heart was beating so loudly it could only be a matter of time before I dropped dead before their very eyes. There was a glass of water in the wings, which rattled against my teeth as I sipped it, for my throat felt so dry I could hardly swallow. I listened to the other acts, and how good they seemed. The audience fairly thundered out their applause, it seemed to me, and I was certain that they too would have no strength left for a good clap by the time my turn came up.

And then I heard Carroll Levis say, 'And now, ladies and gentlemen, give a warm welcome to a wee Glasgow lassie who is going to entertain you with some impressions'. Somebody pushed me on to the stage, and under the blaze of blinding lights and a soft spatter of applause I walked to the mike. Levis asked me my name, 'Molly Weir', I replied huskily, and heard this reply booming round the building. 'And what do you do for a living?' he asked me. 'I'm a shorthand typist'. Unconsciously I had stepped back from the mike a little for the second reply, and this time the sound seemed much more natural. There was a bit of clapping from my office friends up in the gods, which was instantly 'shushed', and suddenly I was in control and determined to be as good a 'turn' as it was in my power to be. The film star impressions were well received, the Gracie Fields one and the Dietrich one with ripples of surprise, but it was the Tommy Morgan one which brought the house down. I had only put this one in at all to demonstrate the real broad Glasgow accent against my 'posh' office voice, and not only was the contrast very effective, but at that time no female had ever thought of impersonating a man, and the sheer surprise sent the place into an uproar. It was pandemonium as they demanded an encore of the Tommy Morgan piece, so I just had to do the same bit again, for I had no more patter, and after that reception even I knew that it was a forgone conclusion that I was winner for Tuesday and would go on to the heat the following Saturday.

Tommy appeared not to be surprised when he heard of my victory. 'Tellt ye they were juist like they stars, didn't I?' he said. My mother was less enthusiastic. 'My Goad, have we to go through a' this again on Setterday night?', she demanded. 'Then I'm gaun oot afore ye, and ye can have the hale hoose tae yersel' to march up and doon, and go through to the toilet as often as you like'.

The office were wildly enthusiastic and kept asking me to 'do' Tommy Morgan for those who hadn't been able to be at the Savoy. Always willing, I must have gone through Tommy's throat-searing voice a dozen times until I was in danger of losing my own voice, and there was Saturday still to come.

The Savoy was packed. For everybody wanted to be in at the death, and the queues had stretched right round Renfrew Street on one side, and right round the lane on the other side, hours before the doors opened. They had added another act from the closely fought tie of Friday, so that made six of us in the running for the first three places. It was better than the originally planned five, I thought, for it would be rotten to be left one of a losing pair, whereas half winners and half losers didn't seem nearly so terrible.

Everybody seemed very sure that I would win it, but I shook my head and refused to believe anything was a foregone conclusion. And it wasn't. The first prize was taken by a bus conductor who did great whistling sounds with his larynx and his cupped hands, and whose Corporation pals nearly lifted the roof when he won. I was voted second, and a singer was third. We were all presented with our cheques—which was the first time I'd ever had a cheque in my own name—and we all made a little speech. I thought I'd make them laugh by using the voice of Tommy Morgan, which turned out to be a terrible faux pas. As an experienced performer told me afterwards, 'Don't you see, you should have used your own nice, well-modulated voice, which naturally makes the Morgan accent all the more impressive. Now they will all think that Tommy Morgan's voice was a natural for you, because you speak like that yourself.' I did see. And it was too late. Oh there was a tremendous lot to learn about show business. I blushed with shame that I could have been so stupid and the thought of the London broadcast couldn't comfort me for the flat response to my little speech.

By the time the summons came to go to London I had worked myself into such a state of nerves that the doctor had to supply me with a bromide to make me sleep and comfort my stomach. With the memory of the Savoy speech vivid in my mind, I dreaded to think what other awful pitfalls might await me in a broadcasting studio. My mother was quite stunned that I was making such a long and fearful journey all by myself. She had never been further than Crieff and Stonehaven in her life, and to go south over the border into England was to vanish into alien territory. But she checked that I had a nice clean nightgown, and had put in the wee Japanese kimono auntie had brought for me when she came from Australia and which was nice and light for packing, and my slippers, and brush and comb. The green dress with the green and white striped top which I wore for the shorthand demonstrations would be fine for the show, which was to have an audience. I didn't then know that a lot of broadcasting was done without an audience, so I accepted it as perfectly natural that the studio at St. George's Hall in London would be filled with people. I was so frightened of getting lost that I sat in my hotel almost the whole day, just contenting myself with a walk along Oxford Street and keeping the hotel within sight. I couldn't resist a visit to Selfridges, which was a magic name to us in Glasgow, and which stunned me by being as big as Copland & Lye, Pettigrew & Stephens and Hendersons, all rolled in one. I felt I had walked miles in the hour I had allowed myself, and even then I hadn't seen all the counters or been in the basement. I bought a pair of gloves and a vest with the money I had brought with me, and a truly glamorous nightdress in another little shop, which was destined for my bottom drawer, for who knew when I would ever have the chance again of shopping in England's capital, where the King and Queen and all the Royal family lived.

Before the broadcast that evening, I seemed to be in even more desperate need of finding the nearest toilet than ever before. I was also growing sleepier and sleepier, and my eyelids felt so heavy I could hardly raise them. The broadcast itself passed in a dream, and I went straight back to the hotel afterwards, fell into bed and knew nothing until thunderous knocking on my door warned me I'd have to hurry for breakfast if I was catching the 10 a.m. train to Glasgow. This was so unlike me, for I am not a good sleeper at the best of times, and certainly not after such an exciting experience as a first broadcast, that I began to suspect that I was ill. A glance at the mirror showed me with blackened swollen eyelids, and my eyes felt so strange that I could scarcely read a word all the way to Glasgow.

Next day when I saw the doctor, he pursed his lips. 'Mmmm', he grunted, 'Let me see that bottle'. He put a tiny drop to his lips. 'Well, young lady', he said, 'Don't let anybody ever think they can give you arsenic poisoning and get away with it, for there are signs of this substance in your finger nails and your hair.' I jumped with fright. It appeared the chemist had mistaken the tiny quantity of arsenic prescribed, and although the dose included wasn't lethal, it was pretty dire in its effect on me as I happened to be one of the people whose bodies absorb arsenic instantly. That was certainly an unforgettable lesson to me for the future, and taught me to look after my own nerves, and not to rely on any old bromide. Fancy spoiling my first visit to London in such a way! I could have had *hours* in Selfridges instead of sitting in my hotel, and I might even have managed a quick shoosh round the zoo before my train if only I'd been more wide awake. I didn't even give a thought as to how my broadcast might have been affected. Frozen terror had obviously numbed my brain, for I found I couldn't remember a thing about my performance. I sighed regretfully and decided that that was probably the end of my broadcasting career.

But Jack House changed all that. During this eventful year when so much was happening to me, Jack was keeping a weather eye on this lass with the assorted talents. He was also in charge of a B.B.C. programme called 'Who's Here', which brought visiting celebrities to the mike in Glasgow after the 6 o'clock news, following a fast sprint round Bellahouston Park where that Empire Exhibition was held, plus, if time permitted, a speedy tour of Loch Lomond. The celebrity of the evening then told us all what he thought of us, of the Exhibition and our beautiful countryside. They had recruited some very big names, all from show-biz. and many from Hollywood, and most of them were flown from London to take part in the programme. One night, due to a tangle of mishaps and bad flying conditions, they were left with no celebrity. What to do? Suddenly Jack said, 'What about having a local celebrity. There's this wee girl who combines the oddest interests. She writes shorthand at 300 words per minute. She has been named as the most promising young actress at the Drama Festival. And now she's just won a place in the Carroll Levis Contest. What about having her as our celebrity?'

With the reporter's zeal it didn't take him long to find out where I worked. My boss was telephoned, and although it was strictly against the rules that we took private calls in the firm's time and on the firm's telephone, he handed the instrument to me. He was impressed by the words, 'This is the British Broadcasting Corporation'. Could I come straight to the B.B.C. as soon as I finished work at five-thirty? I would be on the air just after the 6 o'clock news so I mustn't delay. The tram passed the Botanic Gardens, and I was to waste no time. Nobody suggested I should take a taxi, and I of course would never have dreamed of such extravagance. Luckily there wasn't enough time to get palsied with fear, and this time I was simply burning with excitement. The entire office flew home on the dot of 5.30 to listen to what was going to happen to me at the hands of experienced broadcasters. With a panel of newsmen to see that it was genuine, I took down a dictated piece at 300 words per minute from Mr. McLeod, whom they'd lassooed from his college duties, and then I read them back. Next I did a short scene from the play, the part where it was virtually a monologue, and lastly I did a couple of impersonations from the Levis show, finishing with Tommy Morgan. Then I was asked a few questions about my interests, and that was that. Thinking it over later, probably the most striking tribute to the absolute confidence held by everyone in the integrity of the B.B.C. was the fact that there wasn't a single suggestion from any quarter that the high-speed writing wasn't genuine. It *could* have been faked, after all. On a radio show, who could prove that speeds and shorthand were authentic? We could merely have said that the newsmen were there. Of course we knew it was truly all open and above-board and honest, but for all anyone really knew I could have been reading from the printed page.

This trust in the B.B.C. was shared throughout the civilised world, and in later years when so much lying propaganda came from Germany, we were all certain that if the B.B.C. said it was so, then it was indeed so.

The whole thing had gone off splendidly and my steady was waiting for me when I came out. Now we *really* had something to celebrate—a broadcast from London and one from Glasgow. This was the moment to knock the supercilious smile off that waiter's face in the posh restaurant. We'd march in like lords, and order a mixed grill.

We went to the same table, to make sure the same waiter would take our opulence in, and after a perfunctory glance at the menu to make sure the prices hadn't gone up, we ordered two mixed grills, and sat back to wait, gazing expansively round the dining room, bubbling with excitement and anticipation, but trying to look as though we were quite at home in such an establishment. When the food came, we gave ourselves up to the pleasure of just looking at it for a minute before spoiling its perfection with rude assault by knife and fork.

A beautiful lamb chop, two sausages, a succulent looking kidney split open to look like a flower, two rashers of bacon, a grilled tomato, and perfectly cooked fresh dry chips. A little piece of watercress adorned the picture. It was magnificent.

We'd often eaten a chop at home, we'd also had sausages, and bacon, but never all at once. And we'd never tasted grilled kidney or tomato before. The kidney was delicious, but the tomato seemed wet and squashy compared with the firm flesh of a fresh one and we left ours. I could hardly finish this huge meal, in spite of my ready appetite, and wished I could have spied a bottle of sauce to help the last mouthfuls down, but there was no sauce to be seen on any of those beautifully laid tables, or on the waiter's side table either.

I was thankful we hadn't marred the bliss of this triumph over the snooty waiter by asking for sauce, because next day at the office when they all wanted to hear every detail of the feast, one of the accountants, whose gentlemanly style had always impressed me, shook his head smilingly when I mentioned sauce and said it would have been criminal to have spoilt such perfectly cooked food with bottled sauce. Such condiments killed real flavour, he said, and were only used to disguise poor taste. Besides, they ruined the palate. What a lot there was to learn about eating expensive food, I thought! We had never had any carry-on like this with our egg and chips in Reids. He was also sad that we hadn't eaten the grilled tomato. 'The best part', he declared, 'succulent and juicy and a perfect compliment to the meat'.

Thanks to my belief in this colleague's judgment, I persevered with grilled tomatoes, and learned to enjoy their succulence with the same enthusiasm once reserved for tomato sauce. Incidentally I was glad when I outgrew my need for tomato sauce, because one of Tommy's pals always drowned his chips in my sauce when he came to our house. It was a constant irritation to see his extravagance when I had bought it specially for my own use, for nobody else in our house liked it. Now he would just have to eat the H.P. sauce the others liked, or go without. If only I could stop him devouring my brown bread, leaving me none for the morning, I might quite like him again.

One day in the office the little gentlemanly accountant who'd unconsciously taught me to develop a discriminating palate, asked my great office chum Rita and myself to help him with some work which was urgently required by the director. It made a nice change for us from the eternal tenders and letters we had to type, and as we folded and added, we chatted, which wasn't normally possible over the clatter of our machines. Donald Thrush, the little chap, told us with a sigh that he had hoped to go to a hockey club meeting that evening but he was afraid he wouldn't be able to get along because there were so many black currants in his garden he *must* lend a hand to his sister and pull them, or they'd go to waste. We had always thought hockey was a girl's game, but not the way those posh West End men played it, as we discovered when we went to a match one Saturday afternoon. We knew he lived in a large house somewhere in the Pollokshields area, territory as far removed socially from Springburn as the University was from a Board school. 'Fancy complaining about having to pick black currants from your very own garden', I said enviously. 'We all love black currant jam, and we have to buy our berries.' Donald looked at me thoughtfully, 'Well, if you and Rita would like to come out tonight and pick the fruit, you can keep it, and I'll get to my hockey club meeting. Besides, it will be company for my sister, and it will be nice to know the fruit will be used.'

So after our tea, Rita and I took the tramcar away out to Pollokshields, counting the fares well spent for a keek at one of the posh houses, and knowing there would also be free fruit for our mothers to turn into delicious black currant jam. It was a large grey stone house, with wide front steps, and pillars either side of a beautifully polished mohogany door, but we were taken round the side entrance, straight into the garden and shown the fruit bushes, for Donald was in a hurry to be off to his meeting. The garden seemed huge to our eyes, and we were directed to the part known as 'the kitchen garden' where the fruit and vegetables were grown. The part nearer the house was laid out in beautiful flower beds, and all down the border were what I described to my mother later as big bushes, but which I later learned were called shrubs. Donald's sister, a rather shy plump little roly-poly of a lady, told us we could pick all the berries we could manage, for she had taken all that they needed for their own use. But we weren't to work too hard and we must stop when we were tired. She gave us each a large basket and left us. We giggled to each other. 'Fancy anybody getting tired picking black currants for nothing!', and we set to with a will and steadily stripped the bushes. Robyna, the sister, had to come out to rescue us when it was dark, astounded that we had worked so late. Little did she know that we were so elated with this bounty, we'd have worked through the darkness if she had offered to supply us with torches. When the fruit was weighed, I had gathered just on 6½ pounds, and Rita just over 5.

When we came indoors, I caught my breath at the richness of the furnishings. Dark velvet curtains hung to the floor of the large drawing room window, a matching velvet suite glowed against a pale green carpet. *Pale green!* For a carpet! I had never seen a fitted carpet before, and wondered how she could possibly keep it clean, or how she dared to let dirty shoes walk on it. A roaster of a fire blazed in the fireplace, and was reflected in beautiful little porcelain figures on the mantelpiece, and, sitting on the tiled hearth was a bonnie green and white china plate piled high with buttered toast. And it *was buttered* toast. The very words had a sort of magic for me, ever since I'd read H. G. Wells, *The History of Mr. Polly*, when the hero asks his young love what they will have for tea, and she replies, in her comical accent 'Buttud Toas'.' At home, we all enjoyed toast, but would have considered it a wicked extravagance to have spread it with butter, for everybody knew how much fat the hot toast soaked up, and we and all the folk we visited used margarine. We thought it was just as good. Who could tell the difference on toast? Now, when my teeth met hot toast dripping with real butter, I knew why Mr. Polly's love had thought buttud toas' a special treat. It was *scrumptious!* It was even better than cake. Especially on a cold night, after hours of berry-picking out of doors. And we drank tea out of matching pale green and white china cups, and Robyna told us it was China tea, which seemed scented to my palate, as though she'd washed the cups in scented soap and not rinsed them properly, but remembering my ignorance on the subject of grilled tomato I held my tongue, and told myself it was delicious and far before your ordinary Co-operative Ceylon tea.

We were just finishing our tea when Donald came in from his meeting, and because our baskets were so heavy, he insisted on running us back to the tram-stop. He had a car! No wonder he knew all about grilled tomatoes, and drank China tea out of china cups. He must be rolling in money. We wondered why he could be bothered coming in to our office, but we were very glad that he liked working, or we'd never have been privileged to share this rich life for one evening.

My mother was entranced with my descriptions, but shook her head at such an impractical item as a pale green carpet. 'Aye, she'll have her hands full keeping *that* clean', she flatly declared. 'I widnae exchange my good linoleum and my rugs for all the pale green carpets in Templetons.' Templetons, in my mother's vocabulary, was synonymous with carpets. When Hoeys received their new stock, she drooled over the window display for hours. I could see she was horrified and yet fascinated by the idea of a pale green carpet, and wouldn't rest until she had seen something in Hoey's window which would give her a true estimate of the nightmare of keeping it clean.

But she was overjoyed by the beautiful black currants I'd picked. 'Lovely big dry berries', she gloated, 'Not a squashed one among them. They'll make lovely jam, and be nae bother to set.' My mother made the best black currant jam in our tenement, and a pot of her famous preserve was greatly prized by any neighbour lucky enough to receive one. Pieces on jam were still greatly favoured by all of us, from the youngest to the oldest, for diets were unheard of and we cheerfully filled up with bread, and the home-made jam was a great rich source of sweetness and vitamins. My mother made the most of all the fruits in season, and although we seldom had money for luxuries, we always had a shelf filled with home-made jams and jellies. The very idea of having only one pot of bought jam in the house would have filled us with dismay, for as long as you had plenty of preserves in the press, you needn't be found wanting when the unexpected visitor came to your door.

My mother was always interested in our stories from our places of work, and she followed all the sporting activities and romances of our workmates as though it were a long-running serial. She particularly enjoyed hearing all about my posh fellow-typists, but was dismayed at the number of times I had to fork out a shilling or two shillings, depending on the closeness of the working relationship, for the weddings of the girls who left to be married. Fortunately I didn't know any of these older girls well enough to feel obliged to give a personal present, but I was expected to contribute to the office tribute. The sight of a girl entering our typing room, a long stiff sheet and a pen at the ready, sent me into frantic calculations about my spare money. 'Another bob off my clothing account', I'd groan to myself, as I smilingly wrote down my name and 'one shilling' against it. But we had the fun and excitement of the 'show of presents' at the house of the bride-to-be's parents. We usually went in a body, straight from the office, in our best Sunday clothes, and after gazing enviously at the array of gifts all laid out like a shop counter in the sitting room, we were regaled with a splendid tea. All the mothers tried to outdo one another in hospitality, and we feasted ourselves right royally in exchange for our modest contributions to the wedding gifts.

One mother, far from feeling ruined by all the expense of her daughter's wedding, had actually been so infected by the sight of the new furnishings for the bride's home, that she had completely re-furnished her own. We'd never heard of such a thing. By the time families were old enough to be married in Springburn, parents felt their time on this earth was far too short to have wasted good money on replacing their worn-out furniture. But this well-lined lady clearly felt she was entitled to just the same new setting as her daughter. After looking at the presents, we were shown into a room so splendidly decorated in pale colours that we were frightened to sit down, much less gorge ourselves on tea and sandwiches and cakes. Rita and I, balancing our cups on our knees, gazed fearfully at one another. We were the youngest, and we were very overawed. The mother encouraged us each to take a fragile cream meringue, but just as we laid the cakes on our plates on our knees, somebody squeezed past us, the plates slithered down our sloping legs, and the meringues burst open with a horrifying splashing of inches of rich cream all over the brand new carpet. We daren't look at one another as we fell to our knees and started to scrape the mess up. Hot cloths were brought, knives came into play, while tears of mortificattion sprang to our eyes. We were only saved from howling with shame when the sister of the bride was hurriedly asked to oblige with a song to cover the embarrassing situation, and sent us into suppressed hysterics by screaming out 'One fine day' so stridently that the very ornaments on top of the piano rattled.

What with the meringues and the need to keep a straight face through that aria, we were shaking wrecks when we emerged into the street. We both decided that there was a lot to be said for a nice shabby house, where you could be at your ease, and that it was simply asking for trouble to serve sticky food in a room so perfect that you became a bundle of nerves and were practically hypnotised into dropping things.

The fathers usually kept well out of sight during the shows of presents, which didn't surprise me at all, for Springburn husbands would have been seen dead before attending such feminine affairs. However, at one show, held in a very grand house which seemed a fitting background for the bride-to-be whose rich clothes we all envied, her father, loud and gross, was present.

As we typists sat in a circle, sipping our tea, and nibbling at dainty sandwiches, he went round inspecting us all, as though judging a beauty contest, and said, 'Now, I wonder who will be next to follow my Jeannette to the altar?'. Pausing briefly before a rather elderly, but very ladylike member of the typing pool he said, to my horror, 'Not you anyway'. I gasped, and choked over my sandwich. How could anyone be so destructive of an elderly spinster's serenity? Poor Miss Parkinson flushed and bent her head over her tea-plate, while I broke into a torrent of chatter to drown the embarrassment which threatened to choke me. This vulgarian's coarse insensitivity was proof positive, if ever I needed it, that money did not necessarily confer gentility on its possessor. No wonder my mother laid such stress on gentleness and put it far above mere money. And I agreed wholeheartedly with the little elderly typist when, on the tram going back to town, she said to me, 'How could such a sweet girl have such a pig for a father?' We weren't really supposed to call people pigs, but I had to admit to myself that it was the exact word on this occasion. We maybe had boozers in Springburn, but, as my mother said when I told her of the incident, 'They widnae hurt your feelings for the world'. Exactly.

It was a change to hear about Willie's work-mates for he worked with men in a machine shop, and he had a lively eye for their idiosyncrasies. The man we liked best was the one who took mince and tatties every single day of his life for his lunch. The works' canteen provided quite a wide choice of dishes, which we enjoyed hearing described, but this man told Willie that he had lived so long in digs where all he had was tatties and margarine, or tatties and Lorne sausage, that mince represented for him all that he could desire for his dinner. 'Aye', said my mother, pointedly looking at me, 'Some folk's easy pleased. You widnae get him spending a fortune on a mixed grill'. She hadn't forgotten my extravagant nerve in dining so richly in that swell restaurant, although she herself dearly loved a visit to the La Scala.

4

WHAT the Royal Restaurant was to me, the La Scala Cinema restaurant was to my mother. It was absolutely unique, and she adored it. This was a little restaurant laid out inside the cinema itself. Tables were ranged on a raised dais to the right of the stalls, which brought them a little below the level of the circle, so obstructed nobody's view, and the diners could enjoy the luxury of eating and watching the performance at the same time. Discreet lighting illuminated the food they ate, but didn't distract the main body of cinema-goers. It seemed to my mother a marvellous arrangement, and to the Glaswegians in general it combined the best in the way of their preferred entertainment—dining out and going to the pictures.

For any special treat, my mother chose the La Scala. She was vivacious and she was a lively red-head, so she wasn't short of escorts to provide such entertainment on birthdays or at Christmas, but she didn't go often enough for it to become an everyday thing. It was very special, and had for her the glamour that the Ritz might have for a Londoner, or Maxims for the Parisienne. I rather fancied the idea myself, but I didn't want to rob her of her triumph that this experience was unique to her, and only went once to celebrate when the B.B.C. followed that first Who's Here appearance with a small part in their Radio Cartoon series which Robin Russell and Jack House were producing.

They had apparently regarded my Who's Here engagement, when I did the high-speed writing and the impersonations, as a sort of unofficial audition, and it wasn't too long afterwards that they asked me to come along for a small part in Radio Cartoon. The neighbours were very excited that wee Molly was going to be heard over the wireless, and they were all determined to listen, for this time they had plenty of notice. They had been very disappointed because the Who's Here programme had been a last-minute engagement and they were too busy getting the tea ready to keep listening when the news had finished, and so had missed me. This time, they would all be listening, to hear me put Springburn on the map. Mrs. McFarlane down the stair didn't own a radio, having continually put off such an expensive purchase until she won the Irish sweep. However, this was different, and she sent up to the Co-operative, and had the man deliver one and put in an electric point and the whole thing cost her eleven pounds, a vast sum for an elderly widow. A waste of money, she declared to all who would listen, for she hadn't even recognised my voice! And no wonder. I was playing a little boy, and I had exactly five words to say. 'Hullo daddy'. 'Kazoo'. 'Londonderry Air'. But I was acting with real radio actors, and although I didn't know it at the time, they were among the 'greats' of Scottish radio. There was Jimmy McKechnie, later to be recognised as one of the most accomplished broadcasters in the country and with whom I worked often in London in after years, Ian Sadler of the many voices, dear Meg Buchanan one of Scotland's finest actresses and destined to be my beloved antagonist in 'The McFlannels' where she was of course Sarah, lovely Grace McChlery later, Mrs. McCotton of the McFlannels, and splendid Jean Taylor Smith, a contemporary of Meg's, and a fine actress when she wasn't busily engaged in her career as a dentist.

I was handed a script, given no instruction of any kind beyond being told that I was playing a wee boy, so I just watched the others like a hawk. I noted where they stood, how they held their scripts, and hoped my heart beats wouldn't be heard by every listener in the land. I was far too shy to speak to anyone, and too terrified to ask questions. There were three lights, like little traffic lights, high up on the studio wall, and I wondered what they could be for. Radio was done 'live' in those days, and when it came near zero hour, the red flashed on, so I guessed this was a warning light. Then the green flashed, and it now made sense to me that when, during rehearsal, the director had said 'On a green', he meant that when the green light flashed we would speak. The last light was a white one, and it was ten years before I learned that this was the silent indication that the telephone was ringing for someone in the studio! Nobody told me, and I never asked.

When I came home, my mother said 'Don't tell onybody the next time you're oan the wireless. I was black affrontit. Fancy Mrs. McFarlane gaun tae a' that expense for nothing. Naebody knew who you were.' The office were similarly disenchanted. After my solo performance in Who's Here, they imagined I would be playing the lead. After all, I'd been on once—surely the B.B.C. knew by this time I could do it! Little did they or I know that progress would normally go at a snail's pace, with a sentence more here, a little scene added there, as producers learned to trust the performer's reliability to perform coolly under the tension of live broadcasting.

None of us outside the B.B.C. took into consideration the fact that my five little words had gone out to the widest audience any of us could have envisaged. It just all seemed disappointingly feeble, measured against the strong comedy parts I played for the Pantheon, and the solo performances I was also giving now on the concert platform. Temperance Associations, church concerts, Guides, all provided audiences eager to be entertained by my elocution pieces, and I could have been out doing concerts every night in the week if I had said 'yes' to all of them. I even took part in cabaret at some of the dances, but I detested this, because I felt nobody really wanted to listen. They liked watching a line of chorus girls, because they could sip their drinks and chat without concentrating, but who wanted to listen to an elocution piece in the middle of an evening's dancing?

The first time the Pantheon provided a cabaret for a big affair at the Central Hotel in Glasgow was when I was in the dancing chorus and, having danced that particular routine in the musical for a whole week, not to mention having rehearsed it for over three months, we were reasonably certain we could provide a lively, smart dancing programme. But pride went before a fall. We had never danced on a polished floor before. And, to our utter shame and confusion, we went down one after another like ninepins! The audience was in an uproar by the end of the first chorus, and we were in a tangled heap on the floor. When we got to our feet, we were so nervous of the floor surface, we daren't let ourselves go and kept our legs stiff as pokers, and made our exit to tepid applause. We suffered less from the bruises to our legs than the hurt to our conceit. *How* could we have been such idiots as not to have foreseen what a polished floor would do to our tap shoes! We were very ashamed, and felt we could never hold our heads up again.

Another Pantheon dancing chorus was provided for a special occasion at the Odeon cinema. We came on in the interval, clad in heavy sequin trousers, bare midriffs, and little chiffon tops, as houris from the harem. As we danced, the weight of the sequins pulled my trousers lower and lower, and during the dance I glanced down and to my horror saw the elastic top of my bloomers clamped firmly about two inches above the trouser band, adorning what was supposed to be my bare midriff. I prayed that the strong pink light would disguise my shame from the audience, but a growing ripple of laughter confirmed my worst fears that my bloomers had caught every eye, and I finished the dance with jaw muscles which ached from trying to disguise the tears of mortification behind a wide professional smile. Oh there were terrible hazards in appearing before the public, and I was learning new ones every day. The other girls were mad that I had ruined the seductive effect of the dance with my schoolgirl underwear, and the memory of this incident gave true sincerity to their congratulations when I was promoted out of their ranks to become the company soubrette.

Somebody who wore school bloomers with harem trousers was clearly not going to be missed too much. Who would have thought it would have been necessary to explain to any self-respecting chorus girl the sort of undies to be worn in a harem? It just showed them, you couldn't be too careful. In short, they were delighted to be rid of me.

The part which lifted me out of the chorus was that of Susan in 'Desert Song', playing opposite Eddie Fraser in the part of Benny. Eddie was later to be head of Light Entertainment at the B.B.C., but even in the Pantheon he seemed frighteningly professional to me. He had done a lot of musical comedy, and had a name in Glasgow as an outstandingly good light comedian. I was very shy of him at first, for I had done no solo dancing since I was at school, but he was enthusiastic that I had the makings of a good 'hoofer', and we rehearsed every spare second we could get away from the 'book' rehearsals. This was a very exciting production, for the Pantheon had, with great imagination and daring, decided that as we were now all regarded as practically of professional status by the Glasgow public, we would engage a real full-time actor as the Red Shadow, and we would go for the one who had created the role many years before, Harry Welchman.

It didn't mean so much to me as it did to some of the older members of the company, for I had never seen him, and when he did turn up a week before the show, I was dismayed to find that he seemed quite an old man. I was also perplexed to find he didn't seem all that sure of his words, for I had been told he had played the part for years and years all over the country and abroad. I was far too inexperienced to appreciate that a professional actor can get inside the skin of a performance very easily, if it is one he has established, and that the words themselves aren't important until the moves have been settled. And so it proved with the lovable and delightful Harry Welchman. He was delicately built, but his voice was still sweet and thrilling, and in his Red Shadow robes he looked romantic and handsome, and quite unlike the rather fragile old man who had walked into rehearsals. Watching from the wings one night during a performance, I was stunned to find he could sing romantically to the heroine and give us in the wings a saucy wink. Fancy being able to be so detached! Oh would I ever be other than in a fever of excitement or fear when I was on the stage? I doubted it. And would I ever learn to know what was the right thing to do on all occasions? Sadly and with some cause, I also doubted it. Because I had done a terrible thing, quite unwittingly. In one scene, where the Red Shadow's Riffs captured me and blindfolded me, I was carried, screaming, to his hide-out. While he sang one of the show's big numbers, the blindfold was removed from my eyes, and I had merely to register bewilderment at my surroundings and remain silent till the end of the song. When it came to the performance before the first-night audience, it seemed to me quite unnatural that a young girl would find herself in the unexpected presence of such a romantic figure as the Red Shadow and not register something, so I rolled my eyes flirtatiously, and puffed up the sleeves of my dress in feminine vanity, to demonstrate the fluffy female in Susan's skittish character. Never for a moment did I think an audience would look at me with any attention when Harry Welchman was singing. But they did. And my actions sent waves of amusement from stalls to gallery. I froze with horror, but it was too late. They were watching my every move. It was my elocution teacher's play all over again, when my comedy had spoilt the older girl's dialogue. I felt sick. Like the gentleman he was, Harry Welchman realised it was sheer inexperience which had led me to spoil his number. He told me with great gentleness, and after tactfully complimenting me first that I was the best Susan he'd ever played opposite, that it was absolutely essential *not* to move on the stage when the spotlight was supposed to be on someone else.

When I tried to explain that I hadn't realised the audience would bother to look at me when *he* was singing, he smiled sadly. 'An audience will always look at a pretty girl in preference to an old man'. I could have wept for my stupidity. But the lesson burned itself into my heart. And I can truthfully say that never since that occasion have I twitched so much as a muscle when any other character is speaking or singing.

I didn't tell my mother how badly I'd behaved, and she couldn't understand why I wasn't more pleased about all the nice things the press had to say about my performance. 'By jings', she said, 'It wis worth a' thae weeks and weeks o' rehearsals. Fancy them takin' a' that notice o' you when Harry Welchman was on the same bill'. I gave a jump, for she was using practically my own words of the night before. 'Aye', she went on, 'I'm gled he's gettin' such praise for his Red Shadow. He must be gettin' on, but he's a real gentleman, and that aye tells.'

I gave a gulp. Would anybody ever say I was a lady? Would I ever achieve what grannie and my mother desired for me above all else, to be really genteel? Or would it always be obvious that I was no such thing?

My mother's favourite word, in fact, tenderly spoken in praise of someone whom she admired, was 'gentle'. 'She's that *gentle*', she would say, fixing me with an accusing eye, because we were both aware that that was the last word anyone would use to describe me. I was always puzzled that she found this quality so admirable, for she was no more gentle than I was, with her fiery red hair, and her tough independent spirit. Although she had a natural timidity in the face of authority, she was the opposite of gentle. She told us hilarious tales of her various jobs, in the sweetie factory where she ate herself sick in the first two days and then never touched another chocolate; in the pottery, where she painted exquisite designs on the china; in the machine shops where she and Lizzie, her partner in crime, seemed to spend half their time dodging the foreman and breaking all the rules. And although she herself had had innumerable jobs, she invariably reacted with emotion, as in the bible, 'Oh sharper than the serpent's tooth' was my ingratitude when I wanted to change my job. I suppose there was a difference. She changed jobs because she was 'laid off' and had to seek work elsewhere, but she had never handed in her notice to an employer in her life. Whereas, skipping nimbly up the business ladder, and remaining in each job only long enough to acquire more experience or skill, I had no qualms about announcing that I was leaving to find a better situation. I think she was terrified that I would walk in one day and announce that I was giving up my job in the big city office, and would live to regret such folly. She need have had no such fear. I was ecstatically happy. There were enough departments and opportunities to satisfy the most ambitious shorthand typist (we did not call ourselves secretaries then, until we truly reached that exalted post), and when I compared it with the strange little job which had occupied one trance-like month during one restless period, I hugged myself with delight that I had fallen on my feet.

That little job was a mistake in every way. Not that there was anything wrong with the company or with the people with whom I shared the office. They were kindness itself. The entire set-up was just wrong for me. For a start, instead of being in the centre of Glasgow, it was out in the country, near Bishopbriggs, territory which I associated with Sunday walks after church and not with earning my daily bread. My sense of propriety was further confounded by discovering that the little factory, in whose office I was to work, was in the middle of a field. Offices, I felt, to be real offices should not stand in green fields, they should be on concrete. Four other females shared the office, two who appeared to me very old indeed, and even the youngest member was about 20 years older than myself. The factory produced baby food, and my first task in the morning was to perch myself at a high desk, go through the births' columns in all the morning papers, type out on labels the names and addresses of newly blessed parents, and then tie up little bunches of heather with ribbons, which I finally enclosed in a box with a sample of our baby food, leaflets explaining its virtues, and a little card of congratulation, before transferring the box with its label to the post basket. White heather with a green ribbon was considered tasteful for baby girls, purple heather with red ribbon for baby boys.

The first morning, I had thought this little game with heather and ribbons was merely the prelude to more serious work, but to my dismay nobody all day rang a bell to summon me for notes. When I asked the older ladies what I ought to do, they sent me out for hot pies from the home bakery nearby. These were consumed with great gusto at 11 a.m. and we didn't even require to hide the teapot, for nobody bothered to enquire whether or not we had enough work to do. At 3 in the afternoon, I was sent out again for cream cakes. They were delighted to have a young pair of legs not unwilling to run messages for them. When I asked where the boss was, I was informed he was out of town on business, so I breathed a little more easily, and decided this lack of work was just because of his absence.

After the second day's pies, the older ladies looked a bit more closely at my small proportions and decided they were all too fat and would I show them some exercises. Thankful to have something to do, I bade them clear the middle of the office, and drilled them in bending and stretching and high kicking until they fell, panting against the desks, exhausted. So, each day afterwards, before their orgy of pies and cakes, they lined up in front of me and I led them in a knees-bend, knees-stretch, arm-flinging and toe-touching routine, ending up with them all lying on the floor doing imaginary bicycling. At the close of each session, they fell on the pies and cakes with a will, sure that they had earned them after all those exercises, and certain that they would not gain an inch.

It was all so different from any work I'd ever done that I felt I was living in a dream, and I was fretting because I wasn't earning my salary. One day, gazing out of the window, I was astounded to see a group of men rolling up turf in the specially green field next door. Each roll was laid aside like a carpet. 'What do they *do* with grass rolls?', I asked in great surprise, for I'd never thought of grass being transportable. 'Oh it's sold for bowling greens', was the reply. And so it was. No wonder my mother described bowling greens as 'like a velvet carpet', for that was exactly how they were bought. This was the most interesting discovery I'd made since working in this strange organisation, and I longed to be able to cut a swathe myself, and to examine how it was possible to cut grass in ribbons like this, without it all breaking up into pieces. But it was a skilled job, and I wasn't allowed near the cutting spades. I was very impressed, though, that anybody could have thought up such a brilliant idea, and could make a profit out of selling God's good green grass.

The boss returned before the end of the week, and at once I sat poised, ready to run the moment a bell rang. On Friday he dictated half a dozen letters, and the rest of the day was mine. On Saturday morning, he didn't come in at all, and after the heather ceremony and the pie buying, plus some token exercises, I had nothing to do. I ground my teeth in frustration. It was playing at work. I felt I was wasting away. Me, with a speed in shorthand of 300 words a minute, and secure in typing with my place among the top three in the country. It was ridiculous. And yet, they were all so nice.

I stuck it for an interminable three weeks, then without a word to my mother, marched in to my employer and handed in a week's notice. 'But why Molly?', he asked me in some bewilderment, 'Aren't you happy with us?' His use of the word 'happy' made me gulp with embarrassment, at the thought that I might be hurting anyone's feelings. But I just *couldn't* let my talents wither away in this backwater. With my eyes on his polished shoes I said flatly, 'I haven't enough to do'. He shook his head in perplexity and said it was the strangest reason he'd ever heard for giving up a job. My eyes flew to his face, and I could see he was genuinely puzzled, so I forced myself to say that I was nervous that my speeds might vanish like fairy gold if they weren't used, and that it was a terrible waste of somebody like me to employ me to sit tying up wee bunches of heather. A smile crept round his lips, 'Yes, I can see you wouldn't want anything wasted', he said. With a sigh, he added 'Of course you do need a bigger office, I can quite see that. But it's a pity, all the same. It was nice to see a bit of young life about the place.' He accepted my notice and at the end of the week we bade each other farewell. I shook hands with all the rest of the staff, told them to keep on with the exercises, and sped home on wings of joy, filled with relief that it was all over. I could begin to live again.

After this experience, it was no wonder I loved my large busy office with passionate zeal. I soon became known as the Flying Scotswoman, because when any of the girls fell ill, in any department in the building, and there were urgent left-over notes in their books requiring transcription, these were given to me for deciphering and typing. I thoroughly enjoyed my visits to unfamiliar strange departments, and soon got to know everyone in the building. I wasn't yet eighteen, which was the earliest I was allowed to sit my shorthand teacher's examination, and I gloried in the challenge to achieve a correct transcription of notes which hadn't always stuck strictly to the rules. This was part of our study at college anyway, for it was necessary not only to know the correct use of the rules, but also the incorrect use so that one could teach properly, and diagnose where a pupil was failing to understand the logical progress of the system. What with the college training and the extra experience gained through reading other girls' notes in the office, I grew to anticipate every possible deviation of outline a careless writer could commit. The worst shorthand was an open book to me, and years later I astounded the caretaker at Ayot St. Lawrence by being able to read George Bernard Shaw's diaries, written in his own individual style of shorthand.

In my previous jobs in little offices, I had had to look after my own typewriter, and used to spend every spare moment cleaning it, brushing the keys with specially provided tools, and extracting stubborn ink accumulation from e's and p's and o's with a nice smelly putty ball which was pressed into each key and drew out the blob like a blackhead. I dropped oil into the right holes, used a special spirit to clean the little rubber caps protecting the keyboard, and used a duster over the rest of the machine until it shone. I looked after it as lovingly as a boy with his first new bicycle. To my surprise, in the large office, they didn't trust us to do this, but they shrewdly valued the efficiency to be obtained from machines kept at full concert pitch, and so the representatives of a typewriter company appeared once a month and serviced all the machines in the building. I couldn't lose the habit of keeping my beloved typewriter in immaculate condition, and the rep. constantly praised me for the cleanliness of my machine. He actually tuned it up to take my specially high speeds, rather like a racing car, just to please me. He would nod approvingly at the absence of eraser droppings from the oiled works. He would note the smoothness of the patten roller, unsullied by any tell-tale pattern which would have told him that a careless operator had not used the all-important protective backing sheet when working without carbons. In short, his arrival at my desk was the signal for a nice quiet interval for him, thanks to the immaculate condition of my machine. But, alas, all this loving attention to my typewriter was my undoing. For, when at the end of my service in that office I wanted to buy it second-hand, that ungrateful wretch of a rep. told the firm that he couldn't in all honesty place a second-hand value on it, for it had been kept in such excellent condition that it was actually probably a better, smoother-running machine than when it had been sold, and would have to be charged at the full price! It was a bitter blow. I told myself that in future I would be more careful, and, like the Chinese, would not over-praise something of which I was fond. But I never did learn the ways of China. I could never hide my enthusiasms. And I found I preferred to go along with Shakespeare's Polonius, 'This above all, to thine own self be true'.

My life was falling into a most delightful pattern. The office provided non-stop opportunities for advancement, and at the same time the behaviour of my fellow-typists was teaching me genteel and refined ways, for I observed their every move and was determined to stamp out any sign of vulgarity in my own behaviour. But I was constantly amazed at the numerous ways which could give offence to those thin-skinned creatures. There was a terrible row one day because the director's secretary had come into our cloakroom and had apparently been nauseated by the sight of grubby soap bubbles drying inside the wash-hand basin instead of having been properly rinsed away. She questioned everyone until she had found out who the culprit was, and the word 'SLUT' was hissed across the typing room with such venom, that we all shook with fright. The protagonists didn't speak to one another for days, and I used gallons of clean water for weeks afterwards, to make sure I for one wouldn't sin in this way. I hadn't even known it *was* an awful thing to have done until that terrible afternoon.

Another newcomer drew gasps of horror when she dabbed at her perspiring under-arms with the towel we all had to use for drying faces and hands. The wordy battle over what was and was not good taste waged furiously, ending with 'It's easily seen you have had *no* upbringing.' If I had given the matter any thought at all, I just might have brought myself to a fine sense of outrage over drawing a perspiration-stained towel over my face, but, coming from a tenement where five of us shared a towel until it was considered fit for the washing-tub, I wasn't so easily moved to shouts of horror over such a trifle. I'd have to be careful though. Who knew what terrible thing I was capable of, which would cancel out in a minute my newly acquired acceptance by those delicate creatures?

From two sisters in the office, I learned that middle-class, sophisticated mockery could be far more effective than callow jeering in taking somebody down a peg. The younger one had once had the conceit to enter a beauty competition, and the family had found out. She had lost, but instead of the sympathy or laughter she would have met in Springburn, this 'good' family called her 'Our Beauty' ever afterwards. And when anybody asked why they used this expression, the whole story was told all over again. She was never allowed to forget her vanity. Not as long as she lived. I decided such polite sarcasm was far more deadly than our rough and ready reactions, and that Springburn could maybe even teach those refined ladies a thing or two about letting sleeping dogs lie. For although I was now speaking with greater care than most of my Springburn friends, none of them bothered to remind me any more that I had swallowed a dictionary. And at least one mother decided that the road to success might be achieved through shorthand and asked me if I would teach her daughter. I was elated. We fixed a sum of half-a-crown an hour, and I walked down Parliamentary Road on air. This was far better than class teaching. There was something special about private coaching, and I would pour all my knowledge into this girl who had come to me unsought. She proved an apt pupil, and when she had gained her essential speed certificates, I further gladdened her widowed mother's heart by finding a job for her in my own splendid office. They took her on my recommendation, for I knew she was good, and she never looked back and stayed with the firm until she married. And I derived a wonderful bonus from this friendship. Jeanie's mother proved to be a marvellous dressmaker, and turned all my bargain remnants into stunning outfits. We plotted and planned together to transform odd pieces of material into works of art, and when customers disappeared during the various Glasgow depressions, I somehow contrived to pick up little pieces of material to keep her busy, and the few shillings which changed hands kept her afloat. She seemed to enjoy my enthusiastic co-operation, and my appreciation of her skills, and one day, when funds were very low and I had insisted on giving her an extra shilling on her bill, she said to me, with tears in her eyes, that if ever she left her tenement and went as a 'living-in' housekeeper to remove the worry of the weekly rental, I would have first chance to buy her beautiful mahogany sideboard. She had been much amused that anyone so young as I should appreciate its beauty, but I wasn't my mother's daughter for nothing. My mother had taught me to appreciate the quality of fine wood and expert workmanship, and although I hadn't known the sideboard was a relic of richer days and a family heirloom, I was aware of its beauty.

True to her promise, she broke the news to me one night when I went up to have a dress fitted, that she was leaving Springburn, and did I want to buy the sideboard? I had to ask my mother if she would find space for it until I married and had a house of my own, but I had no doubts in my mind that I would treasure this fine piece of furniture if only it could be mine. When I went back and said yes, I would have it, this dear little dressmaker told me that both the doctor and the minister, the only two professional men who ever entered a working class tenement, had asked if they could buy it. This exciting news set the seal on my good taste! 'What did you say?', I asked her curiously, for I couldn't imagine myself saying no to such exalted characters. 'I said Molly Weir was getting it, because she was the only one who had ever given me a helping hand and a word of encouragement when I needed it.' I gasped. 'Och but I didn't!' I protested. 'You paid for Jeanie's lessons, and look at all the lovely clothes you made for me at such modest charges'. 'I know what you did', she said quietly, 'And I'm glad your mother is going to keep the sideboard until you need it for yourself. I like to think of it being in your house.' I had often wondered what the bible saying meant, 'Cast thy bread upon the waters, and it shall return to thee after many days'. Now I knew. I have the sideboard still, and every time I polish it I think of my fine little widowed dressmaker, her industrious serious little daughter, and of days when half-a-crown meant so much to all of us.

5

Now that I had passed my teacher's examination for shorthand, I had a glorious amount of free time for other activities. I decided I'd take some cookery classes, for although I had acquired my cookery badge in the Guides so easily, because of grannie's good teaching in the kitchen, I felt there were a lot of refinements I could profitably achieve. The classes were great fun, and as I provided the ingredients from home I was allowed to bring the finished results back with me at the end of the evening. My brother Willie and his pals soon decided that their Friday outings would end up in Weir's house, and when I arrived home from my class I would find them sitting up licking their lips, ready and eager to sample the results of my cooking experiments.

I was highly flattered by their appreciation of my apple pies, and sausage rolls, soups and cakes. But my mother grew increasingly annoyed when, if she happened to be a little late in getting home, both brothers would say, 'Och, let Molly make the tea'. There were some dishes she made superbly, but, truth to tell, she wasn't really a dedicated cook, whereas I had inherited grannie's interest in this art. They say it often skips a generation, and the daughter of a splendid cook has little interest because the competition is too close, but in the granddaughter the enthusiasm surges up again. So it proved in our family.

Anyway, at this time my mother had the fanciful notion of trying her hand at golf. Some man in the works had offered to teach her, and as she had always enjoyed a round of putting, she thought this a great idea. One round of golf with this workmate convinced her that this was her sport, and the very next week she acquired a set of clubs at the barrows. She had no idea of numbers of irons or the

the finer points to study when buying such things. The man at the stall kept her right, and she was well pleased with her natty bag and few clubs, which she purchased for a pound. She can have had little competition, I feel, from other tenement females for such equipment. When I asked her, with some amusement, if it was difficult to play golf, for I simply couldn't imagine her playing the game so glamorised by Bobby Jones, she said in genuine surprise, 'Whit's difficult aboot it? It's juist the same as putting, only you hit the ba' faurder.'

I joined the Y.W.C.A. for the sake of its verse-speaking classes, and I went to the University for German, and for drama classes under Parry Gunn. Although I was acting for the Pantheon and reciting at concerts, I wanted time to study drama in a detailed way, and to analyse the whys and wherefores, and Parry Gunn's classes were a revelation. I learned the difference between conveying distant memory and recent memory, and how to express by the tilt of my head and the stillness of my body that a noise had disturbed concentration. I was taught how to convey by my use of body muscles, a feeling of weight and strain in picking up a heavy suitcase or parcel. I was encouraged to observe and utilise characteristics in others to create a rounded personality, and to use every experience in my own life, good or bad, to help me to be a better actress.

I absolutely adored those classes, and they were a marvellous light relief after the concentrated work in the German class. But German, I found, was amazingly akin to broad Scots as far as pronunciation went, and the reading of it much simpler for me than French. I didn't acquire an impressive vocabulary, but I did achieve a good accent which, in later years, brought quite a few compliments when I travelled abroad and which enabled me too, to my surprise, to chat in German to Lilli Palmer's mother when she preferred her own language on the 'phone.

The office friend who had encouraged me to join the Pantheon had a beautiful contralto voice, and was a member of the Orpheus choir, and we used to have long talks about the speaker's art and the singer's skills. She knew how frightened I was of solo singing, although I loved all singing, and now that I had been roped into the Pantheon musical shows as soubrette I had to face the nightmare of solo stage numbers in real theatres. So she took me along to her singing teacher, Ian MacPherson, a noted Scottish baritone, and I enrolled with him for a winter's work, and had lessons one night a week, which was all I could afford. Thanks to all my elocution coaching, he was delighted with my diction, and declared that in his opinion all singers could profitably study elocution, and all speakers study singing. In later years, I found that all American drama students followed this practice, so Mr. MacPherson was ahead of his time.

He knew I had no aspirations to the Orpheus choir or anything so musically exalted, but that I merely wanted to make the most of what I had in the way of a voice. Soon I was warbling to him, 'Wild strawberries', and 'Hey ho, come to the Fair', and feeling exceedingly hilarious inside as I aped all the gestures of a real soprano.

Between whiles, I took another class for dancing lessons, but this again was sheer fun, just to keep me up to the minute with tap steps, and so that I would be upsides with my male partner in the next musical for the Pantheon. This turned out to be 'The Belle of New York', and, backed by the confidence the singing lessons had given me, I sang out the numbers like a lintie and enjoyed it from beginning to end. Jack Laurie was my co-comic, and I was flattered beyond words when he told me he would leave the precision dancing to me and he would just go through the motions, as I was so expert! By jove, all those lessons had paid off. With Eddie Fraser, I was the pupil, with Jack the teacher, and with both their humble slave, for they had much to teach me in the way of timing laughs and 'business'. My dear ma-in-law-to-be always declared my partner and I were 'just as good as Fred Astaire and Ginger Rogers', and while we didn't believe a word of it, for we had enough sense to know that amateurs always think they are up to professional standard, it was nice all the same to hear such encouraging words.

I hadn't heard from the B.B.C. for ages, and then one day I had a letter from Robin Russell asking if I would come along after work the following night, as he was doing a recording of a series called 'The McFlannels', and he was considering me for the part of Mrs. McLeather. When I arrived I found that Meg Buchanan, (whom I had met on my very first broadcast for Robin that radio cartoon item where I had the five words), was in the studio. She greeted me coolly but kindly, and I discovered she was playing Mrs. McFlannel, while the other lady whom I recognised from that first broadcast, Grace McChlery, was playing Mrs. McCotton. I didn't know anybody else, but I was later to get to know them all intimately, after I met the brilliant writer and creator of the series, Helen Pryde, and she wrote for me the part which made me a radio name in Scotland, the gallus Ivy McTweed. But all that was to come. As all Scotland who heard the series will know, the characters were named after materials, prefaced with Mc. So we had McVelvet, as well as the others I've mentioned, and I thought these invented names a stroke of genius, quite apart from the hilarious comedy of the show itself. I wasn't greatly excited over Mrs. McLeather, who was a fairly lugubrious character, but it was great to be in a studio again and working for the B.B.C.

This engagement was followed by a part in 'Wee McGreegor', again with Meg Buchanan as the mother, and almost immediately afterwards I was booked by the schools' department to play the part of a little boy. I was destined to play boys' voices for quite a long time after this, for my husky quality was considered just right, and I was quite a 'find' apparently, as such parts were fairly difficult to cast satisfactorily. Incidentally, one of the best little boy voices I ever heard on radio, on either side of the border, was that of Elsie Payne as Ian in 'The McFlannels'. Meg Buchanan and I used to be wide-eyed with admiration of Elsie, and shaking with laughter over the perfection of her maddening mimicry as the wee pest.

My 'steady' and I now had plenty to celebrate, but we weren't spending money too freely, for we were saving up for an engagement ring. I wasn't in any hurry to be married. Oh I knew the happiness of having someone in my life who could make my heart turn over, and for whom I seemed to make the sun shine, but I had no great desire to shut myself away in a wee house all by myself just yet. It had its attractions of course. I remember my mother sending me round to collect a package from a friend's house. This girl had been one of the big girls at school when I was in the baby class, but she lived round the corner from us and I knew her quite well by sight. It was the first time I'd visited a house where the lady was somebody I'd known as a schoolgirl, and I was very curious to see what it was like. It was a bitterly cold winter day, and I was instantly struck by the warmth and the quietness of her kitchen. A coal fire glowed brightly from the shining kitchen range, her little boy played quietly with some drawing paper and crayons at the table, and Pansy was washing out some things at the sink. The picture etched itself on my retina. It was a scene of complete domestic cosiness, and yet I was aware of a sense of loneliness. It seemed so cut off from the bustle and excitement of everyday living. I gazed at Pansy with some curiosity for signs that this was what was meant by being 'married and living happily ever after'. Yes, I had to admit it. She seemed quietly content, and hardly aware of what she must surely be missing. When I saw her eyes when she looked at the little boy, I knew this was the source of her greatest joy. But oh! how soon it seemed to me that she had retreated from the stir and competition of the world outside. It was beautiful in a way. But it was not for me. Not yet.

But getting engaged was something else again. For months, our favourite pastime when we were out walking, or coming from rehearsals or classes, was poring over the ring trays in the jewellers. My mother used to say, observing the stir round such windows, 'Isn't it a funny thing, hooever poor folk are, they aye like looking at jewellery.' It was true at any time, but especially exciting when one was actually contemplating a purchase. I went through agonies of indecision as to what sort of ring I would have. The number of diamonds all carried their own special meaning. Five denoted 'Will you be my wife', one word for each diamond. Three meant 'I love you'. A solitaire uttered the dramatic 'Mine', and the old fashioned REGARD was depicted by a ruby, an emerald, a garnet, amethyst, ruby and diamond. A cluster ominously reminded the fiancé she was possibly only one of a crowd! Not for me that one. The solitaire was my true choice, and I just hoped there would be enough money, without going mad, to get one of respectable size. When the final weeks came round, we haunted the Argyle Arcade, running from one shop to the next, to see which gave the best value, for all Glasgow knows that the Arcade was like Aladdin's cave with expensive jewellers' shops, and the choice was wide. We eventually settled on the shop of our choice, and the ring of our choice, and, with beating hearts, walked in one Saturday afternoon and asked to see their diamond engagement rings. We knew exactly the one we wanted, for we had studied it in the window for weeks, but I wasn't going to miss this glorious opportunity of trying on an assortment of classy diamond rings. After all, it was the one and only time we'd be in the market for diamonds and I was determined to make the most of it. I had a half-hour's pure fantasy, slipping diamond rings of every style and degree of magnificence on to my engagement finger, holding my hand up to the light, and studying the effect with affected seriousness. The salesman seemed to be stifling a smile, and I had a feeling he knew exactly what I was up to. At last we asked for the solitaire tray in the window. He brought it in. I went very still. There was no excited playing at buying now. Suppose I didn't like it on my finger after all? I'd maybe have to buy one of those I'd already tried on, and I hadn't even properly noticed whether or not they suited my hand. I'd have to buy this most important jewel in a hurry. I held my breath as the salesman extracted my ring from the tray and slipped it over my knuckle. It was *gorgeous*. It was *perfect*. Well, it was maybe a wee bit on the loose side, but that could easily be adjusted, he assured us. Ah, but I could wear it over the week-end if I liked, because it wouldn't go to the workshop until Monday. If I liked! Of course I liked! I could hardly bear to have him take it off to get the number and all the other details.

My fiancé was far more easily pleased when it came to buying his gold signet ring. I was amazed at how easily a man could forgo the fun of trying on everything in the shop. He even left his ring to have his initials and the date engraved, instead of wearing it for the week-end, like me.

I danced up Buchanan Street on air, terrified to take off my glove in case the ring would come off with it, since it was just that shade too large for my finger. But when we reached the Ca'doro and ordered our 2/3d. high tea in celebration of this milestone in our lives, I flashed the ring all round the tearoom, as I gesticulated and acted the whole purchase all over again while we waited for our fish and chips.

The Scottish National Players were doing a play at the Lyric and my friend Meg Buchanan was in it. The only seats we could get at the last minute were in the sixpenny gallery. We were delighted with our bargain seats, for we were by this time a trifle scared with our extravagance that day, and sixpenny seats were more than welcome. And when I held up my ring in the rays of the beaming light which shone down on to the stage, it glittered far more magnificently than it would have done down there in the dull stalls.

We walked home afterwards and my fiancé came in for supper. My mother, always a reliable and shrewd assessor of values, was warm-hearted and satisfyingly enthusiastic over the beauty of my ring. It had been a marvellous day.

It isn't my intention in this book to delve too deeply into the strong personal happiness I've known with my 'steady' down the years. Incidentally, my mother always described him as 'As steady as the rock of Gibraltar', and in her and in my eyes he truly deserved her favourite description, 'gentle'. I always remember reading in Winston Churchill's autobiography, 'We married and lived happily ever afterwards'. I thought that was a marvellous and economic sentence to use, to describe the happiness of a lifetime. He said not a word more, implying that the rest was their own private concern. So it is with us. I am the extrovert. My husband the quiet one. In deference to his feelings, and because this book pursues the course followed from Springburn to the bright lights in search of a career, I am confident the reader will understand why I choose simply to borrow the words of the great man, and echo his telling phrase with joyous sincerity, 'We married and lived happily ever afterwards.'

I'm telling you this now, so that you won't be disappointed in finding no minute details of wedding bells, orange blossom, and the rest!

Even if I hadn't been guided in my feelings about such private matters by the great Churchill, I would have been influenced by a holiday in Girvan after grannie died when some neighbours took me with them for a fortnight, to bring the roses back to my cheeks. I had to share a bed with one the daughters, who was in the throes of wedding plans, and full of romantic tales of her best beloved. At first I was thrilled to the marrow to be the confidante of her whispered secrets as soon as the light went out, but as night followed night and her enthusiasm showed no signs of flagging, right into the wee sma' 'oors, I had to seek refuge in snoring to nip the flow of words in the bud! I had had no idea love could be so tedious in all its wearisome details. That experience undoubtedly gave me a preference for the Churchillian way of dealing with romance.

I had almost forgotten that the Carroll Levis contest win also carried with it the promise of a stage show at some future date, when a letter arrived informing me that the Discovery Show would be going on at Glasgow Empire twice nightly, for a week, and as one of the Glasgow winners I would be added to the company's strength. I was going to be a 'turn' in Glasgow's biggest variety theatre! Excitement, fright, and stunned surprise that my made-up 'act' could be accepted in a professional theatre fought for supremacy. But everything now had a sort of inevitability, as though I were following a selected path and had no alternative but to do as I was told.

The first half of the bill was to be composed of established variety acts, and we Discoveries would occupy the entire second half of the programme. We were called to attend the theatre on the Sunday to go through the running order of the show, and when I arrived I found that the bill-boards were being pasted up, telling all Glasgow that we would be appearing that week. I noted with interest that there would be jugglers, a dancing act, Jimmy James with his drunk sketch, and a ventriloquist. Then, in huge letters, in flaming scarlet, came the words 'CARROLL LEVIS WITH HIS DISCOVERIES, INCLUDING GLASGOW'S OWN MOLLY WEIR'. There it was. Up on the bills. And for the first time, I was 'Glasgow's own'. Nerves crawled up and down my spine, and there was a taste in my mouth like metal polish at the mere thought of having to live up to that description. But what had happened to the first and third prize winners? Oh yes, their names were there too—thank goodness the Glasgow public wouldn't be coming just to see me.

Inside, there was the strangely familiar smell of all back-stage theatres. A sort of compound of heat and dust and greasepaint which grips an actor by the throat and is more potent than drink or the finest perfume. I drank it in, and found it so heady that I was off in a day-dream of bringing the house down with my performance and heading straight for Hollywood. I was brought down to earth by being asked to attend the 'band call' on the Monday morning, for I knew my boss would have a fit if I asked off work again. I assured Carroll Levis that I didn't need any music, and that for the closing music and the song 'Stardust', which the entire company was required to sing, I was word and note perfect and needed no rehearsing. He enquired when my lunch-hour was, and suggested I look in then, and I would get an idea of the final line-up, and where my dressing room would be. I was to share with one of the Discoveries who was doing the tour of the entire country with him and she would show me the ropes. Fancy! A real dressing room for just the two of us. Marvellous.

On the Monday, when I reached the Empire at lunch-time, having run all the way from Argyle Street, the queue for tickets was right into the street. Discoveries were a great novelty, and of course for Glasgow there was the added attraction of three examples of their own talent being on the bill. This, I discovered later, happened in each town the Levis discoveries visited. The local prize-winners were added to the company's strength, and so whipped up local fervour, and made sure of good houses. A very shrewd arrangement, I had to admit. But at the time I thought it was the simple honouring of a promise made to us as prize-winners—I didn't see it as a business move at all.

The people in the queue paid not the slightest attention to me as I made my way round to the stage door. But I looked at them. They were my public. They were a true variety audience. They were used to real acts, for at that time the cream of the variety world visited Glasgow. Florence Desmond was their idea of an impersonator. Layton & Johnson had sung for them, Leslie Henson clowned for them. And the big bands filled their ears with music. How would they react to a bunch of amateurs?

Back-stage, a group clustered round the pianist, running over the words and the key for 'Stardust'. I was just in time. Levis, genial as ever, without a care in the world apparently, went through each entrance and exit with us, placed us for the final chorus of 'Stardust', and told us to sing out and smile radiantly when the moment came at the end of the performance. In the empty theatre you could hardly have heard our voices behind a car ticket, but nobody seemed worried, and I hadn't even time to see my dressing room, for my whole lunch-hour had been swallowed up and I had to run like the wind to get to my desk for 2 o'clock. I nipped into Fergusons in passing and snatched up two Bourbon biscuits, and that was my lunch.

At half-past-five I left the office, carrying my little case with my make-up box and my knitting. Thanks to my work with the Pantheon, I knew to store my grease-paints in the traditional cigar-box, for no self-respecting aspirant to the theatre would have been seen dead using anything else. I had a tin of Cremine, big enough to have removed the make-up of the entire cast, bought through a colleague who could get it wholesale, and which lasted me for about 15 years. The larger the tin, the greater the economy, I was told, and in the following years when such pure fats were impossible to buy, many an actress rejoiced in my prudence as she enjoyed the smooth efficiency of that Cremine in removing her make-up. A box of powder, cotton wool, and talcum completed my equipment. Unlike the Pantheon, which was all chatter and running about backstage before a performance, the Empire was strangely muted. This was the normal working background for most of them. The musicians were tuning up their instruments. Two men chatted quietly outside a dressing room door. A woman came from wardrobe with a freshly-pressed dress over her arm. I seemed to be the only one who had any nerves about the evening ahead. The girl with whom I was sharing the dressing room was very blasé about the whole thing. She was sitting filing her nails and reading a paper when I arrived. Fancy being able to read a paper at such a moment! I spread my freshly ironed towel on the dressing table, and laid out my things. How professional it all looked. The row of greasepaints inside the cigar-box. (I hoped the girl realised I knew about such things.) The huge box of Cremine to the right. The powder box and talcum, with the cotton wool to the left. My brush and comb dead centre. One of the things I can't remember at all is what I wore. Nowadays it would be almost my first concern, but with my limited wardrobe I expect I just wore my best dress, and, secure in the knowledge that it *was* my best, never gave it another thought. I know my hair was clean and shining, for I washed it once a week, and I had done this as soon as I had reached home after the Sunday rehearsal. It was naturally curly, and bounced round my head in finger-pressed waves.

The other girl seemed in no hurry to apply her make-up, but I always liked to get dressed and made up first, and then have all the time left to do as I wished, so that if some unforeseen disaster struck everybody on the stage and I had to go on early, I would be ready to face the public.

The other girl, Jessica her name was, lifted an amused eyebrow as she watched me. She had been doing the show twice nightly since they had left the London area weeks ago and regarded the whole thing as a slightly boring job of work. Boring! 'Calm down', she said, observing my excitement, 'You'll have nothing left for the performance.' She was aghast to discover I worked at an office desk from 9 till 5.30. She herself never rose much before noon, now that she was working in the theatre. 'Och but it's only for a week', I told her, 'And it's only a wee turn. Not nearly so hard as doing a whole musical after my work'. She stared at me. 'You do whole musicals as well as a day in the office?', she gasped, 'Good grief, you must be as strong as a horse, for all your small size.'

Oh I was glad I had brought my knitting with me, for it was going to be an endless wait till the second half of the programme came on. I was too nervous to watch any of the show from the wings for this first performance, and there would be another long wait between the houses and before our second appearance. So my knitting would keep me quiet and stop me running about demented. I have always found the therapy of the hands has a calming effect on me. Nowadays the house is full of fire-screens embroidered by me during the long hours and days of waiting in rehearsal rooms and dressing rooms. It's not only Satan who is kept at bay by busy hands. Nervous tensions are effectively chased off too. Well, up to a point anyway.

Jessica wrote letters while I knitted, and then all at once it was time for our part of the show. A call-boy knocked at the door. 'Curtain up—your call ladies'. The nation-wide winners went on first. Jessica, who had seemed such a friendly simple ordinary girl in the dressing room, was transformed into a striking and dramatic soprano, elegant in black evening dress, and with a voice like an angel. I watched her from the wings, and applauded enthusiastically with the audience at the end of her Grace Moore selection, and was equally delighted with her encore rendering of a Strauss waltz. She was good, oh she was better than good, she was terrific. In fact they were all terrific. They were the pick of the contests after all, and I trembled at the thought of being judged alongside such performers. Levis bounded on after each act, and described where each performer had been found, asked a few questions, and then galloped back beside us back-stage, checking that we were all where we should be.

And then I heard him say, 'And now, give a big hand to a wee lassie from Glasgow—your very own, Molly Weir'. And I found myself walking on shaking legs towards the mike. The theatre seemed enormous, with as many faces as on the terraces at Hampden Park! The applause took me right to the microphone, and only died down when Levis started his questions. I had been praying hard for the last five minutes. 'Oh God, let me be as good as it is possible for me to be. Not necessarily a genius, just let me do my best.' I had to stop praying now, and tell Levis and the audience that I was Molly Weir from Springburn, and that I was a typist in an office, and that I was going to do some impersonations for them. I stiffened my legs in a silent command to them to stop quivering, steadied my voice, and away I went into the 'act'. My mimicry was most cordially received, but as usual it was the Tommy Morgan one which brought the house down. After the experience of the Savoy demand for an encore, when I could give them none, I had written an extra little piece of typical Morgan patter, and so I was able to give this generous Empire audience a second good short punchy piece of characteristic Tommy Morgan comedy when they asked for it. My mother would be delighted to know I'd had an encore. No turn worth its salt got off without having to give an encore. I skipped happily off the stage to enthusiastic whistles from the gallery, solid applause from the other seats, and a beaming smile from Levis. My face was burning, but my heart bursting with joy. 'Thank you God', I sang to myself in my head, 'Thank You for not letting me make a fool of myself out there. Oh Thank You!'

For the finale we all came on and sang the familiar theme song of the Levis show 'Stardust'. And then it was up to the dressing room and the long long wait before we did it all over again for the second house. Some of the acts went out between the shows, indeed most of them did. But not me. I couldn't have left the atmosphere of the theatre. For me it would have destroyed all the magic of this never-to-be-forgotten evening when I had been accepted as a 'turn' with a professionally booked company in my native city.

A few nights later, Levis called us all together for a pep talk. He looked as stern as his merry face could manage and told us we weren't singing the words of Stardust enthusiastically or loudly enough, and it was vital not to leave it all to the orchestra. We must have verve, and sing and look as if we were enjoying ourselves. I was indignant. 'I was singing as hard as I could', I protested, my sense of injustice overcoming my shyness of him. He patted my arm reassuringly. 'Of course I didn't mean you Molly', he said, 'You are always bursting with enthusiasm. It was some of the others.' The ones he stared at so pointedly now threw me derisive looks, and

I heard one of them mutter 'For the peanuts we're being paid, why should we flog our guts out twice nightly'. I stared in absolute dismay. Fancy letting mere money dictate the integrity of the performance! In the Pantheon we got nothing, and it was far harder work. I was delighted to be paid anything at all—I would have done it for washers! In fact the only people who had paid me up till now had been the B.B.C., and I was quite surprised that they felt it necessary to pay me on top of letting me loose in their studios, and giving me the use of their microphones. £4 10s. for the Levis show seemed quite a lot of money to me. It was far more than I earned as a top typist, and I thought those other turns were very grasping, and it would serve them right if they came 'to want' some day. My mother and my grannie had taught me great respect for those who paid a steady wage, and although I later learned to discuss contracts and money with the best of them, I have never allowed my performance to be affected by the size of the fee. Whether a handshake or a cheque was handed out at the end of a show, I've always given of my best. Bebe Daniels was to say of me, much much later, 'That little Molly is always in there pitching!'

Before the end of that week in the Empire, I simmered down enough to be able to watch all the other acts in the first half from the wings. No wonder people say jugglers deserve better attention than they get from all those late-comers pushing their way to their seats. It is a very skilled act, and when one watches them so closely, admiration almost suffocates, for their concentration has to be absolute while at the same time they smile and skip and joke. Jimmy James was hilarious, and his lurching leering muddled delivery in complete contrast to the quiet man who stood so still while waiting for his cue in the wings.

But the act which I've never forgotten was the ventriloquist with his doll. Not the stage performance. That was good of course, but I felt my heart turn over when the curtain came down and the ventriloquist tossed the little man-doll on to a bench. There was something so life-like and so pathetic about that small still figure that I went over and took its hand to let it see it hadn't been entirely abandoned. I've been slightly frightened of those puppets ever since. And one of the films which scared the life out of me in later years was the story of the ventriloquist and his doll, where the doll absorbs all the man's life and takes control. It was brilliantly played by Michael Redgrave and was, for me, too much a reflection of my own feelings to be comfortable entertainment.

On the Saturday night, I had thought there would be a sort of 'end-of-term' feeling, with maybe even a wee party to celebrate the end of what had been, for me, a wonderfully exciting experience. Not a bit of it. The second-house curtain came down. Everybody disappeared to their dressing rooms. Jessica called 'Cheerio then', and vanished with her make-up box, and I was alone. It had been just another working week for them. That was my first experience of the sense of anti-climax which follows the excitement of sharing nerves, tension, happiness and success with a company which at once goes its own ways, and vanishes as unemotionally as though the whole thing had been a dream.

Maybe it was a dream.

But no, the posters were still there to reassure me it had actually happened. And my 'steady' and I walked home, and he wondered how I'd settle down again to 'auld claes and parritch'. I found I was starving, and somebody in the fish and chip shop recognised me and slapped me on the back for being such a 'rer wee turn', especially at good old Tommy Morgan. That, I think, was the first time I was genuinely recognised as a performer by someone who was a stranger to me. It was a pretty exciting moment.

6

THANKS to the Empire engagement, I was now becoming fairly well-known in Glasgow. Both the drama public and the variety audiences were mildly aware of my existence, and my 'turn' must have struck other critical ears as being reasonably good, for the next engagement I received for the Empire was from Jack Hylton. His was a legendary name to us in Glasgow. He was very much a star of the 'big band' era, and the sound of his opening music slowly swelling behind the closed curtain could send any variety audience wild with excitement. The applause would grow and grow, and every eye would be riveted on that curtain, which at last slowly parted and revealed his 'boys', ranged tier upon tier on stage, filling our eyes and our ears with the magic of their presence.

And now this great man wanted me. At our first meeting on that Sunday morning (it always seemed to be Sundays for such work), he sent my heart skittering into my throat by saying to his musical director, 'Have you made sure she does that impression of Harry Gordon? That's the real kernel of her act.' 'I don't do Harry Gordon', I called out in alarm. Surely he hadn't engaged me in mistake for somebody else? It didn't dawn on me that possibly our Scots comics weren't such household words to him as they were to us. The ash dropped from his cigarette down his fine waistcoat, as he gazed at me enquiringly. 'I do Tommy Morgan', I gulped. 'Oh well, if that's the one you did for Levis, that's the one I want', he said. I was amazed. Fancy a famous band leader like him not knowing the difference between Aberdeen's own Harry Gordon, and Glasgow's own Tommy Morgan. I'd never have believed it if I hadn't heard it with my own ears. It was my first intimation that the great figures of stage and screen weren't gods after all.

My mother decided that this time she would risk coming to see me perform. She dearly loved a dance band, and she felt it was high time she saw for herself how I got on in front of such a big audience. Variety audiences were real audiences to her. She knew all about the big turns. Florrie Forde, Gertie Gitana, the Chocolate-Coloured Coon. She spoke of them as though she had been on intimate terms with them. She thought of herself as a shrewd critic, but she had adored them all and had nothing but praise for their beauty, their voices, their magic. She couldn't really believe anybody would judge me on that level, but she was curious to see how the rest of the audience would react. When I asked her afterwards if she had given me a good clap, she was aghast at the very idea. 'Of course I didnae', she said, 'Everybody would know I was your mother, and I wouldnae be seen clapping one of my ain family.'

My mother could never see us as anything but her own children, and couldn't hide her amazement that we could reach positions of importance in the world where we could be taken seriously by the adult population. When brother Tommy later became a mountaineer of International reputation, welcomed by the Alpine Society as a lecturer, not to mention the Geographical Society in London, and became a climbing colleague of Sir John Hunt on many hair-raising expeditions, he was seen in quite a different light by my mother. 'Back fae thae hills', she'd say in irritation, 'A sink-full of wet socks, and torn shirts', and then, warming to her theme, 'And his pick (her name for his ice-axe) and a' that rope falling oot the press every time I open the door'.

When she was sorting through his socks she would cluck despairingly, 'Look at that', she'd exclaim, 'All odd socks. A blue one a brown one a grey one and a heather mixture one—My Goad they must a' borrow each other's socks and they don't give a docken whether they're wearing the right ones or not'.

She had a strong sense of possession and was baffled by this sort of carelessness, and with his lack of regard for his other clothes. 'Pays a fortune for them', she'd tell me, 'And then catches his shirt in the middle of the back and pulls it over his head. And as for his tie—never loosens the knot—just pulls it wide enough to slip over his ears.'

Even when he was recognised as an authority as a writer when anything of particular reference to Scotland was required, she could never get over the fact that he didn't go out to do a daily job of work. It didn't feel right to her that he didn't don city clothes and catch a bus or a tram to a place of business, but merely wrote from a little room in the tenement house they shared. 'He goes into that room at the back o' nine o'clock', she'd say to me wonderingly, 'Just as if he was going to his work, and he stops regular as clock-work for his morning coffee and his lunch'. 'But mother', I'd say, laughingly, 'It is his work'. She'd give me a pitying look. 'Hoo can it be his work', she'd demand, 'When it's at hame, and naebody pays him a regular wage?'

The casual nature of his profession terrified her, and she could never believe he could earn enough by wee bits of scribbling to keep body and soul together. She was quite certain he would live 'to want' in his old age, and her not there to keep an eye on him.

Once, when he was giving a lecture in Edinburgh to an audience of over 2,000 she was there, sitting in the front row, clearly baffled that all those people should have gathered to hear what he had to say, and had paid good money to look at his colour slides. He always used a long pointer to indicate the various interesting and focal spots of the climbs, and as the lecture was about to begin, she sensed at once from his frowning searching glance round the platform that he couldn't locate this vital prop. She was in an agony for him. He was her wee boy looking for his collar stud or his keys, notoriously careless as always in her eyes. All the audience were waiting. Suddenly her whisper went sibilantly round the auditorium, 'Tommy! It's in the corner behind you. At your back!' The audience rippled with laughter. Tommy turned—found it, picked it up, and the evening began. She sat back with a satisfied sigh. He might be the grand speaker, but it took her to keep him right.

She wasn't above teasing him either. She invariably infuriated him by pronouncing the Himalayas 'The Himullas', however much he corrected her. When a card arrived from him from India, she laughed as she described the pantomime of his packing to go off on that expedition. Then she added, 'I know fine Tommy gets mad at me saying the Himullas. Of coorse I know it's the Himalayas, but I *like* Himullas better'. I was astounded. I had always thought the mispronunciation accidental, but now I realised it was simply her way of asserting her independence. She wasn't going to conform just to please her own wee boy. Not she.

She hated it though when he was late in coming home at nights after climbing or lecturing to societies, for she felt his unworldly interests were no match for any possible thugs who might be lying in wait. She saw him an innocent abroad, and wasn't happy until he was safely home and the big outside door locked. This despite the fact that he travelled through Tibet and Morocco and in many wild territories where bandits were not unknown. 'I don't like it when he's oot so late', she'd confide in me, 'There's that many bad rascals hanging aboot, and oor Tommy would never see them, he's that busy thinkin' aboot his mountains and his birds'.

She was terribly proud that he had climbed with Sherpa Tensing, and delighted when they met again in Scotland, and she saw the Sherpa's 'lovely face and smile' in her very own kitchen. But lovely smile or not, she persisted in calling Tensing 'Tinsling'. She wasn't going to be overawed to the extent of giving the correct pronunciation!

But she showed no pride of any of us in public. She was much more likely to say of Tommy 'Fancy not waiting till I sewed that button on his shirt—I could see his semmit a' the time he was speaking up there on the platform,' and of me 'Aye, it's a peety you hadnae a pair o' wings, and then you could nearly be in two places at once'. Whatever the public eye saw in us, she made sure we understood we were her children, to be kept in order by her watchful criticism. There was no fear of any of us 'fancying our barrow' while my mother was there to impress a sense of reality and to make sure feet stayed firmly on the ground.

In spite of this attitude though, she grew so used to my ability to tackle anything I was asked to do, that it was less of a surprise to her than it was to me when my college telephoned one day and told me they'd recommended me to attend a great church debate in Renfield Street church, to take verbatim notes of the proceedings. I felt very honoured, but also very nervous of my responsibilities, because till then I had only done high speed demonstrating for comparatively short periods, and this was to occupy a whole evening and there would be proper names to cope with, religious sects, arguments, and there would certainly be no guaranteed evenly-paced delivery, but bursts of accelerated speed as tempers rose. Goodness, there might even be interruptions from the platform party, or from the body of the hall, and how would I ever know all their names? But I was to be paid a guinea for my services, and it was an irresistible challenge to try my hand at being a real short-hand reporter like the ones we saw in the pictures. I felt secretly rather elated. Nobody nowadays was telling me I was too wee for anything. I'd been accepted as a real theatre 'turn'. Now here I was being accepted as a real reporter. Life was so exciting that my feet scarcely seemed to touch the ground as I raced home on the night of the debate to collect pens and pencils, plus an extra notebook, before setting off again for the church.

I was led to a little table on the platform, at right angles to the main long table, and at 7.30 the debate began before a packed audience. As I was entirely unused to such work, I felt it essential to take down every single word, just as I did my pieces in college and in the office, and I thought my hand would drop off as page after page of notes were filled. Arguments raged back and forth for hours, with hardly a pause for breath. Everybody seemed to have lost all sense of time, and they certainly paid no attention to me sitting there frantically trying to get every impassioned word down. There weren't even refreshments, for it wasn't a social after all. It was a debate. I hadn't the slightest idea what it was all about. There wasn't time to think. The words hit my ears, and were transferred to the notebooks, with no comprehension on my part. I didn't even notice the audience thin out, as people must have left for their trains or cars or buses, but by the time those religious maniacs had finished their arguing, it was 1.30 a.m., the place was quarter filled, and I was absolutely exhausted. It was the Carroll Levis audition all over again, with me walking home in the wee sma' hours, and my mother demanding to know this time, 'Whit kind o' folk are they church men then, to keep a young lassie oot o' her bed till this time in the morning?'. She took one look at my white face and put the kettle on, 'My Goad, your eyes are staunin' in yer heid', she said, 'It's a good thing the morn's your Setturday off, and you can have a long lie'. We had every fourth Saturday off in my fine big office job, and usually this was a treasured treat. But there would be no long lie for me this time. 'Oh I can't have a long lie, mother', I said, as I began to riffle through the pages of notes, 'I've to take these down to the college and type them out, for' they're wanted as soon as possible'. 'DON'T start looking at thae notes the night', my mother implored, 'Drink yer tea and get to your bed, or you'll no' be fit for anything in the morning. It's a good night's sleep you need.'

On the Saturday, I typed without pause till the college closed at 1 o'clock for the week-end. I went back every night after work the following week, and I thought I'd never come to the end of this nightmare task. When he saw the amount of work involved, my nice kind shorthand mentor pursed his lips and said one guinea was totally inadequate, and I must ask the church authorities to make it at least three. 'Och I could never ask them to do that Mr. McLeod', I protested. But when I added it all up, I realised there was as much work in that marathon as I did in a week at the office. And I had supplied all the paper and the carbons. So, when I handed the bundle of transcript over, I found courage to say, 'My college feels this work is worth at least three guineas'. I couldn't look the man in the face as I mentioned this enormous sum, and I felt a bit mean in case these church folk didn't have enough money. But some stubborn streak supported me and gave me strength to stand my ground. For good measure, I added, 'The bible says "The labourer is worthy of his hire", and my college says it's worth it'. The man's lips twitched when I raised my eyes to see how he was taking my bargaining. He weighed the paper in his hands and smiled, 'I'm sure it's a bargain. You've done a very conscientious job, young lady'. I must have been getting used to being called a young lady, or my bargaining had paralysed my emotions, for I never turned a hair at these once-surprising words he used to describe me. I got my three guineas, the first and only time I had ever earned extra cash solely from my shorthand speeds. 'By jings, I'm well away', I chortled to myself as I sped home to tell my mother of this bonanza.

Everything was possible. The story of the ten talents was absolutely right. As far as I knew, I hadn't allowed any of mine to be buried and go to waste, but had worked to develop and add to them and they were all gradually being used. There was no knowing where I would end up. There was plenty of time to find out.

It was the summer of 1939.

In spite of my preoccupation with my own absorbing affairs, two menacing figures strutted across the world's stage, and although it was easy and fashionable to laugh at the ranting Hitler and the buffoon Mussolini, I couldn't laugh. We all argued passionately about armaments. I can remember saying, with what I thought was deadly logic, 'You can't give a child toys and then tell him not to play with them. That's what we're doing with this man Hitler', and I was told to shut up. I was just being a scaremonger like that chap Churchill who was trying to frighten the daylights out of everybody. Nobody wanted war.

The war burst upon us, and the country was almost totally unprepared. My despair came from the sick feeling that all the wrong people were in charge. I remember sitting in a chum's garden one lovely sunny day and crying out against those in authority and their feeble decisions. My chum, exasperated by my attitude, said 'But what do you WANT then? What would make it better?' I drew a deep breath. 'That this lot be thrown out, or the whole Government work together with Churchill in charge', I said.

Somebody must have been listening! For the very next day after that conversation in my chum's garden, the papers and the wireless told us that a Coalition had been formed, and the man who would lead the nation to victory would be Winston Churchill. From that moment, and even through the darkest days which followed, I had absolutely no doubt whatever but that we would win the war. With God and Churchill on our side, victory was certain.

I kept waiting for the B.B.C. to summon me to help them on the home front, but they seemed amazingly able to get on very well without me. I couldn't understand it. So I wrote to my first producer, Robin Russell, and told him so and he very kindly replied from his Air Force camp and advised that I write to the new head of drama, Moultrie Kelsall, and he also would drop a note in my favour. When the summons came to meet Moultrie, I found I had to sit absolutely silent while he corrected a batch of scripts. I felt petrified. I saw a lean stern face with a mane of silvered brown hair, and a complete indifference to my presence in the small room we now shared. I hardly dared breathe. At last he came to the end of his reading, and swung round on his chair to face me. 'Well', he said, after a minute or so's silent scrutiny, 'Robin Russell tells me I ought to be able to use you in my productions and that you're fairly versatile. What can you do?' This question is one which is absolutely guaranteed to make every fact fly straight out of your head. What could I do, I wondered. 'Come on, come on' he said impatiently, 'What did you do for Robin?' So, hesitantly, I told him about the 'McFlannels', and the Radio Cartoons, and the schools' programmes. 'Can you sing?', he said suddenly. Why was I always being asked this when I so wanted to be a dramatic actress? Cautiously I told him about the Pantheon, and the Carroll Levis show, and he jotted all the particulars down on a stiff card, and said I'd maybe hear from him when he'd considered his revue scripts.

Next minute I was out in the street, walking along by Botanic Gardens, and wondering if that fierce man would even remember my existence by the end of the day. But he did. And he became a much-loved colleague and taught me so much that I can never cease to be grateful for the trouble he took with me. It took me a long time to penetrate that apparently stern exterior, but when I really got to know him, it was his ability to make me laugh with his tantrums and theatrical scoldings which were most typical of our relationship. The first summons I received from him was to become one of half a dozen actors who were to sing and play all the characters between us in a revue called 'Lights up'. There was Madeleine Christie, Charlie Brookes, Janet Brown, Edith Stevenson, Moultrie's wife Ruby Duncan (a brilliant pianist), and me. Ruby thrilled me to the marrow the first time she heard me sing a solo piece, by volunteering to transpose the number to a lower and more suitable key. For *ages* I'd tried to have this done in the Pantheon, and nobody would listen to me. Ruby, who read music as easily as I read shorthand, actually transposed in her head, even with five sharps! I breathed over her in ecstasy and became her devoted slave. Those who have read elsewhere* of my attempts to master the piano will realise how unstinted was my admiration of this talented lady. And not merely because, thanks to her true assessment of my vocal range, my voice seemed better than it was, but because she was a musician to her quicksilver finger tips. How lucky we were to have this expertise at our service. It was all the greatest fun, in spite of microphone nerves. We did burlesques of well-known numbers, changing the words to our own comedy mood. We did little black-out sketches. I sang duets and solos, and gradually lost my fear of my own solo singing, and I played everything from wee tough boys to elderly refined ladies.

We did all our own sound effects in the studio in those days. gurgling water, marching up and down on gravel, banging doors, rattling tea-cups, doing train-hooters with our throats, and bleating like sheep. Later, when war was a memory, and the sound effects were done from a separate studio, with only a flashing light to indicate that the effect had taken place, it seemed flat and unnatural and took a great deal of getting used to. It was far more exciting to me to be dashing about the studio and clattering things and then rushing back to the microphone to fit in the dialogue.

This was the period known as 'the phoney war', for while we were in a state of war, there was an uneasy lull when nothing seemed to be happening. We had rationing, we had black-out, and men drilled and practised Air Raid Precautions, and there was a body of men called the Local Defence Volunteers who were to deal with local situations as they occurred. I was determined to go down fighting if the Germans parachuted down, and I carried a pepper-pot to blind them if they got within firing distance. For me the worst thing was the black-out, for I have always suffered from claustrophobia, and when the darkness closed down, I felt suffocated. I was certain if poison gas was used, I'd be the first casualty. I used to practise holding my breath as the tramcar passed the Chemical Works on my way to Springburn to see my mother, and I was always the first to cough. I just knew my lungs would never stand the test. In fact I volunteered to walk through a test caravan wearing a gas mask, not

* BEST FOOT FORWARD.

79

only to see if it would protect me against the tear-gas which had been sprayed in the test chamber, but to see whether my claustrophobia would allow me to keep the mask itself on. It didn't. I tore it off, and emerged into the street gasping and choking, blinded by the tear-gas, and made the family promise that if poison gas was ever used by those hellish Germans, they had my full permission to push my head in the oven and get it over with quickly.

There was very little entertainment in Glasgow at that time, and the soldiers were mooching around with nothing to do. Moultrie had the brainwave of putting on a revue in the Lyric, and as it was based to a large extent on our radio revue, I was invited to join the cast. The cast was augmented by the addition of Nan Scott, Willie Joss, Jimmy Urquhart (Glasgow's Jack Buchanan), Grace McChlery, and Alec Ross. Alec and I were the ingénues, and did all the romantic numbers, which sent me into ecstasies because for the first time I was able to wear floaty romantic dresses. Oh and Ian Sadler was with us, pretending to be a foreign soldier to my wee Glasgow hairie. While we were rehearsing, Willie Joss and Nan Scott decided that one of the sketches which had been written for them wasn't working as it ought to do, and Willie felt the part opposite Nan should be played by a girl. I didn't know the stage producer at all, and in fact I knew none of them well enough to be able to ask for the part, but oh how I coveted it. I started praying, always a positive help when I want to move mountains. 'Please God, let the man give it to me. Let him give it to me. Please God'. The producer looked round us all, and I suppose I gave God a helping hand by looking so eager and beseeching that the producer decided to take a chance. 'Would you like to try it Molly?', he asked. Would I! It was a riot from the first read-through. It was called 'The Girls of the old Brigade' and we were two tram-conductresses in the uniform of the first world war, who emerged from retirement to do their bit in the second holocaust. Nan Scott, the knowing one of the pair, was a tall vigorous blonde with a fine physique, long hair which she wore in a little knot at the nape of her neck, and a Cicely Courtneidge attack. I played the little naïve one, to whom she was showing the ropes, and we sang a catchy little song to open and close the act, and made our exit after a snappy tap dance, with me leaping into Nan's arms and being carried off.

We borrowed first world-war uniforms from Glasgow Corporation, with the old cheese-cutter hats, and I may say these clothes were borrowed dozens of times by us during the course of the war, for our 'Girls of the Old Brigade' was played by us all over Scotland.

And it was thanks to that sure-fire duet that I had the good fortune to tread the boards with the great Sir Harry Lauder. There was no entertainment at all on Sundays, and it was decided that to keep up morale, the Kings Theatre would open experimentally for a single Sunday evening, and put on a variety show with all the stars they could rope in. As there was no certainty at any time that bombs wouldn't disrupt communications, and London artists might find themselves miles from the Kings at the right moment, local acts were drafted in, and Nan and I were asked to appear in our Tramcar number.

I was in a fever of nerves that the theatre would be empty, for no advertising was allowed in case the enemy would get wind of the fact that hundreds of soldiers would be under the one roof, and would treacherously drop a bomb on us. I kept pestering Nan, 'But how will anybody *know* there's a show on?' I couldn't see how they could possibly guess, when there had never been such an entertainment before. In my youthful ignorance, I didn't realise that in entertainment-starved Glasgow, the word would get round as though the Fiery Cross had been employed to carry the news to all.

We didn't know who would definitely be on the bill, because again, for safety's sake, we hadn't been told and we only found out when we turned up for Sunday morning's band call. This time I rejoiced in the knowledge that we had play-on, play-off music, just like the real turns, and with all the nonchalance acquired after a week's experience at the Lyric, we bade the orchestra speed up or slow down just where we wanted such change of tempo. Somebody whispered behind a cupped hand 'Sir Harry's on the bill tonight'. I stared in delighted surprise. 'Sir Harry Lauder?', I gasped, just to make sure there wasn't another Sir Harry, and I wasn't building up my hopes for somebody else. 'Who else?', said the informer.

The theatre was packed. The tom-toms had sounded all right. The audience were practically hanging from the chandeliers. I'd never performed for a troop show before, and the deep masculine buzz made the stomach turn over. Bernard Miles was on before us, with his wheel, and his country yokel character and went down well. The curtain rose again with our two chairs in position, and there was a roar of laughter when we pranced on, me up to Nan's elbow, marching in strict tempo towards the chairs, and sitting down right on the down-beat. The troops found us hilarious, and when we came off we hugged each other, starry-eyed. It was then the idea was born that we had an act which we could take anywhere. For the applause came from people who didn't know us, and we were being judged against really top variety acts. 'Molly my girl', laughed Nan, 'We've got an act, we have. Tell the man in the Corporation when you return the uniforms, that he must keep them in readiness for us whenever we want them.' He did too.

Our own turn safely over, we could wait in the wings to watch the great Sir Harry.

I saw a little old man being cossetted and protected by his niece Greta, from whom had come the strict command that none of us must attempt to speak to him for he was very frail, and needed all his strength for the show. He was so tottery, and so obviously dependent on Greta for support that I was dismayed. Would the real presence destroy the legend? I started to pray again 'Oh please God, let the troops not give him the bird. Let them be kind to him. Let them not give him the bird.' What an idiot I was, and how little I knew of true star quality. The moment he heard the opening music Sir Harry, like an old war-horse scenting battle, lifted his head, seized his curly walking stick, and jigged on to the stage. He was greeted by a roar which shook the chandeliers. 'I love a Lassie', was followed by 'Stop yer Ticklin' Jock', then on to 'I'm the saftest o' the family', 'Bell o' the Heather' and so right through a repertoire which we all knew and loved. It was electrifying. It was magnificent. And still the boys roared for more, and we in the wings clapped and stamped and cheered, proud to share this historic moment when we'd witnessed the miracle of an old man re-charged with the vigour of youth, and who was displaying for us all the artistry acquired through a lifetime's experience.

They wouldn't let him go. But Greta was watchful, and gave the signal that this was to be the last encore. She stood with chamois and cooling lotion to dab the perspiration from his face on each exit, and she knew the exact moment when enough was enough. The applause thundered round the roof, and under it a little old man tottered past those of us who stood applauding in the wings. A little man who now looked as though the mechanism had wound down but who, while the magic lasted, had given us a glimpse of greatness. I'd have loved to have spoken to him, but Greta shook her head imperceptibly and we let him go without a word. But I am sure he saw the love in our eyes as we applauded his passing, for he gave a little smile and a nod, before vanishing from our sight. 'Well', I said to myself, 'You might not have said a word to him, hen, but you can always say that you once trod the boards with Sir Harry Lauder, and that's something no' everybody can say!'

That was only the first of many shows we did for the troops. Moultrie and Ruby organised them, and we did shows under various titles, like 'Salute the Soldier' concerts, 'Prisoner of War' entertainments, 'Salute to the navy' shows. We ranged quite far afield, and when Stirlingshire seemed a good central base for our week-end activities, we stayed at Moultrie's lovely house in Blairlogie. His pre-war hobby had been buying and re-conditioning old cottages of charm, and selling them, but whatever his original intention had been regarding the Blairlogie house, the war effectively put a stop to thoughts of moving, and so we all enjoyed staying in this little jewel of a cottage. The feeling of being in real country was a benison in itself, after the dark pressures of Glasgow tenements, when the drone of bombers conjured thoughts of tons of masonry on top of us. In the country, the stars shone comfortingly and all that beautiful untenanted space was a solace to the mind.

But it was really quite a small house, although it seemed large to me after tenement life, and we all had to double up for sleeping accommodation, and I found myself one night with Madeleine Christie. I was snug as a bug, but at breakfast time she stared at me accusingly. 'I will never share a bed with that one again', she said, 'I've spent my married life training my husband never to put his feet near mine. I can't *bear* people's feet. And now, I've had the misery of pursuing feet chasing mine all night.'

I thought she was joking, and gave a shout of laughter at the thought of anybody worrying about a bed-mate seeking warm feet. I'd always done this with my grannie and my mother, and we were all used to coorying together for warmth. 'There's nothing to laugh about' she told me wrathfully, 'I was pursued to the edge of the bed, had to get up and walk round the other side, and had no sooner settled down than the whole thing started again'. I was practically in hysterics by this time, and everybody round the table thought it was a great joke, but not Madeleine, who was sleepless and cross.

I only appreciated how seriously she regarded my conduct when she refused to sleep in the same bed the next night, and preferred a mattress on the floor of the lounge! It was a terrible humiliation. I didn't mind so much about chasing her feet, for after all I was only in search of warmth, but that hadn't been my only crime. It seemed I had also snored. It was unfeminine and shame-making and the memory has haunted me to this day. It didn't affect my feelings towards Madeleine, who has been a dear friend down through the years, but it dejected me to feel I was still miles away from the sensitive lady-like susceptibilities shared by those posh office colleagues and by others nurtured in a more hot-house atmosphere than mine.

But I had a wee triumph when we visited a big military hospital. Madeleine was the acknowledged singer of the company, for although we all shared solos and chorusses, hers was a lovely soaring soprano of a most pleasing quality. She sang ballads and good semi-classical pieces, and had little interest in or knowledge of the 'standards' of the day. So when, at the end of our show, we went round the corridors of the hospital and the boys in the wards were asked to shout out any requests, it was I with my snoring tonsils who knew all the words and music of the pops. The accoustics of the high corridors flattered my voice bewitchingly in my ears, and I belted out 'Paper Doll', 'If I had my Way', 'My Ideal', 'All Alone', and 'The White Cliffs of Dover'. And when I finished up with a soulful 'I haven't said thanks for that lovely week-end', I was met with gratifying whistles and cheers from the unseen lads in the wards.

Madeleine raised her eyebrows, and said, most generously, 'Well, I can see I'll just have to learn the words of that type of song if we are going to do more shows of this sort'. 'I'll teach you Madeleine', I said eagerly, 'If you don't tell anybody I snored!'

7

SHORTLY after this troop concert, I was invited by Ronnie Munro to join the girls who sang on radio with his B.B.C. dance orchestra. That really put a feather in my hat. Fancy me singing with a dance band! There was Janet Brown, who later became so well-known as an impressionist, Ann Rich, who also sang with the Locarno dance band and later was in ITMA, Edith Stevenson, and me. Ronnie and I sang all the duets popularised by Elsie Carlisle and Sam Brown, and I did solo swing versions of the Scottish songs. Ann and Edith sang the romantic ballads, and Janet and I did the comedy numbers.

Ronnie particularly cherished my deep hearty laugh, and wrote songs for me, where I did nothing but laugh in tune and to the rhythm of the music all the way through. It was the first time I realised how exhausting laughter could be. Really strong laughter is quite a violent assault on the diaphragm, and it also uses up a tremendous amount of oxygen. After some of those laughing sessions, I used to reel from the microphone, dizzy and spent. But everybody seemed to enjoy them, and I'd never have dreamed of saying anything was too much for me. It was all tremendous fun, and even if I had never learned to play the piano properly, those sixpenny lessons were now paying off, for I could at least read music, something absolutely essential for quickly learning new tunes. I could hardly have asked a band leader to translate the numbers into doh-ray-mees!

Meg Buchanan had a lovely old Scottish saying, 'A gaun fit's aye gettin',' and so it proved with me as far as working for the B.B.C. was concerned. Somebody would spot me in the canteen and would be reminded that I was around, would ask for me for their next production, and soon I seemed to be working for everybody, from schools to the variety orchestra. All this was in addition to looking after a house and a job, for nobody at that time considered that mere radio work was helping to win the war, or indeed was work at all. And looking after a husband, which had once seemed a full-time occupation, was now taken on the wing as it were. We were all getting married.

Brother Willie was first from our house, and vanished into the bosom of his in-laws, who had a nice little house with a garden not too far from Springburn, and as his was a reserved occupation my mother had no worries about him being killed by 'thae black-guards of Germans'. She herself returned cheerfully to munition work, and was quite rejuvenated at finding herself in dungarees once more, and working with machinery. Like me, she hated the black-out, but she worked on night-shift quite frequently and preferred coming home in the light of morning, never giving it a thought that she was in much greater danger of being hit by bombs in the munitions' works than in the unwar-like tenement where she usually shared a shelter with the other neighbours.

While he waited for his call-up papers, Tommy decided to accept my offer to teach him shorthand, which we both felt would be a great asset to him as an embryo writer, and I also taught him to use the typewriter efficiently. He came out to our house on the other side of Glasgow for those lessons, for I was now married to my Sandy, and we had taken the enormous plunge of starting to buy a house of our own. Considering the state of our finances and the times we were sharing, it was a tremendous gamble, but I had lived in a tenement all my life, and I flatly refused to consider adding a wedding ring to that engagement one unless the offer included a house with a garden. I didn't care how small the house was, but it must have a place where I could grow things, and feel the soil between my fingers. I think I inherited this love of growing things from grannie, whose skill with sick or wilting plants was the envy of our tenement neighbours, and who could prolong the life of cut flowers beyond all normal limits it seemed.

Our budget was as tight as a drum, and if we bought a bar of chocolate, then we had to walk into town for there was no extra for fares. I remember the very first meal I ever cooked cost a shilling. I had gone down to the local butcher intending to buy a nap bone and a half-pound of hough, to make soup and potted hough. The butcher, sensing I was a new customer, held up an enormous bone hanging with meat and said 'Sixpence to you, hen'. I gazed it with a calculating eye. There was enough meat there to make the hough.

86

I took it and bought no meat. Sixpence-worth of vegetables in the shop next door were more than enough to make a grand pot of broth, when added to the beautiful hough stock after the meat was cooked. That soup was the first course, and a shining mould of hough was the second, and few things have given me more pleasure than the sight of that mound of shimmering jellied meat achieved without even a hint of artificial aids like gelatine, and costing only the price of the gas which cooked it to that tender stage. For of course a bone like that would have cost sixpence anyway.

However, I set an impossible precedent for the rest of our budgeting, because however economical I was in later years, my husband would say with a smile, 'Aye, but you've never come up to that first shilling meal!'

I was so keen on the idea of a garden, that before we even had a stick of furniture, I had obtained hedge cuttings from somebody in the office, and broom cuttings from my fiancé's colleague, and there we were with an empty house, digging away at the virgin soil and planting our little gifted treasures. I could see from the corner of my eye our future neighbours gazing at us in astonishment from upstairs windows, for most newlyweds scrubbed out the house before they thought of the garden. But I didn't care how eccentric they judged us. I was working in my very own garden—at last! The hedge drooped and perished but, undeterred, we planted another and it survived.

And what a boon that treasured garden was when vegetables became as scarce as hen's teeth as the war progressed. Neighbours used to come in and help themselves to the leeks, enormous beauties with thick white flesh as broad as a fair-sized wrist. They reasoned, quite rightly, that I'd never get through that lot by myself, for my husband was by this time in uniform, far away, and very pleased with the rows of golden wonders and fine onions he'd left to eke out my meagre rations. Black currants provided jam made with the precious sugar saved from my one ration book, and wallflowers filled the vases in spring, and graced the tables of neighbours when husbands came home on leave.

I planted fifty crocus bulbs in defiance of Hitler's bombers, and my proudest moments were when people stopped to admire the display. They were like a brilliant flag painted by nature, shouting defiance and proclaiming that this tight knot in the stomach wasn't fear. Few people had had the heart to plant bulbs during that awful autumn, so ours stood out and gladdened many hearts at that particular time when other gardens were bare. Never have a few shillings

87

been better spent, even though I knew really I couldn't afford them.

The neighbour's little boys, toddlers, brought their little spades to 'help the lassie' dig for victory, because, as they told each other, she hadnae a man at hame. One 4-year-old, a Jehovah's Witness, sternly took me to task one Sunday for picking black currants, and refused to help the little team I'd gathered around me. I explained solemnly, controlling my amusement, that God had grown the currants, that it was a sin to waste anything in war-time, and that as I was out working during the week days, I must pick them when I had the time for such work and also the time to make them into nourishing jam. He listened with great seriousness, then left to consult his parents. He was back in a few minutes with a bowl, 'It's all right', he assured me, 'My mammy says God understands.'

Incidentally it was this same wee lad who ferociously crushed my one and only surving anemone and scattered its petals to the wind. I was quite shattered. Surely the devil must have got into him. I gathered my little band of toddlers round me and put the culprit in the middle. I told him he had done a very naughty thing, for he had destroyed the pleasure for all of us in a beautiful flower, for a moment's destructive satisfaction. That now nobody could enjoy its beauty, and all the waiting for the moment of flowering had been in vain. I was fairly carried away by my sermon, and said that God meant his garden for all to enjoy, and that we were fighting the Germans to keep our homes safe and happy, and God had made the little anemone flourish to encourage me to be bright and happy. Now it was destroyed beyond all recovery. They all listened intently, and I finally forbade the vandal from playing in my garden for 24 hours. God banishing Adam couldn't have had a more powerful effect. I had to harden my heart when the little figure accepted the verdict with dignity and turned and walked slowly down the path, while the others returned to their play round the currant bed. But I felt he would never forget how hurtful it was to destroy living grow-ing flowers meant for all to enjoy. And I know I was right. After a day had elapsed, he was back, with no hard feelings on either side, and when his dad came home on leave it was his mother who picked my flowers without permission! Not the boy. He had truly learned his lesson.

Even with a war on, the builders had managed to keep back a few essential men, mostly judged Grade C by the powers-that-be, to attend to the multitude of little repair jobs inevitable with any new estate. My mother never ceased to marvel at this arrangement. 'Fancy no' having to wait for the factor for a' thae wee jobs', she would say, 'and that smert wee man at yer beck and call'. The smart wee man she so much admired had a running battle with the foreman, for as well as all the official jobs he was employed to do, he earned an honest shilling on the side for all the countless tasks which only a man seemed able to tackle. What did newly-weds know about cracked cement, or stiff window fastenings, or a boiler which wouldn't heat the water?

On top of all this, he was always delighted to tell us how rotten the houses were. He hadn't built them. He'd just been called in when the damage was done. It was he who had alerted me to the unsafe state of the concrete slab at the foot of the front-door steps. He'd seen me working in the front garden, cast a furtive eye up and down the road to make sure the hated foreman wasn't lurking anywhere, then dropped his hammer with a hollow thud on the concrete. 'D'ye hear that?', he'd asked conversationally. 'Hear what?', I asked in bewilderment. I couldn't hear a thing except the wireless next door. 'Hollow', he spat, expertly, right into the centre of the lilac bush, 'Absolutely hollow'. I was alarmed, and I could see the look of smug satisfaction in his eyes as I asked him what I ought to do about it. Again came the darting glance right and left I was to learn to know so well, 'If you keep your bl . . . . ., eh, your mooth shut, I'll get the stuff and make a right job of it for you'. This was followed by a scowl, 'But nane o' yer talking to the other neebors noo, if you don't want me to get the sack'. He was only 4 feet 8 inches or thereabouts from the top of his wee bald head to the toe-cap of his tackety boots, but his energy was so ferocious that I gladly swore utter silence, and crossed my heart and hoped to die to prove I would keep my word.

'That's a' right then', he said, and in due course the slab was strengthened.

That was only the first of the many 'side jobs' he did for me. For if I didn't find anything for him to do, he found it for himself. And he made sure I appreciated the quality of his craftsmanship, and didn't overlook the finer details which an ordinary woman couldn't be expected to observe unless an expert like himself pointed them out. 'See that red stuff ah've put roon' yer windaes?' he would ask, cocking a loving gaze towards the mess round the glass. 'Well, that'll keep oot a' the damp this winter. Dear stuff mind you, but there's naething' tae beat it.' With a vice-like grip of my arm, he whispered hoarsely, 'I don't put it in every hoose, ah can tell you'. I had a feeling he liked me because I was so close to his own height. I'd hardly ever met anybody as small as myself, and I could appreciate his pleasure in finding somebody with whom he could literally see almost eye to eye.

But if I was a favourite, this didn't mean he was going to buoy me up with false hopes about the property. 'Rotten hooses thae', he would say pensively, gathering ammunition for another satisfying spit, 'I've been on many a dud job, but thae hooses . . .' When I found the spirit to argue back that the building society couldn't have thought so or they wouldn't have lent us so much money, and that anyway it wasn't very nice of him to condemn so heartily the bricks and mortar to which we'd pledged our financial future for the next 25 years, if we lived that long, he was all sweet reason. 'Whit else could youse dae?', he would say, throwing his arms wide in a dramatic gesture I couldn't have bettered myself on the stage, 'Youse canny get a Corporation hoose. And if you MUST have a modern hoose and a garden, well, youse have just got to pey oot braw saut for the trash they've put up for mugs like youse'.

Before I could stamp off in annoyance at being called a mug, he would launch into his adventures in the Kaiser's War, when he'd been in the Bantams and when, according to him, he'd sent the troops up the line wi' a guid hert because of the excellence of his cooking, and the unfailing supply of hot cups of tea at any hour of the day or night. It seemed he never slept. And the lads appreciated it.

He told me with great relish of his strength and his toughness. 'Aye, there was wan time when ah wis the only man oot o' the hale regiment that hadnae the 'flu. And nae wunner they a' had it, staunin' in a' that water by the 'oor. Water up tae their oxters, so they had'. I smothered a smile, which I disguised as a cough, as I imagined that with a normal-size soldier this would have been about knee level. He would smile nostalgically, 'Aye ah wis in the Bantams. Wan o' the toughest regiments in France'.

I thought there was no such regiment, but when I asked my mother, she said that indeed there was, so maybe it was all true although I could hardly really believe he sent regiments of Bantams into battle, their innards lined with his special Yorkshire pudding.

But the best laugh he gave me was when he confided in me about his romance. This confidence was only exchanged after he'd done about a dozen little unofficial jobs, not one of which had reached the foreman's ears, so he felt he could trust me. He had been courting a widow for three years, it seemed, 'Seeing her regular, every Setturday night, takin' her tae the pictures, and staunin' her a fish supper'. He would never have spent such sums on ony wumman unless he had been deadly serious, he told me. And I believed him. Anyway, one night arriving unexpectedly early, he had found a rival sitting in his favourite chair. The Jezebel had been deceiving him. Him! The pride of the Bantams! 'What did you do, Jock', I asked, 'Was there a fight?' I expected to hear he'd massacred the other man, for, after all, I'd listened to tales of his toughness for weeks. 'A fight?', he echoed incredulously. 'For a craitur' like yon? Not on your nelly'. 'But you must have done something, Jock', I protested. 'Dod, I just turned on ma heel and walked oot o' the hoose and doon the stair, and I never saw her again fae that day tae this.' I clapped my hands in delight. I could just see him do it too. He smiled at me loftily, 'Oh she wrote and tried to get me back'. The lilac bush quivered under the assault of another fierce jet of spittle. 'Aye, she knew a good man when she saw him, but nothing doing! Once bitten, ye ken'.

In spite of my approval of the way he'd handled the whole affair, the memory seemed to infuriate him all over again and he included me in his contempt for the whole unstable silly sex. 'They're a' the same', he said bitterly, 'If they're no' cheatin' you, they're talkin' too much an' getting ye the sack'.

'I like that!', I said indignantly, 'You're just as big a blether as I am'. He gave me a prodigious wink and a dig in the ribs, and I wish I had known this was to be our last conversation, for I'd have managed a wee tin of tobacco for him somehow. 'They'll have been thinkin' you and me were winchin' wi' a' the cracks we've been havin', eh?' We both laughed in slight embarrassment at this almost personal witticism, the first he'd ever knowingly made, and I might have guessed then that the Grade C's had been called up, and he wouldn't be left on the estate on his own. He balanced his tool-bag on top of his workman's bunnet and walked leisurely up the road and vanished over the crest of the hill. Wee Jock, the only Bantam I had ever had the pleasure of knowing. I kept waiting and waiting for him to reappear during the following weeks but he never did. And when the foreman's little hut disappeared, I knew I'd seen the last of Jock. It was terrible to know that there was no spare man to whom I could turn if I was in trouble, for by this time practically all the husbands had gone, and those who were at home couldn't be expected to chase round after all the rest of us with problems on our hands.

I was very frightened of going into the house alone in the black-out, and this fear led me to the daftest adventure one night. It was very late, because I'd been at the B.B.C. in a play which of course went out 'live', as everything did in those days. With London under constant bomb attack, we in Glasgow were liable at a moment's notice to be told to take over because the studios or the artists, or both, in the South were unable to go on the air. Working in the garden, I'd hear the 'phone ringing. The acquisition of the telephone was a great adventure, and a great expense out of my small salary, but it was an essential item of equipment for me living mostly on my own, and it also attracted B.B.C. work because they could get me on the line. Often the call would be from Moultrie. 'Get here as quickly as possible', he would urge, 'We're on the air tonight'. I'd rush out of the house, and catch a tram to town and then to Botanic Gardens, and many times we went straight on to the mike without rehearsal, pages being handed to us as they left the roneo machine. No wonder I learned to be able to give a performance at first read-through. These skills were acquired figuratively under fire, the fire that was raging many miles south in London. On my way home on this particular night, it was pitch dark. Not a star to lighten the sky, and not a sound on the hill but my own footsteps. Every window blacked out, with not a chink of light to betray us to any cruising enemy 'planes. And then as I drew near to my own house, I could see a soft glow in the living room. I stopped dead outside the gate. What could be making such a peculiar light? The house was empty. Was it a burglar with a torch? In my rush out to the B.B.C. I hadn't drawn the curtains, and in the surrounding blackness that small light looked menacing. I couldn't knock anybody up, and frighten the life out of them. What would I do? Suddenly I heard footsteps coming over the hill. Never giving a thought to the idea that the approaching stranger might be as menacing as the imagined one in the living room, or that I might be scaring him half to death, I rushed up to him and gasped 'Oh will you come in with me, there's a light in my living room and I'm afraid it might be a burglar!'

It didn't dawn on me either that a grown man could be afraid, but his voice wasn't at all steady as he said, 'I beg your pardon, madam, what did you say?' He was English. He clearly thought he had a nut case on his hands. So I repeated my question. We couldn't see each other's faces at all in the darkness, and if I'd met him in my porridge I'd never have recognised him again. What I *did* recognise was that he wasn't at all willing to enter a strange female's house at that time of night, and risk being bashed over the head by a burglar. And I had imagined *all* men were to be trusted to behave gallantly to a frightened female—except the Germans of course. Anyway, I was getting impatient in spite of my fear, so I said crossly, 'Oh all right, you needn't come in, but stand by the door so that if I shout for help you can raise the alarm'. Would you believe it, he let me go in ahead of him, while he stood cravenly on the door mat. With panting heart I tiptoed cautiously through the tiny hall into the living room, and at once burst into relieved laughter. The small glow which had so scared me came from the radio! I had rushed out in such a hurry I'd forgotten to switch it off, and because I'd left the house in daylight, the light in the cabinet hadn't shown itself.

At the sound of my laughter, the man turned and ran, without waiting to hear another word from me.

But it was a symptom of the nervous tension of the times that a little unexpected light could cause such a situation. I often wonder, though, if that man thought I was an abandoned female trying to lure him into her parlour! When I told my mother about it later, she was scandalised. 'My Goad, he might have been a murderer. If you werenae sae faur from ma work, I'd come oot and stay wi' you for a wee while, but I'd never manage the travelling. You'll just have to get a lodger.'

While I was turning this novel idea over in my mind, an army officer came to the door one evening and said he was looking for private accommodation for some of his men who wished to have their wives up to stay with them for a short spell. It would be good for morale, for the men were getting very bored. Had I any room which I would let? He was an English officer and all his men were from the Midlands or Wales. It was army policy to station men far from their own districts, to ensure there would be no temptation to run home, so the Scots were stationed in the south, and the English in the north. Cautiously I said I didn't want permanent lodgers, but if it were only for a week or so, I would try it and see how we all got on with one another. He arranged for his sergeant and the sergeant's wife to move in the following Friday. Everything in the house was brand new, of course, and he was very flattering about the excellent accommodation I was offering, and regretted that the financial reward must be so small. £1 a week, to be precise, plus the cost of the coal used. £1 a week seemed a wee fortune to me, for they would be supplying their own food, doing their own housework, and I would be coming home to a warm house at night.

When I arrived home that first Friday night, the first thing I saw was a sheet of newspaper spread on the hall linoleum, and a man was sitting on the bottom step of the stairs taking off his boots 'not to make a mess', he told me. The boots were placed neatly on the newspaper, while he changed into slippers. That small incident illustrated my lodgers' attitude to everything. They were fanatically clean and tidy. I've never met a man so well-trained, or a wife so house-proud. In fact, much as I appreciated their careful regard for my possessions, I came to feel she was *too* house-proud. I'd been told by the salesman not to vacuum the new carpets too often, for fear of removing all the soft fluffy top pile too harshly, but that woman vacuumed them every single day, until I could swear I saw the under-threads before she'd been in the house a week. She was pale and thin and dark, and obviously taken aback that I was so young. I wished that I had been a bit older myself, so that I could have had the confidence to ask her to stop bashing our irreplaceable carpets so enthusiastically! This couple seemed almost elderly to me, but I imagine they were in their mid forties.

As there was only one of me and two of them, I quickly came to feel that I was the interloper. I'd dash in from work, swallow my tea, and dash out again, whatever the weather. I didn't like to sit with them in the living-room, as I felt they only had two weeks together and they wouldn't want me there playing gooseberry. One night, as I skipped past the bathroom, I solved the mystery of the little piece of towelling I had noticed lying on the edge of the bath. I couldn't think what it was for, because I had proper cleaning things up there, but now all was revealed! The sergeant was using it to catch the drips from his elbows as he shaved! Was there no end to their carefulness? Fancy thinking of drops of water in a bathroom! I noticed too that they used old gloves when they brought in the coal, and not a thing was put down on the carpet without a paper being placed underneath. I realised much later that it was surely because they were childless and theirs had been a late marriage, that they could follow this pattern of perfection. No young life had ever disturbed the orderly neatness of their ways. At that time I thought it was because they were English, and old.

One pouring wet night as I retreated to the kitchen to allow them to enjoy their meal in privacy in the living room, the sergeant followed me, took me by the shoulders and turned me towards the chair by the fire, very gently. 'Madam', he said, 'Will you *please* sit down at your own fireside. You've never sat in a chair since the day we arrived. You won't bother us'. I wasn't so sure when I glanced at his wife, who was silently serving the vegetables. But I was tired, and I sat down and gratefully stretched my toes to the blazing fire. Coal was strictly rationed, and in very short supply, and we could only have a fire in the evenings, but oh it was pleasant to have it glowing strongly so early, because somebody was there

94

to light it in good time for us all to enjoy its comforting cheer with our meal.

I almost fell into a doze as I sat quietly there, for it was the first time for weeks it seemed that I had actually taken time to relax, and afterwards while the wife cleared the table and washed the dishes, the first time I think she had done this task unaided, the sergeant knelt on the hearthrug and showed me all their family photographs. Their little house and garden, his folks and her folks, holiday groups, and a small snap of their wedding taken outside the church. It was then that I saw they hadn't been married very young, and it was also then that I learned they had had no children. Not only was I relaxed, and rather touched that this serious man was so enjoying showing me his home background, but for the first time his face had lost the look of pathetic anxiety it usually wore. Suddenly his wife's voice cut across his story of his best man, 'Will you please go out and fetch some coal', and as he rose obediently she added 'You've been talking to her for half-an-hour'. There wasn't the slightest reason for it, but I felt guilty. In my own house. Looking at snaps. So I rose and said with as casual a tone as I could muster, 'Oh is that the time? I'm due at my mother's soon. I'd better get my skates on.' I avoided the sergeant's eye as we passed each other in the hall, but I knew these were the one and only lodgers I'd take under my roof. I couldn't endure such an atmosphere, and this if you please on top of not feeling free to sit at my own fireside when I felt like it.

When the army officer came back again to see if I would take another lot, I was pleasant (I hope!) but firm. Impossible, I said. They were extremely charming, the couple he'd sent, and it was probably my fault that I felt like the interloper, but anyway my husband was probably coming home on leave and we wouldn't want strangers around. This wasn't exactly true, but it was as plausible an excuse as I could produce without hurting anybody's feelings and it was strong enough to save me from being talked into something I was determined not to do.

It was after they left that I had my nightmare. Because of my claustrophobia, before I went to sleep I always wound up the thick tarred paper which was my black-out in the bedroom, so that only the curtains and the open window were between me and the night air. And before I closed my eyes I always repeated, in case sirens went in the night and I'd switch on the light before remembering I had no black-out in place, 'Don't switch on the light if the sirens go. Don't switch on the light. Attend to the black-out first. Attend to the black-out first'. So that I know it wasn't a nightmare at all, and it all actually happened. How else can my lack of fear be explained, I who was terrified if so much as a mouse scampered across the kitchen in the dark.

I had put out the light, wound up the black-out paper, and realised with pleasure, half-mixed with fear, that it was a bright moonlight night. I loved the clear washed light it shed over the countryside, but I also knew the bombers liked it too, for it lit up their targets, and moonlight and sirens had come to be synonymous.

I fell asleep almost at once, I think, and when I wakened it was because something had broken into my sleep. I looked towards the curtains moving slightly in the night breeze, and without the slightest fear, but with intense interest, I saw the figure of a man appear through the curtains, pause on the ledge for a second, and swing into the room. He was smoking a cigarette and I could see the drift of the smoke in the moonlight, and smell the tobacco. I propped myself on my elbow, and my heart gave a great bound of pleasure, for I saw that the figure was that of Leslie Howard. Now one of my strongest reasons for ever wishing to become a film star was to meet Leslie Howard. He was my idol, gentle and cultured, a marvellous actor in my opinion, and all the films in which he appeared were the sort of stories I adored.

He came towards the bed, sat down on the edge, and gazed into the moonlight with the dreamy abstraction I'd observed so often in his films. He was so close to my vision that I could see the tweed of his jacket, every thread of it magnified at such close range, and the buttons on the sleeve almost brushed my nose. Not a word was spoken. This trance-like stillness must have lasted for about five minutes, and then with a sigh he rose, moved towards the window again, swung his legs over the ledge, and vanished. I calmly accepted this feat of acrobatics, for my bedroom was about 20 feet from the ground and, strangely comforted and honoured by a visit from my favourite actor, I fell asleep again.

In the morning, the wonder of the visit was still with me. When I opened the back door, my neighbour caught sight of me. She was reading a newspaper. 'Oh, isn't it awful, Molly', she said, 'Leslie Howard has been shot down in a 'plane coming from Lisbon'. It appeared that enemy intelligence had supposed Winston Churchill was on that 'plane, although there were others who said that Leslie Howard himself worked for Army Intelligence and was quite a prize for them, even if they hadn't got Churchill.

I have absolutely no explanation as to why this visitation happened to me. But I am as sure that it did happen as I am of knowing that we won the war. And I never forgave the Germans for robbing me of my chance to meet him in everyday life. I did meet his sister in the casting studios much much later, but I didn't like to tell her of this extraordinary thing which had happened, because I felt it would be tactless to let her know he had chosen to appear to me who hadn't even met him, and not to his own family who loved him.

Apart from the black-out and the air raids, the most frightening one of which was the intensive bombing of the Clydeside shipyards and Clydebank itself, when the sky was ringed with fire and which I spent huddled in brother Willie's shelter in Robroyston with his family, the worst thing which happened to me was having to go into hospital. I had a blood disorder which required hospital treatment, and the whole thing was a nightmare, from being carried downstairs to the waiting ambulance to the weeks of near-starvation and sleeplessness.

I had never been accustomed to enormous meals at any time, but in hospital I cried from hunger. The food was so tasteless, and half cold when we received it, that my stomach rejected it. I longed for something tasty, and one night the nurses promised they'd share their midnight feast with me. It was to be black pudding, fried, with a wee potato to eke it out. I drooled over it all during the visiting hour, and my mouth watered in anticipation as the smell drifted from their little kitchen through the ward. I waited and waited, not liking to mention it in case anybody else heard me and would want to share the feast too. Ambulances arrived, feet flew up and down the ward, and at length all quietened down. When a nurse came to take my temperature, I whispered, 'Where's my black pudding?' She stared at me in dismay. 'Oh we forgot all about you', she said, 'We had an emergency, and we've eaten it all.'

I turned my face from her, stifling an anguished cry of disappointment, and cried myself to sleep, my stomach gnawed with hunger, emptier than ever before, because it had expected the delight of fried black pudding. It was a bitter moment, not least because mingled with my empty disappointment was shame for my childish tears.

The nurses obviously thought I was a cough drop. This was because I had answered the matron back, something nobody else dared to do. She was a tiny, black-haired woman with a face of stone, who strode swiftly through the wards each morning and evening, her one concern apparently being to check that all the beds were in perfect line. I used to tell the nurses that if we were a row of corpses, she'd never have noticed, so long as all beds presented a symmetrical picture.

After the episode of the black pudding, I abandoned thoughts of help from the hospital kitchen, and begged my ma-in-law to bring me in a wee pie-dish with a morsel of steak buried in mashed potatoes and turnip. When she smuggled it to me, I persuaded a nurse to heat it on top of the kitchen boiler. As I lay there, wearing a smile of happy anticipation for the feast to come, the matron swept in like an avenging angel. She stood dead centre of the ward and called out in icy tones, 'WHO has dared to bring in food, and asked that it be heated on OUR hospital boiler?' Anybody would have thought it had been a bomb which had been brought in, from her manner. I sat up. Shades of Oliver Twist, I thought. In spite of my quivering fear that the wee pie-dish would be swept from my lips as had been the black pudding, I faced her bravely, 'I dared', I said. She stared at me, then came up to the bed, 'And what do you suppose would happen if everyone did such a thing?', she asked, 'The hospital would be in chaos'. This roused me to a biting defence. 'I don't suppose it would occur to anyone else to do such a thing', I replied in tones as icy as her own, 'And I cannot really see what the fuss is about. I find the food abominable, and I am starving. The food is mine, and I demand to be allowed to eat it.' There was a frozen silence. Everybody was terrified of this wee dragon. Our eyes met and locked. 'Very well', she said at last, 'For this once only. But don't attempt to do it again'. I promised nothing, but I knew I wouldn't get away with a second time, although I hadn't really realised I had done anything so dreadful. But the wee pie-dish filled with home cooking was worth the battle. It was delicious. I savoured every tasty mouthful, and at that moment wouldn't have exchanged it for a mixed grill from the Royal Restaurant, not if the chef had brought it to me with his own hands.

My next clash with the matron came during the night, when I had to rise to go to the toilet. I wasn't supposed to do this, but I avoided bed-pans whenever possible. We only had a tiny night light to illuminate the ward, and because of my phobia about cats and my fear that the ward cat might be prowling around in search of scraps, lifted my long nightdress in one hand, and held out my other hand in front of me in readiness to shoo it away if it came within purring distance. All the nightdresses were the same size, and it depended on the shape and size inside as to whether it was tight or loose, long or short. Mine was long by a good six inches. I must have looked like a sleep-walker, with my hair streaming down my shoulders, my eyes fixed fearfully for a prowling cat, hand stretched in front of me, when the doors of the ward were flung open and in walked the matron with a doctor and the registrar. They stopped dead in their tracks, speechless at first, no doubt afraid to waken what they imagined to be a sleep-walker. 'Good evening', I said serenely, hoping to carry if off by sheer calm acceptance of the situation. The matron came to life. 'Get back to bed immediately', she ordered, 'You have no right to be up'. 'I'm on my way to the toilet', I said, 'And I might as well carry on now. It will be quicker than calling a nurse.' And I did. She was furious, and I had a spasm of sympathy for her that I had been so disobedient in the presence of her two male colleagues.

The only time I saw her smile was when she was in the wee cubby-hole in the ward one morning and the light failed. 'Now I see through a glass darkly', I intoned. She lifted her head in quick surprise, and a smile twitched her lips. 'You're well in noo', hissed a nurse out of the side of her mouth when she passed my bed, 'She's awfu' good-living' and you're the first person she's ever met in here who kens her bible'.

Everything is mixed with mercy. I learned one valuable lesson in that hospital which was to serve me in good stead in tricky situations in the future. It was, that if you say anything with sufficient authority, people will believe you. The soldiers used to come round the ward to move the beds when the floors had to be polished, and this sudden lifting movement always made me sick. No amount of pleading to be left in peace had any effect. So I worked out a plan.

Next time, two new recruits appeared and the moment they laid hands on my bed I said firmly 'My bed must not be moved. It stays where it is'. They left it alone. They assumed, as I knew they would, that the order had come from the doctor. And the bed was never moved again all the time I was in hospital. The maids just polished round it, and nobody knew the difference. Except me. On polishing days my breakfast now remained where it was intended to stay, in my stomach.

After that success, I used the same voice of implied authority for everything which I knew upset me. I lay flat, undisturbed by queasiness, when all the ward had to sit bolt upright after lunch. I ate dry bread instead of being forced to accept the oily war-time margarine, and I knew the keenest sense of victory when I won the right to keep my rationed butter in my locker, ready to smear on the waxy potatoes to make them more palatable. It was a heady success, and helped to make me well.

8

WHEN I came out of hospital, although I only had one ration book, I was deliriously happy to be able to buy food of my own choosing once more. All the economies I'd learned in childhood from grannie served me in good stead now, and I could make tasty dishes from the scraps which served as our permitted food allowances. My brother-in-law flatteringly said I was the only person he knew who could make dried egg powder taste something like the real thing, instead of the usual sickening flavour of metal polish. I simply mixed the stuff with milk and seasonings, but blended it with great care, and added the optimism I usually brought to my gardening efforts, and the results were happily palatable.

I used packet soups, like everyone else, but I added rich bone stock to transform them into a tasty and nourishing brew. This passion for bone stock brought my ma-in-law's wrath upon my innocent head, though. My kitchen tended to look like a laboratory, with pots of different sizes full of bones and vegetables which were carefully brought to boiling point daily, all ready for adding their nourishing strength to the basic powders and packet foods which formed such a large part of our war-time diet.

Naturally, when I was whisked off to hospital, the last thought in my mind was of stock-pots, and everyone else was too upset even to think of food, or of checking on my kitchen. Consequently, when my poor ma-in-law visited the house about three weeks later to collect some towels and other items for me, she was nearly knocked flat on her back with the stench of sour and mouldering liquids bubbling in nauseating gassy decay. She was furious. Her normal gentle manner was transformed. I might have prepared the trap deliberately to poison her, from her angry reaction. She banged the towels down on my hospital bed. 'A kitchen fu' o' stinkin' soup', she fumed, 'It was enough to have given me the jaundice'. Every time I tried to explain, 'But ma, how was I to *know* I was going to have to go to hospital', I'd burst into helpless laughter. Which infuriated her all the more. Other people's anger always makes me laugh. Giggling helplessly, I tried to tell her she was being unjust, for nobody enjoyed my soups and stews more than she did, and the secret of their goodness was in the now despised stocks.

She and I were the perfect examples of the wise and foolish virgins. I was always hoarding a wee something for another day. I used to tell her she would turn in her grave if a bomb dared to get her while she had a tin of beans in the larder. She had never been known to keep a single thing for a rainy day. She hated the thought of anything going to waste, so she ate it at once to make sure of it. She was a darling, and I loved her, and it was typical of her large-hearted generosity that she couldn't keep a thing back for what might be a hungrier moment. With ma the time was now. She simply couldn't understand my fears of 'coming to want' and my being so much against eating everything on the ration book at once. I *had* to know there was something left in the larder. I incensed her again, I'm afraid, when I refused to bow to authority and accept what they thought I ought to have for my rations one month. There was a dearth of lean bacon, and an abundance of fat, so the powers-that-be decided that every family must take 2 oz. of fat with their ration. This was all right for a family with several books, but I only had one book and 2 oz. of fat represented half my allowance. With infinite patience and with what I saw as clear logic I tried to explain to the grocer that with four books, 2 oz. of fat was only one-eighth of the allowance, but that with my one book 2 oz. was one-half, and that a single slice of fat with my lean would be just. He kept repeating stubbornly, 'You must take 2 oz. that's a Government order'. Food was getting so short by this time that nobody in their right mind refused anything, but I suddenly felt the time had come to show the strength of my determination, and to demonstrate once and for all that we still had a choice. Greed and hunger weren't going to be my masters. There was a principle at stake. I heard myself saying, 'Oh no I need not take 2 oz. of fat, whatever you or the Government says. I can choose to take nothing'. And I walked out of the shop triumphant, leaving a gaping grocer and a group of murmuring women to shake their heads over my folly.

My ma-in-law was outraged when she heard of it. 'You should

have taken it and given it to me', she said. Maybe I should, but the sight of that grocer's face was worth the gesture. I showed the same royal disdain the month 'they' decided we had to take one pound of rhubarb jam with our ration. Again this meant my entire month's allowance had to be spent on this unpalatable mixture. Home-made rhubarb jam is one thing, the war-time concoction was a waste of my tiny resources. Again the unfairness of such sweeping decisions overcame hunger. With four books, three pounds of varied preserves were possible, and the 1 lb. of rhubarb was merely a fourth of the ration. With me it was 100 per cent. It wasn't fair. I waited until the grocer brought it out from the shelf and started to tear out my jam coupon from my book. 'Wait', I raised an imperious hand. 'I don't want my jam ration this month. I'll wait till next month and have two pounds.' This manoeuvre wasn't really allowed, but the grocer was now becoming nervous that I'd simply vanish down a drain from sheer cussedness in my fight for fairness, for he knew I'd been in hospital and my thinness alarmed him. Or maybe he was just tired and couldn't be bothered arguing. And that month's abstinence was gloriously rewarded for the next month there was a shipment of tinned jam from Australia, apricot and pineapple, and great was my rejoicing when I carried that treasure home. The tins only came in 2 lb. sizes and if I hadn't spurned the rhubarb, I'd never have qualified for one. This tiny victory fairly put new heart into me, and I knew I must be well on the way to good health when my fighting spirit was returning so vigorously.

I was glad to be able to share that jam with my ma-in-law for she had a particularly sweet tooth, so sweet indeed that if I had taken it into my head to have refused sugar, for whatever reason, I think she would have shown me the door! She used to put sweeties in her tea as a last desperate resort when there wasn't another grain to be scraped out of the sugar poke. We were so used to sharing what little we had with each other, that I was astounded when I went to Nan Scott's house one day to rehearse our Girls of the Old Brigade act for a special concert, found that she, her husband and sister all had little separate butter plates and sugar bowls. Because I was Nan's visitor, I shared her rations, and when I inadvertently took a wee piece of butter from her sister's plate during the meal, there was such a howl of correction from all of them that I hastily put it back. I couldn't see our family accepting such strict rules at the table, for if one of us didn't take sugar, it was a piece of luck for the others that they got a spoonful more, and visitors shared the lot.

However, this determination to enjoy their entitlements gave me an idea. The one ration I really hated to eat was the war-time margarine. I hadn't tasted bread and butter as a regular part of my diet till I was 13 years old, but now I loved it, and I didn't mind how thinly it had to be spread so long as it was butter I was enjoying. I knew I could make my two ounces last a week if I kept it solely for my own use so, spurred on by the Scott household's example, I decided that from henceforth my precious 2 oz. was sacrosanct. Everything else I shared, and shared gladly, but my butter was strictly for greasing my own wheels! *What* a difference this made to my attitude towards friends who enjoyed the orgy of devouring their butter ration in one fell swoop. They were now welcome to indulge their taste in this abandoned way without a hint of criticism from me, for when they visited me they ate margarine, and I no longer had to feel resentful watching them devour my butter as well as their own. Fairness was all!

Everybody in war-time had her own particular shortage which was intolerable. With some it was sugar, like my ma-in-law, with others tea, while some people felt a constant craving for bananas and oranges. With my little niece it was what she called 'shell eggs'. To watch her scoop out the contents of a boiled egg was to be reminded of the 'Hums of Pooh' for she hummed joyously as she extracted each spoonful, and only stopped singing long enough to swallow the delicious mouthfuls.

One week-end I told her grannie I would call for Maureen and bring her back to spend Saturday night and Sunday with me, just for a wee change. Travelling with on her the tramcar to my house, we found the lower deck packed and we had to go upstairs. It was a Saturday afternoon, and the entire upper deck seemed to be filled with men, for there were still football matches being played at selected pitches, and they were all obviously on their way to watch the game. Maureen couldn't sit still on my knee, so excited was she to be travelling away from home, and she stood leaning against the far door of the tramcar facing everyone. She carried a string bag which clearly revealed a bottle of a sticky fruit drink, and another which held her milk ration, for she was barely three. 'By jings hen', said a large man surveying the bag, 'I see you've got yer boatles wi' ye. That's no' a wee hauf ye've goat there, is it?' Maureen pressed her lips together, and shook her head. Then in a burst of confidence she announced to the top deck, 'I'm sleeping with my Auntie Molly tonight, and I'm having a shell egg for my breakfast'. There was a moment's silence, then a roar of laughter as an Irish voice said reflectively, 'Begod, I could be doin' wi' both!'

Maureen's face flushed with bewilderment at the laughter, and I bent my crimson face and prayed for the floor to open up and swallow me. But even in the midst of my embarrassment, a corner of my mind appreciated that it was as neat an example of witty repartee as I was likely to hear in a twelve-month. The whole atmosphere had lightened on that top deck, and if Maureen's innocent remark had sent every man jack of them off to their match with twinkling eyes, then my blushes were a small price to pay. Laughter was in pretty short supply just then.

I certainly found it hard to laugh when I had to turn down a chance to sing with the B.B.C. concert orchestra. They were putting on a special show, and wanted me to do some of my quick-tempo Scottish numbers, but my brother Willie had seen me in hospital, decided it was far too much of a strain just then when I wasn't fully recovered, and threatened to ring them himself if I was mad enough to accept. I was quite impressed by this forceful attitude from easy-going Willie, who knew nothing of show business, and so I meekly bowed to his decision. But secretly I felt I had burned my boats, and the B.B.C. would never ask me to do anything again. Never.

But I was wrong. Shortly afterwards Moultrie rang and asked if I would come to the B.B.C. one Saturday afternoon to meet some film people from London. Film people! Magic words to me. I'd always longed to work in films. What could it be? Over tea in the canteen I learned from the youngish couple to whom I'd been introduced that they were starting a Government sponsored documentary film on the life of a young war wife whose husband was fighting overseas, leaving her to work in a factory, to live in overcrowded digs, and who was expecting a baby. The story was meant to illustrate the harsh facts of everyday living in war conditions, as well as the young wife's ignorance as to how long she could safely continue working. Then would come the birth of the baby in the hygienic conditions of a hospital, and subsequent transfer to dirty tenement digs. The film people accepted Moultrie's recommendation that I could act, and they found my looks just what they wanted. It was all to be shot in two weeks and I was given time off work because it was a Government effort. I was to be a film actress! Not on a glamorous set with Leslie Howard. Up a close, and in a house filled with dirty kids. But a film actress all the same.

When I arrived on the first morning at the empty two room and kitchen tenement we'd been lent for the picture, I was terrified to find that it required about a dozen men to shoot the film. And I had never done a film in my life. I would have to learn it all in front of this critical, technical audience. There were men on the lighting, on the camera itself, on the sound boom, men to haul the camera back and forth, one to load it with film, men to move furniture and props around, to instal the cooker from one part of the kitchen to another as the angles changed, and even a man to make the tea. The simplest action became fraught with tension. Even lighting a match and applying it to the gas stove became unnatural, I shook so much. We rehearsed each short 'take' and then shot it. At the end of the first day the director took me aside. 'Molly', she said, 'In rehearsal you're marvellous'. (I wasn't, but she had to say something encouraging to stop me bursting into tears), 'But when it comes to a "take" you stiffen up and all the naturalness goes. What can we do to help?'

I was mortified that I was doing so badly something I had always wanted to do. 'Well', I blurted out at last, 'I'm so frightened I'll make a mistake, and waste all that expensive film, and there's the wages for all those men having to be paid if I don't do it right the first time'. She laughed in genuine amusement. 'Good God', she said, 'Is that all? Look Molly, *they* will make mistakes too. They'll underestimate the amount of film for a particular shot, and you'll have to do it again. They'll ruin your best shot because the sound boom will come into vision. They'll do a dozen silly things because we're all human, and in filming nobody expects you to get it right the first time. This isn't Shakespeare, it's a piddling little documentary, which we must do as well as we can, but it won't lose the war if we spend a few bob extra on it.'

We had stopped for the day, and when she said goodnight she said, 'Now tomorrow I want you to forget the camera, and just be your own natural self.'

Next morning we hadn't been going half an hour when the camera ran out of film. The assistant had under-estimated the length of the shot. I was charmed. The director had been speaking the truth then, and not just saying those things to comfort me. I never from that moment gave the camera another thought. I let them get on with their part of the job, and I got on with mine, and the whole day's shooting apparently showed such a staggering improvement that she re-shot the first day's work, and it was all sheer fun from that moment on.

It wasn't much fun for the rest of the tenants living up that close though. They were livid that their rather posh building was playing the part of a slum for any film, and they were certainly not putting up with the annoyance of lengths of cable running up and down the stairs like snakes, although they had been told this was necessary to provide lighting from our own generator. They also had strong objections to the crowds of men and actors clattering up and down the stairs all day long, starting at the usual unearthly film time of 7 a.m. When we arrived on the third day, a large policeman barred our way, brought in by the tenants. My heart turned over in dismay, for I was sure my film career had come to an untimely end. However, the director smilingly produced our authority, a buff form imposingly stamped by a government official that we were part of the war effort, and the tenement rebellion was at an end.

We had a real slum mother and her six children for the tenement scenes, for hers was supposed to be the house to which I returned after the birth of my baby. Their ages ranged from about 18 months to 8 years, and they were enchanted to find themselves in a house which contained an unknown magic to them, an inside toilet. Every time we went to shoot a scene, we had to rescue one or more of the children from the lavatory, where their favourite entertainment was pulling the chain. The noise was continuous, like a miniature Niagara, and the sound boom couldn't go into action until the last gurgle had been silenced. The mother of this brood was dazed with her luck at not only earning money for all of them, but in having their food provided. This was a 'perk' we all enjoyed. To be free from the nagging planning of our meagre rations was a bonus to be prized above the modest pay packet. Special arrangements for our catering were possible because we were working 'on location'. We had hot doughnuts and tea mid-morning. Meat and vegetables and a sweet were brought in containers at lunch-time, and we stopped for more tea and buns around half-past-three. Those children visibly filled out during the week we worked in that tenement. The mother gave me my most hilarious moment when she told me of her husband's behaviour when he had been home on leave. She had left him to look after the six of them while she had the bliss of a night out at the pictures with her sister. Just to get away from the house for a night had become a craving, for of course she couldn't leave them when he was away. On her return from the pictures, she found all six children sitting up in bed, three at the top and three at the bottom, each smoking a half-cigarette. Her husband groaned at sight of her, 'My heavens', he said, 'I'd rether fight the Germans ony day than look efter this mob'. 'Smoking, Mrs. Clark', I gasped, 'The baby too'. 'The hale six o' them', she assured me. 'What did you do?', I asked curiously, assuming that she would be terrified by the thought of them setting fire to the bed, or ruining their health at such a tender age. 'I just tellt him that if he wis teachin' the weans tae smoke, then he would dampt well pey fur their cigarettes'. That was all it had meant to her. An expensive habit. But I suppose when you live in a condemned house, with water running down the walls, on the tiniest of allowances, everything has to be measured in terms of money. And in spite of poverty, she was a large placid happy woman, and I rejoiced with her at the sight of those children tucking into all that good food, provided so unexpectedly because of a Government film.

On the Sunday, we were filming at the steam wash-house near Gallowgate. At last I was really going to see the inside of 'the steamie', whose interior had only been glimpsed when I was a wee girl visiting the swimming baths and the slipper baths in Springburn.

Again it was a 7 a.m. start, and the wifies who had been recruited were thrilled to be allowed to do their washings free of charge, to feel they were elevated to the glamorous world of films, and to be paid £1 each for their day's work into the bargain. They smiled self-consciously as they thrust clothes into tubs, and later lifted dripping bundles with strong graceful movements from one water to the next, finally gliding in a smooth swooping movement across the line of the camera, their baskets overflowing with clean sweet-smelling clothes.

They had left husbands at home with the children. They had merely been told by the casting director that they were just to do their washing in the ordinary way. As this was something they could normally accomplish in an hour or so, they had assured their husbands they would be home in good time for lunch. They'd get their washing done buckshee, and £1 for their trouble! It was money for old rope! That was what they thought!

Lunch-time came and went. Tea-time came and went. And still the director hadn't managed to get the shots she wanted for the 'steamie' sequence. Once more the wifies had to swallow their irritation, and put the clean clothes into the water and lift them out again. And again. And again. I could see how this offended their housewifely pride, and that for two pins they'd have thrown the ten-times-over washed clothes in the director's face. I think they would really have mutinied if they hadn't seen that the same thing was happening to me, and that I was having to do several shots over and over again until the director was satisfied it was perfect. One of the women said to me wonderingly, as snow was being brushed off my hair for the sixth time, 'My Goad, dae ye earn a livin' at this? I'd rether scrub flairs, so ah wid'. Another said, 'Ma man'll knock the stuffin' oot o' me. Ah've been oot the hoose since hauf-past-six this mornin' an' ah've left him wi' seven weans. God knows whit he's gi'ed them tae eat'. Disillusionment was complete. Weariness filled their eyes and slowed their movements. The clothes felt like lead as they lifted and rinsed them once more. '£1', one of them muttered, 'Ah widnae dae this again if they peyed us in diamonds'. Who indeed would be a film actress, unless she were truly star-struck?

But in spite of the hard work, there was unexpected cossetting which was very much to my taste. As a rule, I had to make my own way everywhere by unreliable tram or bus, and in war-time it was nothing to have to stand for over half-an-hour in freezing cold. So to me, it was truly privileged comfort to be brought back by special coach from all locations, with never a thought of queueing. At the end of each day I was so happy that it had gone well and that I was at last getting the hang of the technique, I sang all the way. I did impersonations of Barbara Mullen singing 'Eileen Og' and 'I know where I'm going' for the especial delight of the Irish director, who found them 'twee' and amusing. But when I at last got into the house, I was so tired I could hardly find the energy to make the tea. Rising at 6 a.m. and working through to at least 6 p.m. seven days a week was a punishing routine, especially when it was all so new to me. And although we were being fed on location, fresh fruit or vegetables were practically unknown at this stage of the war, and there were few energy-producing vitamins in anyone's diet.

And then, just when the finished film had been taken to London for cutting and editing, I came home from work one night and my husband was sitting in the living room. He took one look at my thinness and my pallor, and as he dried my tears of surprise and relief at the sight of him all safe and sound, he said slowly, 'Aye, it's time somebody was here to look after you.'

I hadn't realised how much being independent and facing all fears alone had taken the stuffing out of me, and oh it was nice having the one I needed most to lean on for a wee while.

It was for a very wee while, as it turned out, for this was embarkation leave. At that time, all troops bound for foreign shores were assumed to be going to the dreaded jungles of Burma. To fool the enemy intelligence, every departing serviceman seemed to be issued with tropical kit, so we all feared the worst. Sure enough, my husband was no exception, and we both felt it was surely Burma for him. He had to go to Blackpool for some more training, and to be issued with his overseas kit, and I vowed I'd manage a week-end there somehow, to wave him off. We were all inspired by the example of Vera Lynn, the sweetheart of the Forces, who sang so bravely, 'Wish me luck as you wave me goodbye'.

We had worked out a little code to fool any enemy spies who might tap our telephone line. When he knew it was his final week-end before embarkation, he would telephone and ask if I fancied some shell-fish, and I'd know that was the week-end of parting. I didn't dare tell my ma-in-law of this plan, for even if the artist Fougasse drew his fingers to the bone with cartoons of Hitler and his minions hiding under train seats, or under beds, or up in railway racks, or even in left luggage shelves listening to our every careless word, ma refused to believe that the woman up the stair could be a spy, or for that matter the man in the Co-operative, and she had to say *something* to them when they asked where her son was. Dear innocent ma couldn't accept that although neighbours might be entirely innocent, a casual remark could travel far and endanger a whole ship. Or a whole battalion. I on the other hand believed anything was possible, for hadn't Hitler's deputy, Rudolph Hess, landed almost at the end of our street and been taken to our very own local police station? If they could find Giffnock, there was no knowing where else they might be lurking. So I was very careful, and I told nobody, not even my boss, that I was bound for Blackpool for the week-end.

It was bitterly cold there, and my heart felt numb as I watched platoons of men in Air Force uniform drilling and marching, my own loved one just a blue blur seen through watery eyes. Although it was winter, the fairground remained open, and we sat in empty roller-coasters and pretended we were having a marvellous, unexpected winter holiday. Those stomach-jolting entertainments usually terrified me, but when all was fear, what did one more matter?

We ate shell-fish in vinegar, holding the little plates in blue fingers at wayside stalls. And that night, when we wakened with the queasy sensation that the house was rocking, we thought it was the shell-fish, or a too vivid dream of the roller-coaster. But it was none of those things. It was a small earthquake, the first Blackpool had experienced in its history. Amidst so much that was strange and unreal, this was just one more item, and we wondered if there would be any future for us when we would be able to talk about our earthquake, or if Burma would be the end of everything.

On the train going home to Glasgow, I began to feel really ill. Surely emotion couldn't have such a physical reaction, I thought. I had to change trains and, standing on the darkened platform, I longed to find the courage to go into the buffet and ask for whisky or brandy. But I lacked the sophistication to go in alone, in December, to ask with a Scottish accent for such strong drink. Instinct told me spirits would be the only thing which would stop this shivering pain that gripped me. Years of Rechabite teaching held my feet in a vice on the platform, but when perspiration started to trickle down my arms in an icy stream, I broke loose and tottered into the station bar—only to find that the hours were wrong and they couldn't serve me. Maybe God and the Rechabites were fighting the demon drink and protecting me from myself.

I was thankful only the dimmest blue light illuminated the railway carriage, for I staggered back and forth to the toilet a dozen times between Blackpool and Glasgow. I was ashamed and felt the other passengers must imagine I was drunk. Somehow I managed to reach home, having to get off the tramcar more than once to be sick, but at last I reached the blessed sanctuary of my own bed, and fell instantly into an exhausted stupor. It was shell-fish poisoning, the doctor said, and gave me a line to get extra milk to help build me up.

Nobody had time to be ill in war-time, and I was glad I had a 'Down at the Mains' broadcast for Hogmanay, to keep my mind off thoughts of convoys and submarines, and men floundering in icy waters. I played the wee servant, Teenie Tawse, in this radio series, with Grace McChlery playing the farmer's wife and Willie Joss a pawky old buffer called Old Cairnallochie, and our signature tune was the lively 'Dashing White Sergeant'. On this particular broadcast, we had to sing 'A Guid New Year', and each time in rehearsal when we came to the second verse, and the words 'And may ye ne'er ha'e cause tae mourn, or shed a bitter tear', thoughts of my husband and a Burma grave swept over me and I burst into floods of tears. I was determined to overcome this shaming weakness, but when we came to the actual broadcast, Grace McChlery took me gently by the arm, and opened the door leading out of the studio. 'Molly', she said, 'Don't try. Just stand outside till it's finished, or you'll have us all in tears'.

The shell-fish poisoning must have robbed me of my strength, for I did as I was bid, and stood on the other side of the door, gazing through the little glass panel at them all singing round the microphone, tears streaming down my cheeks. When the song was over, I dried my eyes and went back and finished the scene.

When the first air-mail letter came, it wasn't from Burma after all. It was from the Middle East. Those sun-hats and that tropical equipment had been a cheat-the-Germans subterfuge right enough.

When the first glorious feeling of relief had subsided, I felt mad at the Government for having given us all that heart-stopping worry unnecessarily, and then I slowly had to admit the wisdom behind such planning. For although I was now beginning to believe I had some qualifications for calling myself an actress, I knew that if a spy had been keeping an eye on me during that time of strain and worry, no histrionics of mine could have been so convincing to an onlooker as was my genuinely haggard appearance between the Blackpool farewell and the arrival of that beautiful air-mail letter.

My ma-in-law had been very hurt by my keeping Sandy's departure a secret until he was well and truly on the eve of arrival at his destination, so I now told her he was in the Middle East but kept the exact location deliberately vague. I still felt that Glasgow was hotching with spies, and I brushed up my German at conversation classes, so that I would be wise to their every utterance if ever their path crossed mine.

With my mind relieved that my husband wasn't destined to perish in Burma, I could enjoy all my B.B.C. work again. Gordon Jackson became a great chum, although he was a nightmare to work with because of his tendency to giggle. I remember when we were doing Bridie's 'The Tragic Muse', where he and I were playing the young lovers, and there was a line of Meg Buchanan's where she had to react to finding a body in her bath. Instead of horror, she had to bemoan the fate of her bath, and in a strident tone she wailed, 'Ma bath! Ma bath! Ma GOOD bath!'. Gordon stood opposite me at the microphone, and as soon as Meg howled out this line, his eye caught mine and he burst out laughing, setting me off too. It was a very dramatic moment in the play and the producer was furious. He bade Gordon to stand where he couldn't see my face, for it was to be a live broadcast, as were they all in those days, and he didn't want the atmosphere of the play ruined at the actual performance. Gordon obediently stood close behind me, to be ready for our dialogue, and when we reached the dreaded line from Meg, he laughed so hard that his stomach beat against my back like a drum tattoo, and I could hardly get a word out through my suppressed laughter. When we came off the air, Gordon gasped, 'Oh I hope the public thought it was emotion which made our voices shake'. They did too. I know they did, because many people told me that our terror was most convincing, because our voices trembled so uncontrollably! But I came to dread working with Gordon after that, because once the pattern of laughter has been set, it becomes increasingly difficult to control.

I remember another time when he was sent out of the studio for giggling, and he sat in the control room till he was wanted for his scenes. When he came back for a scene with me, he was determined not to meet my eye in case an accidental glance would set us both off, so he did something we never normally did—he took his eyes right off the script and gazed into space. I finished my speech. Silence from Gordon. I looked up in alarm, and saw he was dreaming. I kicked him savagely on his shin-bone, and with a start he came back to the play and found his line. But in taking my own eyes off my script, I'd now lost my place! My heart skittered with fright. Wildly my eyes flew up and down the page, and just in the nick of time, as he uttered his final word, I found my next speech. That taught me a lesson. Never again would I lift my eyes from the script, not if every actor at the mike dropped dead in front of me.

And by jove, one of them very nearly did drop dead, thanks to a too realistic sound effect while we were playing 'Kidnapped'. The old chap playing Ebenezer was supposed to be having his breakfast porridge when I, playing the boy, came in to impart some vital news. To get the right effect, our producer had had a thin sort of gruel made up, which Ebenezer supped and smacked right through his next speech. Some of this gruel went down the wrong way, and he stood there choking, and uttering strangled whistling noises, fighting for breath. As he was a very experienced elderly actor, I just thought it was wonderfully realistic acting. Only when he rushed from the studio at the end of his speech, and I could see him through the glass of the control room being thumped on the back, tears streaming down his cheeks as he fought to get his breath back, did I realise it hadn't been acting at all, but near tragedy. Again this was a live broadcast, and the listeners must have been most impressed with the quality of that choking scene!

I had never heard the army advice 'Never volunteer'. So it was my own fault when, during the rehearsal of a play, where one of the actresses had to play a consumptive, I found I had jumped right into it with both flat feet. I had piped up and said to Moultrie Kelsall, our producer, 'That's not a consumptive cough'. This was in no spirit of criticism of the actress, but because I couldn't bear inaccuracy. I knew full well and everybody in Springburn knew only too well the authentic cough, for T.B. at that time was very common.

Moultrie laid down his script and raised his eyebrows. 'Oh?', he said, 'Perhaps you'd like to let us all hear what *is* a consumptive cough'. I gave the little dry rattle which I knew so well. He pursed his lips reflectively, 'Well, since you can vouch for it, perhaps you'd like to do it throughout the play?'

It was ghastly. I had my own performance to do, we were at the mike for an hour, and I never sat down. I had to mark every blessed cough on my script, timing it to the other actress's lines, and then clear my throat and get into the character for my own part. At the end of the performance, Moultrie gave me a sly smile, 'Very nice, dear. Very nice'. I smiled weakly back, my throat raw, reeling from nervous concentration. That would teach me not to open my big mouth in future. But it was characteristic of Moultrie that he trusted my judgment about the accuracy of the cough, and that he knew I could be relied upon to fit the coughing to the lines. He was a great man for stretching the talents of any performer, and we all did broadcasts and stage shows for him which extended our range in ways of which we never dreamed we were capable.

By this time, I was well established in my second regular radio series, which was to become a great joy to me and which was to make me a real 'name' in Glasgow, and in Scotland. Helen Pryde, also from Springburn by the way, had devised the authentic Glasgow family called 'The McFlannels', which I've mentioned earlier in this book. Mrs. McLeather, my original part, had been quietly dropped, to my delight, and I was now that wee Glesca Keelie, Ivy McTweed, and Ivy made an enjoyable contrast to the wee douce Teenie of 'Down at the Mains', which I was still playing. I felt I knew everything about Ivy, from the top of her frizzy perm to the peerie heels of her dance shoes, and I devised a sort of basic gallus laugh for her, which apparently was so true to life that I was unable to convince a man met on a journey from London to Glasgow that I hadn't based it on the neighbour round the corner from his house in Rutherglen. 'But you *must* have copied Sadie McPherson's laugh', he kept saying, 'Fur the hale close recognised it the minute you did it. It wisnae just me'. He refused to believe I'd never even heard of Sadie McPherson, much less her laugh, for he was quite certain nobody, but nobody, could have copied such an individual laugh so accurately.

Ivy wasn't the only one with an identifying laugh. She had a bosom pal, 'Giggling Bella', who never uttered a single word during the eleven years the series ran. She brilliantly varied those giggles to sound admiring, frightened, awed, daring or flirty, as the stories demanded, and she was beautifully played by Effie Morrison, later to reach world recognition as Mistress Niven of 'Doctor Finlay's Case-book'.

I was now doing so much radio that there was scarcely an evening or a week-end I wasn't out rehearsing, and my fellow-actors and actresses had become real friends and were great company.

Between times there were the concerts, and I even took part in one from the war factory where I now worked in the typing pool as my part of the war effort. They were glad of my speeds, and it was within walking distance of my home—a great boon. I had always used trains, or buses or trams to get to work, but with unreliable schedules and black-out it was now bliss to have my timekeeping controlled by my own fleetness of foot. One of the older colleagues used to shake her head when she saw me racing up and down the hill, 'It's not *good* for you to rush about like that', she would say, 'You should allow yourself five extra minutes and go at an even pace.' But I just laughed. At that time I must surely have had the heart and stamina of a long distance runner, and a slow pace was something which simply didn't apply to me.

I taught my big friend Mary the words and music of 'Girls of the Old Brigade', and I borrowed the tramway uniforms, for my colleague Mary was near enough the height and build of Nan Scott, my stage partner. We had allowed it to be whispered throughout the factory, via the office boys, that we were doing a very classical number, and we knew the men and women from the benches where the bombs were made were prepared to be bored to tears. We were from 'upstairs in the office' and in their view we were the posh side of the war effort. So they swallowed our propaganda, hook, line and sinker. When they saw us march in wearing the uniforms of the first world-war conductresses, they couldn't believe their eyes. There was a yell of delighted laughter, and we brought the house down when we went into our broad Glasgow patter. They couldn't believe 'thae yins in the oaffice' had it in them! Mary and I enjoyed their smiles and friendship for the duration of the war after that appearance. And my popularity with the management was sealed when I made up a slogan in the 'War Effort Contest', with the winning sentence, 'NO VIC.ORY WITH AN ABSEN-TEE'. This was painted on the factory walls in letters of vivid blue thereafter. But I never got my prize money.

9

I so despised that rich management for gypping me out of my £5 prize for my slogan, especially when they used it right till the end of the war, that I simply cocked a snook at them and became an Absen-tee myself when I got the chance of an interview with John Mills for a part in a new play he was touring, written by his wife. Strangely enough, I had been recommended to John Mills by Leslie Howard's sister Irene, who was casting director for the famous M.G.M. studios and *she* had heard of me through the film director who had done the little documentary picture up that posh close in Glasgow. Apparently the Americans had been delighted with the picture. It was the first time they had been shown anything of the working-class side of Britain. Previously their mental picture of our country had been of Royalty, old lace and polished silver, of country house parties and riding to hounds. They were enchanted to find we had an earthier side, and declared that the film owed everything to the sincerity of the young couple playing the husband and wife. It was an odd sidelight to me that I never even clapped eyes on my 'husband' during the entire film. He was supposed to be a soldier, of course, and all his scenes were shot on active service. When I did meet him after the war, he had to introduce himself to me, and now I see him practically every time I visit the S.T.V. studios in Glasgow, where he works, and we share nostalgic memories of our 'starring' roles in our very first film.

When I received the telegram from Irene Howard asking me to ring her at M.G.M. studios, my heart gave a hop, skip and a jump of excitement. What could it be? Was I going to star in a first-feature film? How had she heard of me? It was my lunch-hour so I flew to the telephone, only to discover she wasn't there. I had to cool my heels until I had finished at half-past-five, for, short of my house going on fire, I hadn't a hope of being given permission to use the office telephone. After work, I raced up the road to the house, got through to the studios and she told me that John Mills wished to re-cast a real Scottish character for his new play. It was an oldish part, a woman of sixty-plus in fact, but she was sure that it would be useful for me to be seen and that if he liked me otherwise, make-up and costume would do the rest. He was in Leeds, and I was to present myself at his hotel at tea-time the next day, and watch the performance that night. The next day was Friday. How was I to get the time off? Not for a moment did I dream of missing the interview. War-time or no, I was determined to see John Mills in person. It was only the carrying out of my plan which exercised me.

I knew it wasn't the slightest bit of good asking off, because we had had a high old drama only a few months back when one of the lads in the office had asked the boss if he could go home to Liverpool for the week-end, as his fiancée was very ill. He had been refused permission, but he went just the same, and when he came back to the office on the Monday morning he wasn't even allowed to take his coat off. He had been handed his cards, and shown the door. This in spite of the fact that we were desperately short of young men of this lad's experience in accountancy. We had counted ourselves lucky to have him, and blessed his flat feet which had kept him out of the forces.

When I came into the main office that morning, after taking some notes from the boss, I found the place in a ferment. Everybody was denouncing the boss, 'As if dogs widnae lick his blood', as my grannie would have said. As I approached the group crowded round the centre desk, I heard wild words of 'all coming out on strike' to show our solidarity with young Len. 'What do you think, Molly?', they asked me, 'You've just seen that old devil, has he said onything?'

I told them, quite truthfully, that he had said nothing to me but that I thought they had no justification for coming out on strike. They stared at me, furious that I didn't agree with them. Patiently, working it out in my mind as I spoke, I said that if Len had simply taken French leave and gone to Liverpool, and returned on Monday morning with the story that he had had a chill, even if the boss hadn't believed a word of it and had suspected a bit of skiving, without proof he could have done nothing. But because we all knew that Len had *asked* and been refused, and had openly defied the boss's authority, then there was no alternative but to make an example of him and dismiss him. It was cruel, I agreed, but in war-time conditions above all, it was absolutely essential that the man at the head of the affairs should be seen to have authority and to have his decisions respected and obeyed. There was silence for a moment or two. 'She's right', one of the older men said, 'Len was a bloody fool. He should never have asked'. As they drifted back to their desks, the boss, who had opened his door during the latter part of the discussion, rang for me. When I entered, feeling quite a heroine for having saved the factory from a strike, which might have left those hellish Japs free to wreak more evil upon us (we were making bombs for use against Japan), I was stunned when the boss informed me that I was far too dangerous a personality to be tolerated, and had far too much influence over the others, and that for me to encourage a strike in war-time was treason! I could feel myself almost suffocating with righteous indignation. 'Encourage a strike!', I cried dramatically, 'I have just averted one, and it was precisely because I knew your authority must be upheld, rightly or wrongly, that I told them they had no justification for coming out'. For good measure, I added cuttingly, for I was well away by this time and had forgotten he was the boss, who could easily sack me, 'Poor Len was a fool. He should never have asked you. But having asked you and then defied you, you had to sack him'.

There was a silence, while my heart thumped, and commonsense returned and I waited to be told to collect my cards. The boss coughed. 'I see', was all he said. 'I'll want these notes typed by lunch-time', and he returned to his desk without another word. Not even an apology for having misjudged me. We had been standing facing one another like boxers, and I found my legs were trembling when I went back into the main office.

So, with that experience to guide my actions, plus the memory of having been robbed of my fiver for my slogan, I made my plans. As soon as I'd swallowed my tea, I rushed up to Springburn, a forty-five minutes' journey by tramcar, and I plotted with my ma-in-law. She would ring the office next morning and say that I had been up all night with diarrhoea (there was a lot of it about, with all the queer food we were eating), and she would tell them that I would be back on Monday if I felt better. I couldn't ask my own mother, for not only was she unused to the telephone with her deafness, but she didn't go home from her work at the munitions factory during the day and would have had no access to a telephone anyway.

Later, my friend Mary told me that when ma had rung to pass on the news of my unreliable innards, the boss had tut-tutted angrily and had said, 'That mother-in-law of hers simply spoils her. She's as strong as a horse, really'. Mary had been let into the secret, for she would have to tackle my work as well as her own, and she told me she had had a job to stop laughing at the boss's reaction.

With the factory deception safely arranged, I packed a bag, remembering to include the solitary pair of sheer silk stockings that brother-in-law Jimmy had managed to buy for me in France before the Germans swept through, laid out my one and only decent suit, a green Shetland tweed that my husband had bought for me before he left for the Middle East, and set the alarm for the morning. I always kept a few pounds in the house to cover emergencies, so I had enough for my train fare.

Next afternoon, when I arrived at the hotel in Leeds, I went straight to the ladies' room and took off the thick lisle stockings which we all wore at that stage of the war. I took the fine dark silk ones, so prudently saved for just this sort of occasion, it seemed, and started to pull one over my toes, scarcely daring to breathe in case a ragged nail might catch a thread and cause a ladder to mar its perfection. Suddenly I was aware of a rustle of movement around me. I had been too absorbed and excited to notice anyone else in the ladies' room. But they had noticed me, and I looked up to find a circle of faces gazing with awe at the fine silk I was pulling over my knee. '*Where* did you get them?', one lady breathed, looking down sadly at her own clumsy stockings. I started to tell them that my brother-in-law had brought them from France, but they weren't listening. They stood as though mesmerized by my legs. They seemed to sigh in unison, and one of them vowed that when the war was over the first thing she was going to buy was a pair of the sheerest silk stockings she could find. As they drifted away, I heard one lady say to her friend, 'Do you know, I had actually forgotten our legs could ever look like that'. So had I, and as I gazed at my reflection in the mirror, I decided that even if John Mills disliked every other thing about me, he couldn't but be impressed by the elegance of such expensive-looking silk-clad legs.

When I went into the tea lounge, I recognised him at once. I was so excited to be greeted by the famous John Mills that I forgot to be nervous or self-conscious. I even forgot my silk stockings. I was surprised to find him such a finely-drawn man, with small bones, a slim build, and a pale look of tension which vanished the moment he smiled. When he did so, his entire face lit up, the eyes, the mouth, and one felt he was basically a witty, humorous man, but that the strains of touring theatre in war-time were perhaps beginning to tell. He was dismayed to find me so young, and found the same resemblance to Janet Gaynor in my appearance that newspapers had remarked, and which at that time was the nickname the children in Glasgow gave to me. He described the plot of the play, and said that while he would be delighted to re-cast the part with a real Scot, he felt it would be a great pity if somebody so young as I was (he also said 'and so pretty' if I'm going to speak the whole truth!) made her début in London in a part which was really for an elderly woman. I would be able to judge for myself when I saw the play that evening, but he added 'You'd be type-cast for good, Molly. Managements would only remember you as they first saw you, and it would really be better to wait to appear in something much nearer your own age'. I liked his assumption that it was only a matter of time before I appeared in London!

Over a delicious tea of toast and tea-cakes he told me what a perfectionist his wife was as a writer, and how often he had had to rescue her work when she chucked it out in disgust. I blushed when he confided, without a trace of self-consciousness, that once she'd actually thrown a play down the lavatory. And he'd fished it out! We didn't talk like that about lavatories in Springburn. He knew how good her work was, but she was never satisfied—a true sign of talent. I could see he adored her.

I heard all about his early days, of trying to pretend he liked office work, and of his struggles to break into the theatre and films, and I listened with my mouth open, drinking in every word and wishing he didn't have a play to do, so that I could have gone on listening to such confidences, straight from the fountainhead, for the rest of the evening.

Still there *was* the play to see, and I had a 'house' seat in the stalls, four rows from the front, free of charge. I found the play thoroughly absorbing, and very strong melodrama. As well as John Mills, the cast included Elspeth March (then the wife of Stewart Granger), and Elwyn Brook-Jones. In spite of my concentration on the part I was being considered for, I soon forgot to watch out for her entrance, so dramatic were all the twists and turns of the plot. When she did eventually make her appearance, I was terribly tempted. She was an old Scottish nannie, fey and spry, with an agile turn of speed on her entrances and exits, and although the part was smallish, it was important to the plot. But oh, could I endure to cram my hair under a wee tight grey wig for every performance, and sit till the third act before I opened my mouth? And did I want to go on playing elderly wifies before I'd even been seen as a young one in London? John Mills' words about type-casting had given me pause, for this was something I had never had to consider in Scotland, where I played anything and everything from schoolboys to grannies.

Afterwards, I was invited to join the party at dinner in the hotel dining room. Not only were the play's principals there, but Florence Desmond had been included, as she was starring at the nearby variety playhouse. I was nearly swooning with excitement at eating in such starry company. I devoured every word they uttered, as though wisdom had been brought down with the tablets from on high. After all, I was with the crême-de-la-crême. These people had all 'arrived'. They were household names. Their world was the world of show business, and I could learn much if I kept my mouth shut and my ears open.

I was specially interested in the theories of Florence Desmond, although I had enough sense not to mention that I also did impersonations. I could recognise a member of the first league when I saw one! And I knew I was in the third division. She was of the opinion that one should only work with the best. Some variety people, she said, liked to be the big frog in the small pond, and to top a bill of mediocre players, because they thought that by doing so they'd shine all the brighter. 'And don't they?', I ventured to ask. 'No, honey', she said. (Honey! What a nice thing to call me!). 'All that happens is that the audience goes out at the end of the show and says "Well, that was a lousy bill". They *don't* say, "That was a lousy bill, but Joe Doaks was all right". What they go out with is an impression of second-rate entertainment and that goes for every act on the bill'.

'Now', warming to her theme, 'If *all* the acts are first-class, not only does the quality rub off so that everybody gives absolutely top performances, but the audience goes out saying, "That was a *marvellous* show. Not a dud act among them", and every name on that bill shares in their memories the magic of a great night out, when nothing disappointed.'

I suppose it was just another way of expressing Shaw's advice, 'Never associate with failures', but I was most impressed with her clever reasoning, and I never forgot it. Later, when I went into the real West End theatre, I found that managements knew this truth too, for few successes included also-rans in the cast-list.

Before we parted for the night, John Mills said to me, 'Well the part is yours if you want it, Molly. How do you feel about it?' When I had left Glasgow, it had never crossed my mind that the choice would be up to me. If anybody had suggested that I would be offered a chance to appear in the West End of London and would have hesitated for an instant about saying 'yes', I'd have laughed in his face. Now I was all mixed up. The seeds of indecision had been sown with all this talk of typecasting. What was I to do? My stomach whizzed with nerves. Suddenly, inspiration came, and I saw my way out of this dilemma. I would just throw it back to him again. After all, he knew far more about show business than I did.

'What would be your advice?', I said. 'What would you do if you were in my place?' He looked at me very thoughtfully, and I held my breath. My life could easily turn completely upside down, depending on what he said next. 'I'm speaking against my own interests in saying this', he said at last, very slowly, 'For I know you could play this part standing on your head, and I badly want to re-cast it, but for the sake of your future, I would advise you to wait'. I didn't know whether to be glad or sorry. He patted my shoulder, 'Wait for the right part, wait till you can be seen as the lively young person you are. Don't let London's first sight of you be in the disguise of an old woman. That's my advice'.

I took it.

On my way to my bedroom I passed the beautiful Elspeth March and she was speaking on the corridor telephone to her husband. I was fascinated to hear her call him 'Jimmy'. Fancy me hearing Stewart Granger's wife chatting to him, and using his private name, and giving me a friendly wave as I passed as though we were chums. And fancy me having been allowed to choose whether or not I'd accept a stage part! A London career did honestly seem a little nearer now. I had been accepted into the acting scene by professional actors, without anybody turning a hair or thinking it in the least odd that I should be one of them. The entire marvellous day and evening had been like a dream. And wouldn't my mother be thrilled to hear I'd actually sat at the same table as Florence Desmond, Elspeth March and John Mills and indulged in show-biz chat as we passed the chips round? I could hardly wait to get home to tell her all about it.

I'd have to calm down, though, before I returned to the office on Monday morning, and try to look suitably peelie-wallie to convince the boss that I truly had been under the weather. This would be a very good acting test for me, to have to save all my news for the evening, when I'd invite Mary home for tea and would reward her co-operation by telling her chapter and verse everything that had happened since we had parted on Thursday. Was it only

Thursday? It seemed weeks since the diarrhoea plot had been hatched.

But when I did get to the office on Monday, I found that Mary had been laid low by asthma, that scourge which felled her with sickening regularity and which prevented her from adding so much as a pound to her slender frame. So there was no need to do any acting to prove my integrity, for it was all hands to the pumps to get through the work, and nobody was paying the slightest attention to my looks, healthy or otherwise.

By the end of the week, I was well and truly punished for my pretended illness, for half the office were down with various complaints, from gastric upsets to bronchitis, and I hadn't a minute to breathe. It was wages week too, and the wee old-fashioned accounts' clerk, whose thin legs and sallow complexion made her the butt of the office boys' jokes, was frantic that she wouldn't be able to meet her deadline and balance cash, books and Income Tax deductions in readiness for the Friday pay-out. Filled with euphoria at having dined with John Mills and Florence Desmond, and feeling I owed the company extra time anyway, I nobly volunteered to come in at 8 a.m. on Thursday morning and help wee Miss Turpentine to get through the work. Her sharp little face filled with gratitude, and I went to bed early to make sure of being fresh as a daisy when the alarm went off.

Next morning as I slowly drifted to an awareness of the day, I decided I must have had a really refreshing sleep for I was awake before the alarm went. 'Mmmm, I reflected as I snuggled luxuriantly into the warmth of the pillow, how lovely not to be jerked to my feet by the whine of that penetrating electric buzzer. Then I became aware of another sound, that of the murmur of neighbours' voices on the pavement outside. Apprehension gripped my stomach. 'What time was it, when they could stand chatting in such a leisurely manner? It must be after breakfast time!' I leaped from the bed. It was broad daylight. There had been a power cut, and the alarm had stopped at 4 a.m. I rushed downstairs and found it was twenty-five-past eleven! ! ! And I had promised that fraught wee soul that I'd be in at 8 a.m.

I threw on my clothes, and didn't even stop to make a cup of tea, but ran all the way to the factory, and I was so distraught that the aloof glare which Miss Turpentine turned on me changed at once to a touching concern. I shouldn't have run like that, she told me, it was enough to make me drop dead. 'I knew something must have happened', she assured me, 'I knew it, because you are utterly reliable'. I had missed the coffee break, and didn't even have the comfort of a hot drink to see me through till lunch time, but my heart was singing with that heart-warming testimonial. How my grannie would have rejoiced to hear such words spoken of me. I had been taught that loyal service wasn't to be measured by the pay packet, and as I was only earning £3 7s. a week, it certainly wasn't for the financial rewards that I felt it necessary to give unstinted service. But I had given my word, and I had a Saturday morning to repay, and I was helping to win the war after all.

After that, Miss Turpentine and I exchanged many a confidence, and when Mary returned to work we often made a threesome when we went for our canteen lunch. She was full of good works, a regular church attender, delivered the church pamphlets, and cared for an aged parent, and she sent Mary and me into hysterics when she unexpectedly decided that she was so fed up trying to get fixed up with a single room for her holidays at sea-side hotels, she was considering spending a fortnight at a nudist camp! If she had told us she was contemplating living in sin with the boss for a fortnight, we wouldn't have found it more incongruous. It was such an original, as well as such an outrageous idea coming from a docile little spinster like her, that it fairly took our breath away. She sent for brochures, and we laughed ourselves into a state of hiccups at the idea of being served tea by a maid quite starkers. Imagination ran riot when we thought of Miss Turpentine leaping about playing table tennis, wearing nothing but a pair of tennis shoes, and we dreamed up hilarious situations where we saw her passing the vicar on the stair and uttering a cool 'Good morning', with not a stitch of clothing between them. Altogether it was the best laugh we'd had since the factory concert, and although we had intended to keep it to ourselves, the news soon swept the factory, and wee Miss Turpentine received many a thoughtful glance for quite a long time afterwards.

Alas, though, the pamphlets unnerved her, and she ended up having a fortnight at a very ordinary boarding house at Rothesay. It was such a pity. We felt quite defrauded that we weren't to hear unabridged tales from a nudist camp after all.

For my own holiday, I decided to take my mother down to Arran to a little cottage owned by my hairdresser. There were no mod. cons. whatsoever, and it was a wonderful contrast to the tenement life of the black-out in Glasgow, so that for once the war seemed very far away. We went to the stream for water for our cooking and washing, and we built our fire in a huge kitchen range, with wood gathered nearby, topped up with the precious coal ration which was stacked behind the cottage. We felt we were really in the wide open spaces when an inquisitive horse, ecstatic at finding company, galloped round and round the place, and even poked his nose right inside the kitchen where we were having our breakfast. We leaped up in alarm, but we soon grew used to him as he daily popped his head round the door to see how we were getting on, and we actually found courage to smack him on the rump to get him out of the way when we came out with a bucket for water. Who would have believed that my mother and I, both terrified of cats, could grow so chummy with a huge creature like a horse? We felt those women pioneers of the West in their covered wagons, had nothing on us!

But it wasn't long before we met our Waterloo. One lovely sunny afternoon, as we crossed the open field which formed our right of way to the shore, our path was blocked by an enormous bull. We were transfixed with terror. Struggling with my fear was indignation that the farmer had allowed such a dangerous animal into this field, when he knew it was a recognised right to cross it to reach the sea. Trembling with fright, and pushing my mother in front of me, I dashed for the gate, beating the bull to it by a short head.

All too soon it was time for me to return to the job in the office of the factory, but my mother had a few days left, and I urged her to stay on in the cottage, and to make the most of this blessed respite from the fear of air raids among the tenements of Glasgow, and the suffocating feeling of the black-out. It was dark in the country too, of course, but it was a more comforting darkness. One could believe God was on our side in the vastness of that sky, and was keeping a watch over us.

When I reached home, I found a most welcome parcel, handed in by my neighbour. It had been left by some Americans who had seen me in the Lyric Revue and who received my address from the Pantheon Club and had posted it on to me. When I opened it, I found bars of chocolate, packets of cigarettes, some peanuts and chewing gum. 'Corn in Egypt' as my dear ma-in-law would have said. It was the one and only time I had a food parcel, and so thrilling to know it came from American 'fans'.

Knowing my mother's sweet tooth, and being only too aware how lonely she would find it on her own in Arran, I at once made up a little parcel with a selection of the American goodies, ran down to the Post Office and got it off on my way to work next morning. My mother told me later that she had been out for a wee walk, and when she was climbing the hill to the cottage she had been saying to herself, 'My, I could go a wee sweetie', but she hadn't even any coupons left to enable her to buy any, nor for that matter was there a sweetie shop within miles. Once indoors, she had sat down by the window, pondering what she should have for lunch when her eye fell on my parcel. She'd left the window up about six inches, and the postman had apparently pushed the little box through.

She had stared at it, and said aloud, 'Noo, where did that come frae?', gazing all round to look for some human agent. Or even a wee fairy. She couldn't believe her eyes when she opened it and realised it had come from me, for I had only left her a bare 48 hours earlier. 'Manna from heaven', she declared, 'I don't know when I enjoyed onything mair'.

As the sage has it, he gives twice who gives quickly, and I rejoiced that this small gift had given her such pleasure. We both talked of that simple little holiday for years afterwards, and when she was in a low mood I had only to mention our meeting with the bull to send her into reminiscent giggles, and set her eyes sparkling with remembered delight over the boon of that coupon-free chocolate.

Such small pleasures became remembered landmarks of joy in war time. Anything at all which raised a smile was doubly welcome at that time and my mother always gave me a slightly scandalised giggle by her total inability to recognise that the word 'bum' might be considered vulgar in polite society. In company, when she was in a particularly chirpy mood, she was wont to burst into the wee song,

> 'There wis a wee lassie
> She cam' frae Camlachie,
> She hurtit her bum on a wee chucky stane.
> A sojer was passin',
> An' filled wi' compassion,
> He lifted her up an' he carried her hame'

It was the comical words which amused her, and the jaunty tune, and it didn't dawn on her that the laughter which always greeted this ditty was due to her unselfconscious use of the coarse word for bottom.

Another one which tickled her, because she loved the word 'spiflicate', and which was mercifully free from any suspicion of vulgarity was,

> 'Jean, ses I, ye're lookin' smert,
> Could ye spiflicate an aipple tert?
> Noo her wee nose was lookin wat,

So ah handed her ma hanky.
Too-ra-loo-ra-loo-ra-loo,
They're wantin' monkeys in the zoo,
If ah wis you, ah'd go the noo,
An' get a seet-u-a-tion.'

It was quite something to watch my mother leaping into her dungarees before setting out for her job in munitions, warbling this infectious song as she snatched up pieces, hankie and key, with a last look at the black-out before she ran down the stairs to go on the night-shift. I saw all this on the occasions when I went over to spend the odd night with her, and I marvelled at how enthusiastically she was throwing herself into the war effort. She adored Churchill, as I did, and although she couldn't hear his words clearly on the radio, for she was very dull of hearing, she could catch the low rumble of his voice and the defiance which ran like a clarion call through every word, and she'd say, with an admiring grin 'The British bulldog. My Goad, he pits new hert into ye.' She despised Lord Haw-Haw and his lying propaganda and got mad at anybody who quoted him, and as for 'that blaggard Hitler', she and the woman next door took him down a peg by referring to him always as 'Hilter.'

Auntie Tassie had a more childish sense of humour, and I could always send her into chortles of delight, by my fast variety style patter, cultivated for her amusement. She would choke over her tea, as I stood up and rattled off like an old-time comic.

'Ah gi'ed her ice cream,
An' she aye screamed fur mair'.

'A gi'ed her macaroni,
An' it didnae mak' 'er ony better'.

'Ah gi'ed her satinettes,
An' she sat an' ett them a' hersel'.'

She was quite sure I was every bit as good as Dave Willis. We all loved Dave, whose song about the 'Nicest lookin' warden in the A.R.P.' had the whole audience joining him in the chorus and yelling out 'An aireyplane, an aireyplane, away 'way up a kye.' He must have sung this ditty a thousand times by the time I worked with him in a B.B.C. programme, where Ian Sadler and I were doing all the voices in a potted pantomime, and I was astounded that Dave had to have the words chalked up on a board in case microphone nerves would make him forget them. It was a revelation to me that somebody who could hold a packed theatre in the hollow of his hands, without a cue to help him, could find a studio mike such a nervous ordeal. I was very thrilled to meet him, and could scarcely believe that this quiet modest little man was the same dynamo who raced on to the stage of the Theatre Royal dressed in shorts, and sent us into a roar with his 'Whit dae ye think o' the legs? Ah tossed a sparra fur them!' Typical Glasgow humour, which I loved, and which could be found in the trams and on the streets, Hitler or no Hitler. I remember one day I happened to be waiting at the tram stop when a dozen cleaners streamed up from the factory at the end of their day's stint. They were marching in a sort of congo line, each with a hand on the shoulder of the wifie in front. As they marched in a sort of jazzing rhythm they sang,

'Fares please, fares please,
You'll always hear me say,
As I go up and down
The tramcar every day.
Oh Ah work fur the Corporation,
You'll know me by ma dress.
Ah'm Lizzie MacDougall,
Fae Auchenshuggle,
The Caur con-duc-ter-ess.'

I burst out laughing. It was pure comedy. A hilarious example of Glasgow sturdy humour at its best. As they drew up to the stop, another of their colleagues joined them. 'Aye', said she, 'Youse urr ferrly gaun yer Acme wringer the day!,' I'd never heard the rhyming slang for 'Gaun yer dinger' before or, as the English would say, going at a tremendous lick, and I giggled all the way into Argyle Street. My heart expanded in a great wave of love for those women. The salt of the earth. Hitler might as well throw up the sponge. He'd never defeat people like that.

I was still laughing when I went into the B.B.C. and Moultrie was greatly entertained when I told him of the incident. But he had most exciting news for me. Alastair Sim, and J. M. Bridie the playwright were in the building, and they wanted to see me, to consider me for a part in a new Bridie play 'It depends what you mean', which was to be put on in the West End of London after a short tour. We met in the canteen, and over a cup of tea they told me the story of the play, which derived its title from a popular radio brains trust programme in which one of the contestants, Professor Joad, always replied to the simplest question with the words, 'It depends on what you mean by . . .'

127

Alastair Sim took one look at me, and turned with a huge beaming smile to Bridie, 'Jessie!', he said, 'She's perfect.'

It was arranged that I would go down to London at a date to be advised later, armed with all the necessary documents to enable me to do the play. For of course I was subject to war regulations, and with my high speeds couldn't just jump out of a war factory into a theatre without a great deal of negotiation. My stomach was doing its familiar somersault, a mixture of fears that the Ministry would never release me, joy that Bridie and Sim had both liked me, excitement that at last I was to appear on a West End stage and, above all, terror at having to go to London which was under constant bomb attack. Then when my excitement died down, I was filled with a gloomy certainty that I'd *never* be allowed to leave my job for anything so frivolous as a play.

I was completely ignorant of the fact that the theatre was considered a great contribution to the war effort as a morale-booster, and I didn't believe Sim and Bridie, those impractical theatre people, that there would be no difficulty in getting away. But they were right. In a matter of weeks, I obtained my release papers. Shortly afterwards, I had a letter from Alastair Sim's London Agents asking me to present myself at their office the following Tuesday, when I would sign on the dotted line. I would then return to Glasgow, there to await the exact date on which rehearsals were due to start. It might be a few weeks before everything was tied up, but in the meantime a day in London would be useful for signing the contracts and having a read-through of my part with Mr. Sim.

I was able to have a day from the holidays which were due to me, so no deception of the boss was necessary this time, thank goodness, and there was no difficulty getting a sleeper on the London train. It was out of the question to think of sitting up all night, for I had a busy day ahead of me, and I had enough sense to know that the saving of the sleeper charge would be false economy on such an important occasion. As I climbed into my berth, I prayed that no spiteful German bomber would score a direct hit on the train, for I was at last on my way. To London. To the theatre capital. There were four of us, two a side on the sleeper shelves of the third-class compartment, and I didn't care what sort of exploits the others were up to, none of them, I was absolutely certain, was bound for an adventure a quarter as exciting as mine. I longed to share my secret with them, but prudence bade me hold my tongue in case speaking of it would put a jinx on my chances. So I lay quietly and dreamed of the future as we rattled through the uneasy darkness towards my goal.

IO

I WAS far too early for my 10 a.m. appointment with the agent, so I decided to walk from Euston towards the West End and find some breakfast in any Lyons' cafe which happened to be open. I hadn't seen much bomb damage at this time, and was quite unprepared for the effect it would have on me. My heart turned over at the sight of bomb-shattered buildings, at the broken glass and boarded up windows, and, above all, at the sight of the indomitable Londoners, many bandaged, many more wearily emerging from underground shelters with their blankets, but all showing obvious satisfaction at the sight of so many familiar landmarks still standing. I was impressed and humbled by their courage, as I watched their eyes rest on the tall buildings, but I grew so nervous at the prospect of being buried underneath tons of solid stone, that my heart skittered into my mouth at the first sound of a 'plane. They, more used to the scene than I, never even glanced towards the sky, and during that long day I came to learn that only the sound of the sirens would stop them in their tracks to look for shelter.

Lyons was packed with people who had been sheltering all night and were now on their way to work, several wardens either going on duty or coming off their night watch, and a smattering of the elderly who looked almost too tired to eat. What was I doing thinking so selfishly of a career when these people were in the front line, facing the nightly horror of air raids, asking only to live to enjoy a future free from Nazi tyranny. I could scarcely meet their eyes as I ate my toast and drank my tea, and afterwards I felt that looking at shop windows would be tantamount to dancing at a funeral, so I went down into the underground and sat and gazed at the advertisements along the tube wall and sniffed the hot, dusty, human smell which for ever afterwards spelt London to me.

A light rain was falling when I came into the street an hour later, and I checked the agent's address with a helpful London policeman, who didn't seem a bit surprised to find a Glasgow lassie in Piccadilly in wartime, although he did register great pleasure in my accent. 'You didn't bring a haggis with you then?', he enquired, with a friendly wink, and I felt cheered and uplifted as I nipped through a short cut which would take me to the offices I sought. I peeped cautiously round the door marked 'enquiries', and saw a girl sitting tapping away at a typewriter, and a few people sitting around in chairs, obviously waiting to be seen. Were they all actors, I wondered? Would they think I was an actress too, or would they see right through me and recognise that I had never set foot on a stage as a bona fide professional? I was so self-conscious that it was several minutes before I realised that they were quite uninterested in me. Their eyes were riveted on the girl, and their ears on the inter-com. telephone which summoned the lucky one to the inner chamber. I had given my name to the girl, and in about five minutes the inter-com. chattered and she jerked her head towards a door, 'In there, Miss Weir', she said, 'You will be seen now'.

The agent looked me over, glanced at the script on his desk before passing it to me, nodded approvingly, and asked me to sign the various papers he had ready. He had obtained confirmation of my release from industry. There had been no trouble. I was now to go along to Alastair Sim's flat to read the play with him, and we would all meet again when I joined the company for rehearsals in a week or so. He also said that there would be a three months' tour round the number one dates before opening in London. I had no idea what number one dates were, and wouldn't have cared anyway whatever they had turned out to be. If they pleased Alastair Sim and J. M. Bridie, then they were good enough for me. But the thought of rehearsing in a London which was the target of almost nightly air bombardment made me shiver. Still, if other people could do it, then so could I.

I didn't feel quite so bravely defiant later that afternoon when I allowed myself a stroll round Selfridges while waiting for the clock to creep round to my 3 o'clock appointment with Mr. Sim. Suddenly, all the sirens in the capital started up their stomach-turning wailing. Posters all over the shop announced, 'In the event of a warning, remain where you are. Then make your way to the shelters, following the signs'. I did as everyone else did, and stood motionless, while my eyes searched for the arrowed signs which would lead us to the shelters if necessary.

My legs trembled beneath me as I gazed at what seemed to be acres of plate glass and mirrors. If any of those bombs had Selfridges' name written on it, we would be cut to ribbons, and we would surely have enough stone masonry on top of us to build a small town.

I felt sick. But I wasn't going to show fear in a shop filled with English people. Before we could take a step towards safety, we were frozen in our tracks by the unmistakable whistle of a bomb plunging towards its target. I had never been in a day-time raid, and I had never heard anything so terrifying as the whistling intensity of this unseen enemy. My heart filled with wonder and admiration of the long-suffering Londoners as I watched the eyes of shoppers and assistants, schooled to a stony stoicism. I had time to observe all this, even as I wondered whether I should dive to the floor, or make a run for the shelter. There was a 'cccrrump' in the distance, and a long sigh from all of us as we were released from this waking nightmare. It was all over in seconds, but it had seemed like an eternity.

But what terrible morality war induces, I thought, when we could be so glad that the bomb hadn't had our name on it, and show so little sorrow for the target which it had found. I learned later that it had fallen on buildings in Park Lane, not very far from Selfridges, and I prayed that casualties had been few. All the way to Alastair Sim's flat, I pitted my wits against what the fates had in store for me from enemy 'planes. For five minutes I'd run tucked in as tightly as possible to the walls of the high buildings. For the next few minutes I'd move out to the centre of the pavement, and then right out on to the kerb itself, risking splashes on my good thin lisle stockings from the traffic swishing past so close to my legs. The sirens went twice while I played this game, but I heard nothing, neither explosion nor 'plane so they may have been false alarms, and I was a nervous wreck by the time I fell in at the door of that quiet comfortably furnished dwelling. I was very ashamed to be so fearful of my own safety when so many appeared able to take it in their stride, and, looking back, I wonder how on earth I managed to give any sort of comedy reading in such a state of jitters. However, the sight of the famous comedian in his own lounge soon knocked every other thought out of my head, and after I'd taken off my hat, at his request, we plunged into scene after scene of the play. I was a wee bit disappointed at having to remove my best hat, which I thought made me look more actressy, but he seemed well pleased with my appearance without it, and with my fly-away fluffy hair which I wore in page-boy style at that time. He prowled about the room as we read, hunching his shoulders, and arching his eyebrows in the way I'd seen him do so many times on the stage and in films, and once he let out a chortle of satisfaction, as a huge smile lit his face. 'Do that again', he commanded. I read the line once more, and did the deprecating little gesture I had found confidence to include. Again the chortle. 'Now *that was pure comedy!*' he said. 'Yes, you're Jessie all right'.

I think we had some tea together before I left, but everything faded into the background against the blazing joy I felt in his approval of me as a comedienne. To have my idea of comedy endorsed by Alastair Sim was truly a joy devoutly to be wished. I hugged myself with delight as I raced back towards Oxford Street, not bothering this time where I walked. I felt that neither bomb nor disaster would have the cheek to touch me now. I laid the play on the table in Lyons during my modest meal, and started to learn my scenes there and then. A lady and her husband were sitting opposite, and she seemed very interested in my absorbed mouthings as I went over the speeches. At last, unable to contain her curiosity any longer, she asked me what I was doing, and, now that I had the part, I felt I could risk jinxes, and I told her the whole story. She was quite elated, and declared she was an avid theatregoer, and one day when I had 'made it' she would write and remind me that we had met when all was before me. She kept her word. For, years later, I had a letter from her and she told me she had kept every cutting about me she'd come across in newspapers and magazines, and she felt I was her very own discovery.

But maybe I shouldn't have told her after all, for jinxes are not to be trifled with.

When I went back to the office, I told the boss that I would work there till I was wanted to begin rehearsals in London. At home, I hauled the cabin trunk from underneath the bed, and started putting in my few possessions. My typewriter had to go with me, of course, for wherever I went I liked to jot my ideas down on paper, and I also wrote long detailed letters to the Middle East, letting Sandy know exactly what I was getting up to. I learned later that the boys in the squadron dubbed my love-letters 'Sandy's D.R.O'S' (Daily Routine Orders), because in their length and neat typing they resembled the routine orders pinned to their notice board daily. The joke had come about because one day as Sandy was devouring one of my long epistles, several of the boys started reading over his shoulder, thinking he was just studying the daily orders before pinning them up. When he indignantly shooed them away, they laughed and apologised and one of the lads said he'd never seen a letter from home which so resembled official orders. From that moment, when my letters were handed out they were 'Sandy's D.R.O'S.'

Apart from my engagement ring, my typewriter was my most prized possession. I was still writing little pieces for the newspapers and magazines, and I could pour out my heart in long letters to Sandy. Each of us had different highly treasured things which we dreaded would be destroyed by German bombs. Mine was the typewriter. The old lady at the back told me that hers were her false teeth. She took them out and put them in the gas oven every night before she went to bed, using it as a safe. She clearly shared wee Bantam Jock's opinion of the quality of the houses, for she gave it as her opinion that the cooker would stand up to the worst weight which was likely to fall on it. 'Och', she would say, with a disparaging look round, 'There's nae a beam in this hoose that would fell ye. Naw, naw, ma teeth are safe in the oven. They're the only thing I care aboot, for whit would ah dae without them? No' only would ah look a sicht, but ah'd sterve tae death into the bargain'.

So, in preparing for the move to London, transporting my typewriter safely gave me a lot of thought. Eventually I managed to get a stout wooden box, specially made for the job, which had securing bolts which would keep the machine rigid during the journey. Next I spread the bottom of the cabin trunk with packets of foolscap and quarto paper, a box of carbons, and two new typewriter ribbons. My old school pencil-case, an old treasure which I'd hung on to, held cleaning brushes, cleaning oil, rubber, pen and pencils and paper clips. Lastly a duster, and some envelopes completed my office equipment and I wouldn't have parted with any of them for gold. They were far more important to me than clothes, for they gave me something no mere garment would provide—contentment and a release for my imagination.

I couldn't quite believe it, but it was to be my last day in the office. The summons had come from London, and I was leaving Glasgow on the overnight train, ready to start rehearsals in the morning. I had no idea where I was going to stay, and had some vague idea of presenting myself at the Y.W.C.A. and sleeping there for a few nights until I got myself sorted out. The cabin trunk was packed, and I had an empty box in readiness to take the rest of my rations when I'd eaten my final meal that evening. The few men still left in the factory office drifted in to say goodbye to me during their coffee break, and one of them from the drawing office left a sheet of statistics for me to type. I soon rattled through this little job, and took it along to him for checking.

As I skipped along the narrow corridor, which ran like a balcony from one end of the factory to the other, the Tannoy sprang into life, and the voice of Eisenhower stopped me dead in my tracks. General Eisenhower himself! The commander of the Allied Expeditionary Force! What terrible news was he giving us? We had had too much bad news to be sanguine that anything good was going to be told to us at this hour in the forenoon. The Russians had been growing more and more dour about our apparent slowness in wishing to mount the Second Front and relieve the pressure on them. Bickering had been added to slaughter and we were all tired and hungry. At first my ears wouldn't take in the words that the General was saying. I shook my head and listened hard. He was repeating it all, thank goodness. 'Today the Allied Expeditionary Force has landed in France'. I didn't hear the rest. The Second Front had started! And I was leaving for London that night. All hell would be let loose on the Capital, I thought, for the Germans would never take invasion lying down. They'd go for the capital.

Everybody had rushed out on to the corridor, and we gazed at one another with eyes which were a mixture of fear and elation. This was the moment we'd been waiting for, for how many years? How would it all end? This was the beginning of the end all right, and there would be no holds barred by anyone. What was in store for us?

When I went home at lunch time a telegram was lying behind the door. My neighbour had given her signature and put it through. It was from the theatre management. 'Delay departure for London. Second Front opened. No one knows what is going to happen now. All transport strictly controlled for emergency journeys only. Await later instructions.'

I tried to tell myself it was merely postponement, not cancellation, but that part of my stomach which knows the truth long before my head does, felt hideously hollow. If I had been older, and bolder, and more like the Scarlett O'Hara to whom the office wags compared me, I might have ignored the telegram and gone just the same. I could have pretended it had never arrived. But I had not the sophistication for such deception. Truth and obedience were instinctive to me, and so I swallowed my bitter disappointment, and sent off a telegram in reply, 'Message received and understood. Will await instructions as to when I shall join you.'

The trunk went back under the bed. The typewriter was removed from its wooden shroud and, to my boss's delight, I remained at my war job in the factory.

I wrote to Alastair Sim asking when they visualised starting rehearsals. His reply was vague. I wrote to the agent and the management, refusing to listen to the foreboding rumblings from my most knowledgeable stomach. It was only a natural delay, I told myself. If I was right for Jessie before the Second Front, then I was surely just as right a matter of weeks later. It wasn't as if *years* had elapsed, and I was too old for the part or anything. The thought brought me up with a jolt. Up till now, I had always been too young for anything, but I forced myself to realise that one day it would be the other way round. Och I was getting morbid, I'd be hearing from them any minute now, saying the magic word 'Come'.

I did hear. They told me, so tactfully and with such charm, that with the war situation they couldn't take the risk of bringing me all the way from Glasgow, involving leaving my home and finding digs, and that all things considered they had decided it was wiser to engage an actress who lived in the London area and who, if things went wrong, would be able to return to her family. And as though it were an afterthought, would I please return the book of the play as I would now no longer require this.

I didn't cry. I wanted to, but I didn't. Instead I shook my fist at the sky, denounced that blackguard Hitler, topped up the pepper pot in case any dastardly German paratrooper would have the nerve to drop in our garden, parcelled the play and took it down to the Post Office. As I watched it plop into the pillar box, I shook my head, angry at the tears which threatened to spill over, and found comfort in the knowledge that this had been my second chance to go to London. First John Mills. Then Alastair Sim. Surely the third time would be lucky. For now I truly did believe it was only a question of time. How many Glasgow girls had had one chance, much less two? Och the second front was far more important than any piddling little play. My time would come.

We had had enough drama to fill a dozen lives, it seemed. The retreat from Dunkirk, which had been turned into a victory by the use of all the hundreds of little boats which had turned themselves into an Armada to rescue our troops from the pursuing enemy. My brother-in-law Jimmy had volunteered for the later Cherbourg rescue operation, when the Germans had been so closely at their heels that if they had misread a map and taken a wrong street turning, they'd have been cut off. He had arrived home in the middle of the night, filthy, dropping with weariness, and when I quietly let him in, he just patted my shoulder, staggered through to the bed which ma had prepared on the floor in case he got back, and was asleep in seconds.

Next morning, as ma collected his grimy clothes for washing and cleaning, he hushed us with the drama of the tired race they'd had for the train the previous night. An officer had stopped them, observed their dishevelled state with disgust, and rapped out to Jimmy's pal, 'Where's your cap?' Wearily the lad had straightened his shoulders and replied, 'I left it at Cherbourg, sir'. The officer had coughed, then given a magnificent salute. 'Carry on', he said. As they stumbled towards the train, his voice had followed them, 'But get a replacement cap as soon as possible.'

He later thrilled us with his tales of the military operation, and of how his sergeant had become a hero in the eyes of the men when he had drawn not one gun, but two, on the Guards' officer who had attempted with his platoon to crash the queue waiting for the rescue ships. This little sergeant was having none of it. The pier was mined, and bombers flew overhead, and they were all in imminent danger of being blown sky-high if anything had landed on the pier where they stood. Jimmy and his fellow soldiers had been waiting for an hour or so when the Guards appeared.

'Get back', ordered the wee sergeant, and drew one gun on the officer. Jimmy said that the officer, towering above the sergeant, ignored the order and continued marching his platoon forward. 'Back', repeated the sergeant in a voice of thunder, drawing another gun. The men stood completely silent, hardly able to believe their eyes and ears. The officer halted. Stared in shocked amazement at the two guns, then ordered his men to the rear of the queue, and stated for all to hear that it was his considered opinion that the sergeant had gone mad, and he would be reported to the appropriate quarters.

Jimmy's crowd cheered, and a wag among them shouted, 'Noo a' get yer tuppences ready, fur yer pier dues!' From that moment onwards, the little sergeant was 'Two-gun Tony' and the men were wax in his hands. But my own salute went to the lad who had had the wit to shout out the command about the pier dues. Anybody who could find comedy in the grimness of such a situation filled me with admiration.

Later, when the Americans, the Russians and the British were pressing towards Berlin, the succinct vulgarity of General Patton is among my treasured war laughs. The whole world waited to know who would reach Germany first, and reach its heart. A telegram was received at the White House, which merely said, 'Peed in the Rhine today—Patton'. Not a word more. There were some who deplored such unofficial language. Not me. It had the lusty humour of Rabbie himself, in my opinion, and it said everything.

And all at once, almost before we realised it, the first danger was over and we could cautiously allow ourselves a little light in the highways and byeways. For me, this was the end of fear. Oh the sheer bliss of walking through the streets in this period of 'dim-out'. No more claustrophobic gloom. No more suffocating darkness on those nights when no star shone to guide our footsteps. The authorities might call this lighting dim, but for me it was as radiant as the joy which flooded my heart and soul. Victory was in sight, and soon it came, in Europe.

I have never in my life, before or since, felt the utter ecstasy of V.E. night. We all headed for George Square after our day's work at the factory had ended, and we sang our hearts out. Mary and I were the factory harmony duet and we fairly 'gave it laldy', as the Glaswegians have it. We sang 'For me and my gal', 'Let the rest of the world go by', 'It's a long, long trail a-winding', 'The white cliffs of Dover', 'Danny Boy', everything we could think of, and of course 'Auld Lang Syne' a dozen times or more. The square was packed. We danced eightsome reels, making a space somehow for our figure eights and our birling. We hooched and we cheered. The lid was blown off the damped-down furnaces of fear, and we were drunk with relief that we had lived to enjoy our victory. It was years since we had felt such energy charging our batteries. It was Christmas, Hogmanay and Ne'erday all rolled into one, and the Fair thrown in for good measure. It was a spontaneous hymn of gladness and praise. The air was charged with loving kindness. It truly felt that night, that Rabbie's words might yet come true, that 'man to man the world ower, shall brothers be for a' that'. But before that could happen, the war had still to be won in Japan.

Mary and I were on holiday in Dunoon when the bomb went off in Hiroshima. The factory had shut down for a fortnight, for now that the war with Germany was over, the work force was gradually being whittled down, and we had our holiday together in an excellent boarding house, and were blessed with glorious sunshine every day. When the radio told us that the atom bomb had been dropped, we shivered as though an icy blast had cut through the warmth of the day. I remember Mary went white as a sheet and her eyes widened with horror. 'Oh Molly', she gasped, 'Oh Molly. They shouldn't have done it'.

I remained silent, although I felt sick. I remembered those Japanese soldiers who had so brutally massacred the Australians, roasting them alive in their quarters. I remembered the slave conditions of the building of the Burma Road. I remembered those suicide pilots. 'Mary', I said at last, trembling as I spoke the words, 'If it shortens this war and brings it to an end before we dare hope for such a thing, it will have been worth it.'

It was a terrible thing I was approving. But after years of nightmare slaughter. I honestly believed that anything which would end hostilities had to be tried. And this surely was the ultimate horror.

Strangely enough, it was Mary, who had been so distraught by the news of Hiroshima, who lost her sympathy for the Japanese after she met and married a splendid soldier who had been their prisoner for two long hellish years. He was recovering from prison brutalities when she met him, and when she saw photographs of three shrivelled creatures like witches, taken at the camp, she wept. She had thought they were three old crones and they were her fine soldier and his companions under Japanese conditions.

Now it was I who shivered at my acceptance of this obscene weapon, although I believed then, and still do, that by its very nature it would put an end to wars on a global scale.

And the bomb did shorten the war. We were soon rejoicing in V.J. night (Victory in Japan), but it wasn't the joyous outpouring that V.E. night had been. The horror of Hiroshima brooded over us all. We took our pleasures more soberly on this occasion, although we were filled with a deep thankfulness that at last it was all over.

Shortly afterwards we began to make an inventory at the factory of all the goods which the Government would now wish to sell to other industries. I had never before been part of anything which had outlived its usefulness, and although the relief that we were at peace ran like a thread of pure gold through every minute of the day, it was at the same time sad to go to the empty factory each morning, where 'Music while you work' still echoed through the stillness of huge buildings, where not a footstep could now be heard. Indeed this music sounded so ghostly in the reverberating empty workshops that I was compelled to ring up the source of it one day and beg to have it shut off. 'Oh ah thought it wid cheer you up, hen', a warm Glasgow voice said in surprise, 'I knew youse yins in the oaffice were the only wans in the building'. 'We are', I informed the voice, 'But that music is driving me mad. It's like a wake. And anyway, I can't hear the telephone because of the echoes'. So it was turned off. And I got back to my marathon task of listing every last nut and screw and bolt, pages and pages of them to be typed on enormous sheets of lined paper which fitted together finally, and made up a book for distribution to the interested Government departments.

Then the boys began to be repatriated, and all Glasgow threw itself into the jollifications. Tenement streets were bedecked with coloured paper streamers saved from pre-war Christmasses, and huge placards were strung across from opposite windows bearing the proud words, 'Welcome hame Jimmy, after four years fighting the Germans'. Or, 'Welcome Hame Tommy, after two years as a prisoner of war.' But my favourite placard bore the words, with typical Glasgow humour, 'Welcome hame Maggie, after two hours in a tottie queue'.

For of course we still had rationing. And for the backcourt parties to celebrate the warrior's return, everybody pitched in with their coupons which were absolutely necessary if the feasting were to include tins of beans, and tins of Spam, that lease-lent American meat roll which had enlivened our frugal wartime diet, tins of tomatoes, and indeed anything at all which could be scraped together to make a party.

The entire street was invited to each party. Tables were set up in backcourts, and sometimes even in the front streets if they could be cordoned off from traffic, and there was dancing to the music of an accordion, and singing, and old feuds were forgotten, and every heart filled with rejoicing because long-absent sons and husbands were home among their own folk at last.

At these parties, shyness was forgotten, and maiden aunts or grannies were persuaded to sing faintly daring songs parodying hymns, and I won't easily forget the memory of Auntie Jenny standing with sparkling eyes, waiting to be struck dead for her blasphemy, belting out:

'Oh for a man, Oh for a man,
Oh for a man-sion in the sky!'.

She was quickly followed by her sister Mary, who had the company in stitches with her story of the conceited lady who wore a new hat to church, and was delighted when the whole congregation seemed so impressed that they stood up and sang what sounded to her like, 'Glory, Glory, ah hardly knew ye!' This tale was a great success and fell into family folk-lore, so that 'Glory, Glory, ah hardly knew ye' was the theme song whenever a relative appeared in anything new. I even found myself singing it in church instead of the correct words 'Glory, Glory Hallelujah'.

It was a marvellous time of innocent enjoyment and, unlike the Sunday School picnics or the Fatherless children's treats which only took place once a year, these exciting welcome-home parties seemed to take place somewhere in Glasgow almost every night in the week. From the top of tramcars I would gaze down on side streets as gay and lively as scenes of the Mardi Gras from the pictures. Over the tops of wash-houses I would catch sight of coloured streamers, and even the occasional balloon prudently hoarded for just such a day. And always people, laughing and happy, glad to be alive together, not wanting anything more just then but to savour the taste of it, and discover their feelings towards one another all over again. Glasgow was en fête, a happy city, and it reminded me of the description in the hymn of the streets of the New Jerusalem filled with the sound of happy voices. It was a good time to be alive.

Our B.B.C. revue was in great demand at 'Salute the soldier concerts' again, and 'Soldiers' Parcels' concerts, for of course many of the boys were still overseas and although they were now in no danger we still had to look after them and not have them feel they were being forgotten. So we travelled to little village halls, and to big concert buildings, and we did our 'Girls of the Old Brigade' song and dance routine times without number. I also donned a hoarded black net and lace evening dress for two ship's concerts we did at Dunoon, first for the naval ratings and then for their officers, and impersonated Dietrich herself in the seductive number 'Falling in Love again'. I felt a real femme fatale when sailor after sailor came up to me afterwards and said he had believed I was singing just for him! My word, they must have been starved of feminine society right enough if I could hypnotise them so easily!

We updated our 'Down at the Mains' stories for radio, and I was to be 'married off' to Jock Tamson, my lad who had returned safely from the war. We were reflecting the world situation in our little farm dramas, and so I, as Teenie, had a lovely reunion with Jock written for me. I was so filled with innocent romance at the thought of all the other reunions which must be taking place all over Britain that I gave this scene all I'd got. I sighed softly, I paused for long moments, I murmured huskily, and in fact painted such a fearful picture in the minds of those in the control room that Auntie Kathleen burst through the door, horrified at what my silences implied, and told me to speed the whole thing up and be *far* more matter of fact.

So much for romance. But it was a lesson all the same, that more can be suggested by what you don't say, than by any amount of spicy conversation. Strangely enough, when I later came to London and visited Children's Hour, it was this episode of 'Down at the Mains' they remembered, so I must have kept enough ginger in the scene after all!

The Pantheon decided to put on 'WILD VIOLETS' as their first peace-time production, and I was afire to play the part of the French schoolmistress. We were to be produced this time by a new man, and the usual auditions were held in early autumn. This time I didn't worry about how much or how little singing there might be for me with this part, because I felt I was so right in every other way I'd take the warbling in my stride. The first part I had played with any success in Glasgow had been that of a French girl. The critics had found my height and type dead right, and my broken accent convincing. Added to this, I normally used my hands and arms so instinctively to illustrate my speech that it used to be said I'd be struck dumb if my hands were tied behind my back. So, naturally, in my zeal to play this part I couldn't see how they could possibly find anyone else who could interpret it as entertainingly and as faithfully as I could.

I was wrong, of course. Enthusiasm doesn't always mean success. After three auditions—*three*, when I'd never had to do more than one—I was informed they didn't think I was tall enough. I didn't believe a word of it. They could see my height at the first audition, couldn't they? They surely didn't expect me to grow during the course of three auditions? It was the end of college days all over again, when I was either too wee or too young for the jobs I wanted to do.

I just couldn't understand it, particularly as I was now established as a reliable comedienne, and even had a little bit of a name. Rightly or wrongly I became convinced, as I chewed over the matter in my mind, that the new man had had somebody else in mind all the time. He had merely been going through the motions so that fair play would be seen to be done.

He did me a good turn really. For months I had been torn with indecision as to whether or not I ought to have a shot at London before my husband returned from the Middle East. I knew if I waited until he returned, I'd never want to rush off in pursuit of a stage career, and yet I did want to see what would happen if I tried. I had twice been given the chance to go into West End plays. I couldn't risk waiting until somebody came in search of me a third time. I was swayed this way and that, until disappointment over the loss of this coveted part made up my mind for me. I'd found the necessary spur.

I began to make plans. I looked at my Post Office Savings Book and decided I could back myself to the extent of fifty pounds. I would go to London and stay there as long as my money lasted, and if I had no luck, then I would come home. It was a £50 win or lose bet. The factory job would come to a natural end in a few weeks' time, and I would pack and go south to the city of theatres and films as soon as I'd collected my last pay. I had no idea where I was going to stay. I just knew I was going.

I I

I WAS amazed at the interest everybody took when I told them I was London bound. You would have thought I was going to take on the German army single-handed from the way they carried on. Where would I stay? I said, quite truthfully, that I didn't know but the Y.W.C.A. were bound to give me a bed for a couple of nights at least. I was a member of that excellent organisation in Glasgow, and felt confident their London branch wouldn't let me down. And I knew that I would be allowed the freedom of their kitchens, so I wasn't likely to starve. It was vital for me to conserve my small financial resources and I mustn't waste a penny on unnecessary luxuries.

I didn't have the name of a single theatrical agent, apart from the one who had seen me for the Alastair Sim play, but I wrote to the B.B.C. telling them that I was coming. I sent letters both to Broadcasting House and to Aeolian Hall where the light entertainment shows were handled. It really wasn't broadcasting I was after, for I could get plenty of that in Glasgow. It was theatre and films which lured me. But I knew I might be glad of the chance to earn a few broadcasting fees while I waited for my big chance.

I hauled out the trunk from under the bed once more, and this time I knew it wouldn't be opened until I reached London. There wasn't much time wasted on indecision as to which clothes I should take. After years of clothes rationing, my only respectable garments, both for underwear and outerwear, were few and far between. The lovely mossy green Shetland tweed suit which Sandy had bought for me in Frasers before he left for the Middle East was easily the best thing in my wardrobe. It would definitely be my 'audition' and 'interview' outfit.

The short mole jacket from Karters which had been my wedding present would go on top of the suit if the weather was cold, but I had a vague feeling London must be far warmer than Glasgow because it was hundreds and hundreds of miles further south. I was to learn the hard way, during two Siberian winters, that this naïve trust in southern weather couldn't have been more misplaced, and I was to rue all the thick old woollies I'd left behind in damp muggy old Glasgow.

My shabby red coat would do for travelling in, and for knock-about wear in London. A spare skirt, my hand-knitted dress, some jerseys, a blouse, my two pairs of shoes, my raincoat, an umbrella, my short rubber bootees for really wet weather, one or two night-dresses, my fluffy dressing gown made for my trousseaux by dear Mrs. Campbell, my slippers, spare stockings, that was the lot. There was plenty of room in the trunk for the carbons and notepaper. The wooden box with my typewriter safely bolted down, would go separately, specially labelled to ensure careful handling, and I'd pack the left-over food rations in a cardboard box which would sit inside the top inner lid of the trunk, to give me a good start before I had to seek out the nearest Ministry of Food office to change my registration with grocer and milkman and butcher.

I had written to my husband to tell him of my plans, of course, and he gave me his blessing. Well, actually what he said was, 'Go ahead and get it out of your system, for you'll never settle down otherwise.' He was more interested in describing how I was to shut off the water system after draining the tank, and in reminding me to turn off the gas at the main and the electricity. It was December 1945, and bitterly cold, and we couldn't risk all the pipes freezing as I didn't know when I'd be back.

A neighbour round the corner told her English sister-in-law about my proposed departure when she was up in Glasgow for a family wedding. A Londoner herself, this good soul was horrified at my even contemplating arriving at the capital without a place to lay my head. She was certain I would be robbed, possibly murdered, or worse, if I didn't have someone to keep an eye on me, and she insisted on ringing a widowed sister who lived at Sudbury to see if she could provide accommodation. She brushed aside my objections that I couldn't afford full board, and only wanted a bed, for she was sure I'd starve myself just to make my money last as long as possible. Her sister would make sure I ate, she informed me, and that was that. Her niece would meet me at Euston and take me out to Sudbury, and she could now sleep safely in her bed at night knowing I wasn't going to be alone in a wicked place like London.

My heart sank at the idea of eating landlady's meals and at having to be back at set times, for although I hadn't the slightest idea where Sudbury was, I knew it wasn't the West End of London and I guessed it would be miles away and it would take me ages to get back and forth to appointments. My mother, however, was delighted. 'You're that heidstrong', she had kept saying when I told her I was having a shot at London. 'Whit'll Sandy say to you gaun away doon there among the English'. If it had been the cannibals she was describing, her tone couldn't have been more critical. 'He knows', I told her patiently, 'He approves.' She gave me a shrewd look. 'Aye, that's whit *you* say', she said, 'But I'm sure he just knows fine he's nae option, him being so faur away. You've a sin tae answer for, so you have.' Now all was smiles because I was to be in the care of a respectable woman, obviously a right nice buddy at that, when she had a sister who went to the bother of telephoning all the way to London just to make sure I would be looked after. 'Aye she'll see ye get yer meat', she said happily, 'An' I'll know where you are.' My ma-in-law knew London well from her young days, for she had actually worked there, in the nurseries of the great families, and she kept nodding her head sagely and telling me with great solemnity, 'Aye, London can be the loneliest place in the world'. I didn't really believe her, for I was used to the easy friendliness of Glasgow, and how could anybody be lonely in such a big place as London, with millions and millions of folk there. I thought she was just trying to talk me out of going, but time was to prove her absolutely right.

I caught the 10 o'clock in the morning train for Euston, so nobody came to see me off. My mother was working, and the others were busy. I had sent off the trunk and the typewriter by Advance Luggage carrier, and both should be at Sudbury when I arrived. The journey passed in a dream. I remember a sick feeling at the pit of my stomach, a mixture of excititement at the thought of what may lie ahead, and apprehension that I had taken an irrevocable step. I kept checking my Post Office book and trying to work out how long my money would last, an impossible task really, for I had no clear idea of what fares or anything else cost. I knew that for everyday living I would look at prices with an entirely different eye compared with my reactions when I was only down for a brief day.

It was foggy when the train arrived at Euston—over an hour

late—but the good niece Doris was waiting for me, and she recognised me from her aunt's description and from my red coat. We travelled in the underground for over half-an-hour, to my dismay, for I realised this lengthy journey was going to be an obstacle if I were making last-minute appointments. Worse, it cost whole tenpence. This, compared to Glasgow's maximum fare of tuppence-ha'penny, was a fortune and would soon knock a hole in my bank book. But I didn't let Doris see any of this unease and chattered non-stop to her, just the way I did at home. I didn't realise that Londoners didn't speak in trains, and couldn't understand why they all seemed to be listening to me and to have nothing to say to each other. Doris told me long afterwards that she'd never seen such a stunned carriage in her life, for she was sure that to a man they'd not heard such a ceaseless flow of entertaining talk for years. I was glad she said 'entertaining', but I had a feeling she was just trying to be tactful, and was letting me know that this wasn't correct behaviour in public transport in this part of the world. Later observation confirmed me in this, and much later, when my husband came to live in the south, he travelled for twenty years in the train without anyone so much as opening his mouth to him.

Mrs. Horton, my landlady, was a nice gentle soul, whom I took to be in her late forties. The house had a little garden, to my delight, and I had a small but pretty upstairs bedroom which was almost filled with my cabin trunk and my huge typewriter box. She had an enormous meal waiting for me which, in my tired and excited state, I was quite unable to manage. 'Mrs. Horton', I gasped, 'You must have spent all your food coupons and I'll never be able to eat all this. I'm not used to such big meals.' Having had only one ration book for years, my appetite had dwindled to that of a bird. She brushed my objections aside and insisted I took every drop of soup, ate as much Shepherd's pie as possible, and finished off with a decent helping of her special bread and butter pudding, made with a real egg. All this at past eight o'clock at night, when I was used to having my dinner in the middle of the day, with just a tasty wee snack at 6 o'clock and a cup of tea at bed-time. English ways, I was to learn, were very different. They dined in the evening, and had a light lunch in the middle of the day. How long would my stomach take, I wondered, to adapt itself to this altered regime?

Next day being Saturday, with all the London offices shut for the week-end, gave me plenty of time to attend to unpacking my trunk and filling drawers and wardrobe with my belongings. This done, I borrowed a screwdriver to release my precious typewriter from its restraining bolts, and as soon as the machine was in its place on the table, I began to feel quite at home, and I immediately sat down and typed out a letter to my husband, telling him all my news and describing my digs in minute detail.

In the middle of this, Mrs. Horton called me down for coffee. I had been afraid I might be a bit of a nuisance, for she wasn't really used to lodgers, but she seemed genuinely glad to have me in the house. Her twin daughters were both away in the forces, she told me, and she missed their company so much since she had lost her husband. My heart grew lighter with every word she uttered, for I could see she really was pleased to have me there to fill at least one vacant chair.

We went for a walk in the afternoon, and she showed me the local shops, and the Food Office where I'd have to register on Monday to enable me to use my food coupons in the district. I was amazed to find that it didn't feel like London at all. Apart from the English accents, it was more like Thornliebank, or Springburn, with small shops and little houses and not a tall building anywhere in sight. And of course, when I really thought about it, it wasn't London. It was suburbia. It was nice, and it felt comfortingly familiar, but it was a far cry from the world of show business, and I felt in my bones that it was too far from the sounds and smells of theatreland to keep me there very long.

On Sunday, when we sat chatting, I was astonished when Mrs. Horton confided that she was glad it wouldn't be long till she received her pension, for then she would be able to make ends meet without any trouble. 'Your pension!', I exclaimed, 'But how old are you then? I thought you were just forty-something'. She smiled, and passed a hand over dark hair which hadn't even a single silver thread that I could see. When she told me she was in fact coming up for her sixty-fifth birthday, I looked so disbelieving that she burst out laughing. 'It's true', she said, 'I'll show you my birth certificate if you like'. I looked into her face intently, not troubling to make my study discreet or polite. She was a plain, simple, woman and it was absolutely clear that it wasn't cosmetics or special effort on her part which contributed to this appearance of youthfulness. She simply looked an ordinary woman of forty-plus.

I shook my head in bewilderment, and seeing that I was so bemused, she told me a fascinating story which explained this phenomenon. It appeared that she and her sister hadn't aged at all in looks since they were around forty. They'd just accepted it as a piece of luck, which they scarcely even noticed. However, one day her sister had slipped in the street and fallen, breaking an ankle, and was taken by ambulance to a large London hospital nearby. When they took particulars and learned her age, they reacted just as I had to Mrs. Horton's age. So much so, that they asked if they could do a series of tests on her, to check whether or not her physique matched her appearance. She had no objection, so they did blood tests, bone X-rays, skin examination, heart machine, the lot.

Some time later when she went back to have the plaster removed from her ankle, they told her, with some excitement, the result of their tests. It seemed there was a rare Polynesian strain in her physical heritage, and this would slow up the ageing process to a degree which meant she would never look really old unless she lived until she was well over a hundred. I gasped. 'Just like the people in James Hilton's *Lost Horizon*,' I said. 'They had the secret of perpetual youth, but only so long as they remained in the Valley'. 'A bit like that', she agreed, 'Except that of course we're not affected by geography at all'.

What would affect their descendants though, was dilution of the strain through marriage, so her daughters wouldn't be quite so lucky, and *their* children would be a little less so, until after some generations there wouldn't be such a noticeable difference in the ageing pattern from the rest of us.

'Oh', I said enviously, 'What a marvellous inheritance for a woman to have, especially if she were an actress'. But she just laughed. She was so used to the miracle, she took it for granted. As it happened her daughters arrived home on leave while I was with her, and if I, hadn't known they were in their late twenties, I'd have sworn they were seventeen. Both beauties too, and much more aware than their mother that their looks would endure, untouched by the unkind finger of time, well into middle age.

We had great talks together, and I decided that if the south was going to provide such unusual types, I was very glad I'd come. I'd have had to have looked far enough in Glasgow before I'd have found anybody possessing a Polynesian elixir of youth in her bloodstream! Suddenly, home seemed very far away.

On Monday I had an appointment at the B.B.C. with Jo Plummer, a Children's Hour producer. To my surprise, she seemed to know me, and greeted me as 'Teenie' of 'Down at the Mains'. I hadn't realised London took any of our Children's Hour programmes, and so knew some of our names quite well. The very last thing I had expected in London B.B.C. was that Molly Weir would mean anything to anybody. The blood rushed to my cheeks with pleasure, and the cold nervous knot in my stomach melted under the warmth of her friendliness. Although we were from entirely different backgrounds, we were on the same wavelength right away. She was a tall cool young lady, with a ready smile, and clearly out of one of the very top drawers. I learned later she was an honours graduate of Cambridge University, and at one point in her career had assisted the Poet Laureate, John Masefield. She was by far the youngest of the producers in that department, of whom the others were May Jenkin (Auntie May), and David Davis of the gentle voice and brilliant musical talent. I was to come to know all three very well indeed.

As I was leaving Jo's office, she advised me to have lunch in the canteen, which I would find was cheap and good, and she assured me she would get in touch the moment she had anything to offer. I believed her. I followed her advice about eating in the canteen, where I had the great good luck to run into Jimmy McKechnie and Joy Adamson, both from Glasgow, and with both of whom I'd worked in the Glasgow studios. It was marvellous to meet them just then when I felt so far from home, and right at the beginning of the adventure, and to know that I might run into them at any time in the future, for they had both settled in London and worked a great deal for the B.B.C. I coaxed from them, and from others who joined us round the table, the names of various agents to whom I might apply if I had no luck with the one who'd seen me for the Alastair Sim play. At first, nobody could think of a single possible name, but I took out my diary and sat with pen poised until they were forced to rack their brains, and soon I had a dozen names, and a purpose for being where I was.

The lady assistant in the big Agency who had cast me for the Alastair Sim play during the war, was very disparaging about my accent. 'You'll never do anything in London', she said with a sniff, 'Unless you lose that accent'. What did she mean, when there she was, sitting behind a large desk, successfully employed in a top agent's office, and with a voice not very much less Scots than my own! Telling ME to adopt the accents of the Sassenach! I hadn't the guile to hide my feelings, and I was much too inexperienced to know that an unemployed actress doesn't tell the truth to one who holds a position of power in an important agency. 'I have no intention of losing my accent', I said, 'And I notice you haven't been too successful in losing yours'.

I should never have said such a thing, of course, for she may have thought it was good advice she was giving me, but I couldn't bear what seemed to me such disloyal criticism of her own tongue.

It goes without saying that I never got a single job from that agency, or even another appointment!

Apart from that lapsed patriot though, I found it surprisingly easy to make appointments to see people. And, unlike her, everyone else embarrassed me by being almost too free with their admiration for my voice, so that I became very self-conscious about it and started speaking in whispers again, just as I had at school. As I left each interview, I was given another name to try, until I had pages and pages of names in my little diary, and I flew up and down Charing Cross Road and Shaftesbury Avenue like a yo-yo. I learned that I could use the B.B.C. canteen any time, because of the work I had done for them in Glasgow, and as soon as I knew this, I stopped trying to go back to Sudbury for lunch. I could get a meal in the canteen for tenpence instead of spending it on fares, and that left all the more time for seeking work.

I felt I'd been away from home for weeks, but it was in fact only nine days when Doris, the girl who'd met me at Euston, invited me to go over to see her great friend at Clapham Common on the Sunday. We were invited for tea, and Doris would call for me at Sudbury about 4 o'clock.

On the way to Clapham, Doris asked me how I liked living with her aunt. I said, quite truthfully, that I liked Mrs. Horton very much, but that I was worried about the high cost of fares and the expense of having to take full board. I realised it wasn't really pricey, but it was too much for me, and I needed to be free of domestic ties, for I fretted when appointments prevented my getting back punctually for the meals she had ready waiting for me. I hadn't really come to London to be cosy, but to be ready and accessible for theatrical opportunities, and ideally I should be nearer London. Doris was very understanding, but doubted whether it would be very easy to get a furnished room any cheaper, because the nearer one got to London, the more digs cost.

When we turned off the main street into the Close in Clapham where Doris's friend lived, I immediately felt a great sense of belonging, and I knew that this was a good place for me. Everything, for the first time, felt just right, in spite of drifting fog which stung nose and eyes. Although the railings had gone to help the war effort, the gardens in the middle of the square were pleasant and well cared for. The pillared houses were tall and gracious, and had once been the homes of rich Londoners, although they were now fallen upon more stringent days, and were sub-divided among many tenants. The one we were visiting had once been the town house of Sir Godfrey Tearle, I was told.

A flight of steps led to an imposing front door, and a light to the left at street level showed there was a basement flat. I'd read about such places in Sherlock Holmes, but this was my first sight of one. It was a very large house, and the hall seemed vast in the dim light when Doris's friend Lois softly opened the door. A staircase went twisting round and round to the top of the house, and on the third floor, at the very top, Lois had her room. The minute I walked in, I fell in love with it. Not because it was furnished with any great beauty or skill—it was after all just after the war and it was a rented room. But it was *huge*, to my eyes, with a high lofty ceiling, large windows, and a gas fire which blazed cheerfulness from every pulsing jet. A kettle hummed on a gas ring, and beside it stood a trolley with tea things and a plate of buttered toast.

Lois was a civil servant. She worked in the Post Office behind the scenes, a gentle creature (my mother would have approved!), with soft brown eyes, dark red hair, and a shy smile. She seemed surprised by my enthusiasm for her room, and amused when I darted about exclaiming over its appointments. 'A gas ring for cooking', I said, 'Great'. 'A shilling in the meter slot—oh what a good idea, for then you've no bills'. Oh, what would I give for just such a room, where I could come and go as I pleased and cook as little or as much as I wanted, with no time-tables except those of my own making. And all this in a district which felt and smelt like the real London I'd come to find.

I looked imploringly at Doris, hoping she would get round to the subject of accommodation, and at last she understood and wondered if Lois knew if there was a room vacant in the house. 'Yes', said Lois, 'I think there might be, for there was a couple next door and Mrs. Parker doesn't really like men in the house, and would prefer a woman to share the landing with me'.

I had noticed a little sink outside on the landing, and only now realised this was the sole source of water for Lois and the room next door, and that dishwater and washing water would have to be got there. I could quite see it might be embarrassing having a man so close by, especially if tenants were running about in old dressing gowns in the morning. I jumped up in my excitement at the mere possibility of my getting the room on the same landing with this nice quiet girl, 'Can I ask the lady now?', I said, dropping my toast back on the plate and making for the door. Lois decided that wouldn't do. It would be better if she went down and asked Mrs. P. to come up and show me the room. She was very particular, and only took recommended lodgers.

I had to contain myself till we had finished tea and washed up the dishes in the little sink, and then Mrs. P. was brought up to be introduced. She was a plump elderly lady, with swept back black hair, smallish dark eyes, round rosy cheeks, and a habit of rubbing her plump hands together as we talked. We went inside the vacated room, which was now festooned with ladders and buckets of distemper. The walls were a cold grey and the woodwork a sooty black, but I didn't mind the funereal colours. The ceiling was lofty, just like Lois's, the room was large, and there was a broad ledge outside the barred windows which reminded me of a castle battlement. This must have been the nursery when the house had had one single family living there, and the bars were to keep the children safe. I thought of Peter Pan. There was more than just a gas ring in this room, I noted with a start of pleasure. There was also a tiny tin oven, with another little gas ring on top, besides the usual one on the hearth like Lois's. By jove, I would be able to cook a whole dinner here!

I tried to damp down my enthusiasm in case Mrs. P., like my mother, preferred people with gentle ways and might think I was too wild. But she could see I liked the room. 'If I get it when can I move in?', I asked her, trying to keep the eagerness out of my voice. 'Well', she said, 'The painter won't be finished till next week-end, but you could come the following Monday if you like'. 'How much was the rent?' She hesitated, and I saw as clearly as daylight that she was going to jack it up for the new tenant. I later learned that I was right! However, it was barely £1 a week, and with the shillings for the meter under my own control, I could keep my expenses down. There would be no fuel bills, whose hidden totals could strike a lethal blow at my capital. It was less than half my Sudbury digs, and although I would now be catering for myself, I knew how economical I could be. And of course, the fares to the West End were half those from Sudbury. It was corn in Egypt! It was mine! I hugged myself with delight. Who could have guessed that a simple invitation to Sunday tea would end in my future digs being settled for the rest of the time I stayed in London on my own? Such small encounters shape our ways. My stomach, always the barometer of events, told me I had made a wise decision, and I had no cause to doubt its accuracy.

I was so glad that Mrs. Horton didn't mind my moving to Clapham. But she seemed to understand that I had to be nearer my goal, and she wouldn't be alone for long, for she'd had news that one of her daughters would be getting demobbed in a matter of weeks. Everything fitted, and nobody was hurt. We parted the best of friends, and I'll always be grateful to her for sharing her home with me, a stranger, and for making my first week or so in the south so comfortable and happy, a true home from home.

It was a real pea-souper when I arrived at Clapham, and I was thankful I'd sent the luggage on by road haulage, and hadn't made the move by taxi as my landlady had suggested, for it would have cost a fortune to have crawled from Sudbury through fog-shrouded streets. I'd travelled by underground, which was not only cheaper but infinitely quicker and safer on such a night. I rang the bell. Not a sound came from inside the house. Surely Mrs. Parker hadn't gone out? Who else would hear the door-bell if she wasn't in? Where would I go if there wasn't a reply? Maybe she had changed her mind and had let the room to somebody else! My heart was thumping as I pressed the bell a second time, and kept my finger on the button. It was all I could do to stop myself battering at the door with my fists, for now that the sound of my footsteps had ceased, the fog had blotted out all other human noises. A hooter sounded mournfully in the distance. I was alone in London.

I hadn't realised my finger was still pressing the bell until I heard a high Scottish voice calling from somewhere inside the house, 'Hold the line. Hold the line. I'm coming'. Oh thank goodness, somebody was in. The door opened, and a tallish, spare, elderly lady with a fine head of silver wavy hair addressed me in a voice which was a mixture of welcome and irritation, 'Come away in, lassie', she said, 'Don't stand there on the doorstep letting a' the fog in'. With an imperious arm she drew me inside and shut the door. 'They're a' oot'. As I moved to follow her upstairs, she turned, 'Noo, tak' yer time. I'm two stairs up, in the room underneath yours, and it's no' a race we're having. You'll come in to me first. The kettle's on. I was just having a cup of tea'.

Much much later I was to learn that she was only exaggerating the homely tongue of our native land to make me feel at home. Born in Aberdeen, her knowledge of English was encyclopaedic, and when required her accent was impeccable, but she had the right words for a frightened newcomer, which was how I had struck her with my white face and startled eyes when she had opened the door.

Her disdain for polite nothings warmed my heart. It was my grannie all over again, keeping me right. Instinctively I felt we were going to be true friends, and twenty years of basking in the warmth of her affection amply confirmed that first impression. But just then as I followed her upstairs, slowing my pace to please her, I was aware only that I must curb my impatience to see my own room and spend a little time with this kind creature who was making me so welcome.

The bitter fog had seeped into the house, and the first thing in her room which greeted me was her roaring gas fire, turned up to its fullest, with no thought for greedy meters. In front of it stood a wee steel 'winter' such as we had used in Springburn for keeping food warm, and a plate of toast was being kept hot in the reflected heat from the glowing fire. A kettle sang on a gas ring, and in minutes I was sipping a steaming cup of tea, and having toast piled on my plate, 'Tak' it noo', she said, 'Its newly made. And it's REAL butter'. To lavish the butter ration on toast was no small sacrifice, and I knew it, but once she had made her point and made sure that I appreciated what it was that I was eating, she would have no thanks.

She was astonished to learn that I had only been in London a matter of weeks. When Mrs. P. had called up to her, 'Oh Miss Chree, if Miss Weir comes, perhaps you'll let her in', she had assumed I was a Londoner, and knew my way about. She shook her head and wondered what I would have done if she herself had had to be out and I'd had a shut door on such a night. I discovered that it was only a matter of luck that she had been in the house, because she was a housekeeper and they were up to their eyes with Christmas preparations, and she had merely come home for the night to collect a few things she needed over the Festive Season. 'I always keep on my room', she said, fixing me with a fierce blue eye, 'Because that preserves my independence. Once you accept an employer's roof over your head, you're done for if you want to make a change, for it gives them too strong a hold on you.' Wise words which impressed me very much, and which increased my respect for this vigorous, clear-thinking new neighbour. As she spoke, I was glancing round this precious room, whose possession enabled her to choose whom she would serve, and for how long. It was chaos with the lid off! Drawers had been pulled out, stood upright like cupboards, and were used as book-shelves. Papers were heaped everywhere. Clothes lay in bundles, where they'd been removed from the drawers—it was clear Miss Chree preferred literature to mere dress. An upturned drawer with a cushion on it served as a stool. Another with a cloth spread over it was my table. The only colour on the walls (distempered grey, like mine, I noted) was given by two large photographs cut from newspapers. The one over the mantelpiece was of General Smuts, and facing him from the opposite wall was Winston Churchill. I was not only to learn in the months which followed, that they were her heroes, true champions of the right in her opinion, but she could quote extensively the main episodes in both brilliant lives.

On the bed a beautiful faded Paisley shawl was folded, and when she saw me looking at it her blue eyes softened and she told me it had belonged 'to mother'. It was touching to hear an elderly lady refer like this to her parent, as 'mother', without the more usual 'my' we used in Glasgow, and I could sense what a strength this lovingly mentioned parent must have been to the family.

The whole place looked as though a storm had blown through it, leaving disorder in its wake. Everything was clean, but there was a sort of 'playing at houses' atmosphere, because nothing, apart from the bed, was being used for the purpose for which it was intended. But somehow, it all added up to a cosy, lively, welcoming refuge. As I watched her move back and forth with milk-jug and plates, and listened to her soft Aberdeen accent, I found I was smiling in sheer pleasure at having found such a glorious eccentric living in such close proximity. As somewhat of an eccentric myself, I was right on her wavelength, and although she was being very casual I could see from the sparkle in her eye and the flush on her elegantly thin face that she knew it too.

When our friendship strengthened and developed, I was trusted with the crisis which had brought this fine, well-educated Scot to London. She had been secretary to an old established firm of whisky blenders in her native Aberdeen, and her description of the serious art of blending was a poem in itself. The owner was a gentleman of the old school, greatly esteemed by everybody, by none more than Miss Chree who knew quality when she met it.

Everything had gone like clock-work, all tasks properly accomplished in their due season, owner and workers in perfect harmony, and a quiet sense of service and mutual respect graced all their activities.

And then, one terrible afternoon the long arm of the law stretched out and plucked from their midst their chief accountant. He had been systematically cooking the books, and because of the very nature of the trust reposed in everyone in that happy firm, his fraud had gone undetected. Until that moment. Inquiries had been started by creditors and now, when the firm was on the verge of bankruptcy, was the moment of truth.

The disgrace was numbing, and the whole staff grieved that the owner should have been betrayed by one of them, for it was very clear that he had known nothing of what was going on. But he blamed himself, knowing he should have been more watchful and not made it possible for his accountant to have been tempted by easy money.

He felt the disgrace of the loss of the firm's good name keenly, and on top of that he felt guilt that he could have let it happen, and when he had made all arrangements for debts to be cleared, he tidied his desk, went home, locked his bedroom door and cut his throat.

When they came to tell them the news at the office, Miss Chree had been so shocked and so bereft by the terrible thing which had happened that she walked from the office without a word, caught a tram home, packed a bag, and sat in the station until the overnight train was due to leave for London. She never returned.

And because this grief was almost too much to bear, as she travelled south she decided that never again would she allow herself to become attached to any one employer or situation. She would become a rolling stone. She wanted a changed life, with nothing to remind her of the old. As the train rattled through the night, she forced herself to assess what talents she had for earning a living in the vast unknown city of London. She had chosen London because she could disappear there, with no curious eyes to give her a second glance. She would never be a secretary again. It had to be a complete break with the past. She was intelligent and well-educated and as she mentally surveyed the needs of employers, it came to her with a flash of truth that wealthy houses required domestics. They would always be in demand. She had had the good home training of most Scots girls of her generation and she knew she could fulfil this role. That would be her future. She was so certain that she had found the right solution to her problems that she slept for the rest of the journey.

Like me, she knew of the Y.W.C.A., and as a trained secretary she knew where to look to find domestic agencies, so she registered with one which specialised in 'temporaries', and which dealt with the best families. She had a great love of the fine things created by craftsmen. Beautiful furniture, precious antiques, paintings, old silver. She would care for the possessions but wouldn't become attached to the families, for she wouldn't stay with any one family long enough to be hurt. She didn't need to earn a great deal to find peace of mind. She offered herself as a housekeeper with a knowledge of cooking.

By the time I met her, she had seen many of the kitchens of the aristocracy, and had also cooked for Royalty. Her account of this, when they had no soup ladle and she had to transfer soup from pot to serving bowls with a handle-less cup was hilarious. She had even been rung up by Buckingham Palace one evening, when they wished to know if the Duke of Windsor was with her employer! Her knowledge of antiques had made such strides that she had been asked to catalogue the priceless treasures of one of our noble Lords when he had moved house. And of course, trained in an age which scorned typewriters, her handwriting was copperplate, and each item of his Lordship's household carried a label in her lovely handwriting, so that locating a particular item in storage was reduced to simplicity itself.

She was honest as the day, and had a rakish elegance which lifted her well above the normal run of domestics. She must have been worth her weight in rubies to any employer lucky enough to acquire her services. But these rich people all had one thing in common. They hated to pay decent wages. And my dear Miss Chree never earned more than £3 10s. a week, plus her food, in all the years she lived in the Capital. But she had a soul above money. She had a marvellous life. She fell in love with London at first sight and never failed to rejoice in the richness of the passing scene. She taught me to appreciate its markets, its fascinating back streets, and its riches in a way which would have been impossible for me to do in the company of any of the acting fraternity.

But all that lay ahead. Now as we chatted, the voice of Mrs. Parker soared upstairs, and soon she was panting up to show me how to manage the gas meter and to give me my rent book.

I LOVED my room from the very start. Other eyes might have seen only the assortment of second-hand furniture. The easy chair with the stuffing bursting out of its bottom seams, the small rickety table for my meals, the narrow bed with its lumpy mattress, the drunken gas fire with its missing fitments, but to me the place had the very savour of theatrical digs.

It was large and dignified, with lofty proportions, and when I saw it for the first time in daylight I was thrilled to find I was looking right over the roofs of London and could actually see the Tower of London itself. It was as romantic as René Clair's film, except that my exciting rooftop view was not of Paris, but of London.

I gazed round me with calculating eyes and saw where I could put extra hooks for my clothes, which I could later cover with an attractive curtain. (Miss Chree's introduction to the street markets provided a great source for such bargains). I'd look out for a new steady table to hold my typewriter, and eventually I'd coax the landlady to allow me to buy a bigger bed and better mattress so that I could have my mother down to stay for a few nights. She'd never been to London in her life, in fact she'd never crossed the border, and it might calm her suspicions that I was living in squalor if she could see it all for herself. The little tin oven and the extra gas ring had already met with my full approval, and I was so busy planning future feasts in my head that I didn't take in a word of the landlady's instructions about the shilling-in-the-slot meter, and only vaguely heard her tell me to be sure to have a good stock of coins. I was to be sure to ask for shillings when I received change in the shops, for they were very scarce.

I wasn't used to the world of bed-sitters, and shilling meters, but it didn't take long to find out that all Clapham hoarded their shillings for this purpose, so that trying to get these precious coins in change was like expecting to find a sovereign in the gutter.

As well as shillings for the meter, I had to make sure of sixpences for 'toll' telephone calls, and pennies for local calls. I'd never heard of a 'toll' call, and discovered this wasn't quite so distant as a trunk call, but beyond the range of a local one, and that *all* the film studios involved toll charges. I'd be asked to ring a film casting director at eleven a.m. I would do so. 'Oh', an airy unconcerned voice would say, 'I'm afraid he hasn't come in yet. Could you ring about twelve?'. At twelve, another precious sixpence from my dwindling capital would be fed into the box's greedy mouth, and I'd be told, 'Sorry, he isn't coming in today after all. Try again tomorrow if you like'. What with finding sixpences, queueing for a cubicle, hanging about until the agreed hour to ring again, I determined that the first thing I was going to do when I got a job was to have a telephone installed in my room. It was impossible in such early post-war days to have a telephone at all unless the wiring had been previously done in the house for a former user and where, for some reason, only the instrument itself had been removed. One day when I had been wailing about running back and forth to the Post Office, up and down three flights of stairs to my room, to make appointments with those elusive film people, and had vowed that I'd get a telephone in the room or die in the attempt, Lois, the girl next door, told me my room was already wired for one. I jumped with excitement. Only essential workers had been allowed telephones in the war, and the nurse who had earlier occupied my room came into that category, but when she had been drafted elsewhere the landlady had had the instrument removed, as she didn't wish to pay for it, and was afraid a future tenant wouldn't have taken it over. I gnashed my teeth in vexation. Oh *why* couldn't she have left it! Fancy anybody in a rooming house not realising the usefulness of a telephone!

Lois, who was in the Post Office herself you may remember, brought home forms which I could fill in, for she said it would take ages before I'd get to the top of the queue, and if I couldn't afford to have the 'phone connected when the time came, I could always say so. Nothing would be lost. I felt it was an act of faith in my future, so I applied for my telephone, and then prayed every night that I would have a job before the Post Office reached my name.

It was marvellous though to find that the tube only took twenty minutes to get me right to the heart of the West End at a cost of sixpence. I saw every agent I could coax into giving me an appointment, and I enjoyed chats and cups of tea, and told them everything I'd done in radio and on the stage, left a note of name and address, regretted I was sorry I had no telephone, then whizzed on to the next appointment. I went to see the Light Entertainment people at Aeolian Hall, the B.B.C. headquarters for this side of the business in Bond Street, whose name I had had from Moultrie. I had sent him into shouts of laughter over the telephone in Glasgow when I first heard this unfamiliar name and thought he was recommending me to go to see a lady called 'Oley Anne Hall!' He couldn't believe I'd never heard of the place. Leslie Bridgmont saw me there, and was so friendly that I told him of my gaffe over Miss Oley Anne Hall, and laughed, gave me a delicious cup of coffee, and said he'd certainly remember me. I was so elated after this appointment that although I still had no prospects of any sort of job, I was grinning from ear to ear as I cut through to Regent Street, and an American soldier pressed a packet of cigarettes into my hand and said I must have them, as mine was the happiest face he had seen since coming to London! I couldn't wipe the smile off my face like lightning, or he'd think I was a bit dotted. Gosh, I'd have to be careful, or folk would think I was like the poor daft lassie who used to rush down Buchanan Street in wild spurts of speed, alternatively laughing and scowling, a long hat-pin at the ready to repel any masculine assaults. The American refused to take back his cigarettes, gazed long and earnestly into my eyes as he repeated he would never forget my laughing face, shook my hand and went on his way.

My next appointment was with a film director, again introduced by the always helpful Moultrie, but as this man preferred to see me at his flat, I was terrified. Everybody knew that film directors were the wolves of show business. All the movie magazines had told us so for years. What would I do if he attacked me? I had no experience in such matters, and I hadn't even a long hat pin. I walked up and down on the pavement outside the block of flats for a good five minutes before I could summon courage to press the bell and, once inside, I wouldn't remove so much as a glove although the room was like an oven. It turned out he was pleased to see me because I had worked with his wife on radio in Glasgow, and he wanted to hear all about her. In case this was merely to lull my suspicions, I still kept my gloves on, and I was so nervous that any impression I created must only have been off-putting. Anyway I never worked for this man, but it had been quite interesting, in a way, seeing the inside of a posh London flat. It had also been the first flat where the occupant spoke through a little tube which ended in an ear-piece at the door, and when one pressed the bell and gave a name, a mysterious force allowed the door to be pushed open. What a good idea, I thought. It was a pity we hadn't such an arrangement in Clapham, for I couldn't count the number of times I had had to race down three flights of stairs to answer the door, usually to take in a parcel for somebody else, or let the meter man have the keys, or take delivery of the laundry. Everybody else was out working during normal hours, and I often had the house entirely to myself.

My landlady was an ardent Catholic, and as we were getting close to Christmas, she was in constant attendance at the church round the corner. I seldom saw her, but when I did, she fascinated me. Less experienced mortals may have gasped in admiration at the sight of Fanny Craddock performing cookery chores clad in stunning dinner gown, but this came as no revelation to me, because my Mrs. Parker brought the same assured approach to all her household tasks. She was always dressed for the church rather than the kitchen.

In her cubby hole of a scullery I would catch glimpses of her clad in rich blacks, the materials varying from heavy silk to gleaming velvet, even occasionally trimmed with fur, and on her head she almost always wore an elegant toque. Thus attired she might be baking scones, cleaning the oven, or making her stately way towards the door to clean the front steps. For this last task she had the fanciful notion of using a vegetable pot instead of a basin, and her brush might once have served to apply the shaving lather to a departed lodger's beard. I had a notion that she preferred this tiny brush and pot to the more usual cleaning equipment in case a passing priest caught sight of her, and could be allowed to assume she was feeding a needy stray animal. But this mis-use of the vegetable pot filled Miss Chree with horror, and we both felt secretly rather glad we catered for ourselves.

When my mother eventually came down to visit me, she was stunned to find such a regally clad lady performing household tasks without so much as an apron to protect her finery, and declared, 'My Goad, she must be an auld theatrical'. When I laughed, she said, 'I'll bet ye onything ye like that ah'm right. She'll hiv been used tae playin' the part o' a Duchess who has seen better days'.

This was nearer the truth than we could have supposed, for I subsequently learned that Mrs. Parker had indeed 'trod the boards' in her younger days, but alas had got no further than the chorus. But there was no doubt she exuded an air of grease-paint.

Although she had a theatrical background, she was extremely

modest and would pull her dressing gown tightly round her ample curves if I happened to be passing as she was coming from the bathroom in a cloud of steam, after her bath. I had been warned that I must always knock before I entered her room if I wanted anything. She had told me, frowning with distaste at the mere recollection, that on holiday in Italy a waiter had entered her bedroom without tapping the door. She had been stark naked and was about to don her corset. 'What did you do?', I asked, waiting for some terrible revelation of screams, or attempted seduction, or fainting clean away with horror. 'I just turned my back on the beast', she replied, closing her eyes with a shudder. I had to sneeze and pretend to cough to stifle the laughter which threatened to explode from me. She clearly hadn't the slightest idea that a susceptible Italian might have found the sight of her plump bottom quite as alluring as those parts she was at such pains to keep hidden from his gaze. In all our future conversations I had a terrible job keeping that mental picture from flashing before my eyes, for she had a very serious turn of mind and was extremely suspicious of misplaced levity.

One day when I left the B.B.C. canteen and stood wondering who else I could ring, it occurred to me that I had been in London for nearly three weeks and I hadn't yet seen the Thames. It was a grey gritty day, and although all Britain might be getting ready to celebrate Christmas, the Festive Season for me meant only that all the offices would be shutting down and I would have nobody to approach in my search for work. Things were already slowing down, so I might as well have a look at the Thames. But how did I get to it, I wondered. I was at Oxford Circus, and I approached a policeman. 'Could you direct me to the river?', I asked solemnly, not realising the impact of my words. The policeman gazed down at me and smiled. 'What's the matter Jock?', he asked, 'Too far from Bonnie Scotland, are you?' When I shook my head, he said, 'Not thinking of chucking yourself in then, eh?' For the first time since I had arrived in London, I really burst out laughing. The very idea! 'No, no', I assured him, 'It's just that I've been here for weeks and it's high time I saw the Thames to see how it compares with the Clyde. How do I get there?'

Following his directions, I found myself passing the end of Downing Street. Could that wee street really be where the Prime Minister lived? And there was the centre of all the crime-busting brains and the place mentioned in all the detective stories, New Scotland Yard. Somehow the Cenotaph seemed much smaller than when one saw it in the news-reels, but it was a most impressive street, and the buildings were beautiful. And then, before me, was the whole magnificent façade of the Houses of Parliament. What had I been doing all this time, neglecting such historical landmarks. I leaned over the parapet and gazed down at the murky swirling waters. Lights were beginning to pierce the twilight, and the Embankment looked romantic and very beautiful. Across the river, the skyline showed a fretwork of exquisite architecture. There was no doubt it was a wonderful city. Oh I hoped my fifty pounds would last long enough to let me explore it to the full before I had to go home, which I would have to do very soon if I didn't get a job.

I hadn't intended going home for Christmas, which wasn't celebrated to any great extent in Scotland, but when I discovered that practically everything in London would be closing down not for the single day I had supposed, but for nearly a week, I agreed with my landlady that I'd probably be better off at home. Lois was going away to friends. Miss Chree, whom I hadn't seen at all since she had welcomed me to the house, was obviously busy with her employers, and I didn't know anybody else in the place. I looked at my bank book. It would cost me nearly £4 to go home (I had a concession ticket as the wife of a serving man), but maybe it would be a good idea to pop back, check that the water and our house were all right, and see my mother and my in-laws. Yes I'd go, while I still had enough money to come back to London again. My mother's letter next morning confirmed my decision, 'Don't stay down there by yourself for Hogmanay', she wrote, 'Come home for a wee while'.

I caught the 10 a.m. train from Euston, and as I opened the front door of the house in Glasgow the telephone was ringing. It was the B.B.C. in London. Aeolian Hall to be precise, from Leslie Bridgmont's office. He had kept his word and he hadn't forgotten me, but oh if only he'd thought of it 24 hours earlier he'd have saved me such a lot of time and precious cash. They wanted me the next day to play the part of a wee boy in a comedy sketch, and to join in some of the concerted items with the orchestra. Dorothy Carless was the soloist, and the variety orchestra would be featured. Was I free to do it? I was tired and hungry after my journey, but it was my very first offer from a London producer. I couldn't say no. 'Yes, I'll be there', I said. 'What time do you want me in the morning?'

Long long afterwards when she heard this story, Grace McChlery said that that was the moment when she knew I would make a success of my life in London. 'With the strength and determination to say yes, and to be able to turn round and go straight back to London', she told me, 'You were bound to succeed.'

My neighbour thought I was mad, but lent me a kettle of water to make myself some tea to save the bother of filling up the water tank all over again. I took a quick run up to Springburn to break the news to my mother that I had to go back to London right away, but would be home for Hogmanay. She was aghast at the expense and even more so at the thought of the journey, and she cast her eyes upwards, 'My Goad, you must be ambitious, she said, 'Can ye no' juist tell them you canny come till efter the New Year?' As if the B.B.C. planned their programmes round my convenience! I laughed and shook my head. 'It's all right mother', I told her, 'I'm lucky to have my room to go back to. I'll be home the day after tomorrow'.

So that was how my first broadcast from Aeolian Hall came about. I was thrilled to meet Dorothy Carless of the velvet voice, who surprised me by being tall and blonde, when I'd thought of her as being small and dark. She obviously had the sort of voice which conveyed that impression, because when I said impulsively that I had pictured her entirely differently, she said wearily that everybody told her so. She must have been fed up listening to this remark, as I was later to be myself when people met me who'd only heard me on the air and told me they'd imagined me to be a big fat wifie!

It was most exciting finding myself singing with her and the others rousing Christmas chorusses, backed by musicians to whom transposing, re-arranging and brilliant improvisation were child's play. One knew that however one faltered, they would be there to sustain and cover up, and I may say I've found this impressive musical talent in every B.B.C. orchestra with whom it's been my good fortune to work. I have never taken such expertise for granted, and they always seemed highly amused by my open admiration of their talents. I think they were pleased though, for it's always nice to be told you're good, even in the rarefied atmosphere of top entertainment, where you've just *got* to be extra special to have reached that height. It's no accident that musicians are among my best friends in London. As a sixpenny pupil, I know how much hard work has gone into putting them in the top rank!

This was my first engagement as a London artist, and of course as I was supposed to be resident in the capital it was just my bad luck that I had been in Glasgow when the booking came through. So my first fee went to British Railways, for the amount I was paid almost exactly matched my fare, to a penny. But I was creating goodwill and I could now say I'd worked for London B.B.C. After all, you had to invest before you could expect a return. I couldn't expect to show a profit as well, not at this early stage.

So I returned to Glasgow with a light heart to match my pocket, and it was great to be home for Hogmanay. I stayed in Springburn and went first-footing, and nobody seemed particularly interested in my activities in London, which was just as well for I wasn't exactly setting the Thames on fire. It was all too remote for them to comprehend, and they were far more absorbed in knowing who was getting home from the camps abroad, who was likely to be demobbed soon, who getting engaged or married and, above all, in pitting their wits against food and clothing shortages.

We were still strictly rationed, and the big fruit cake that year was once more heavily fortified with grated carrot and a dollop of stout to make up for other missing ingredients. But there were promises of whiter flour any month now, promises which had us agog with anticipation, for we all longed for the taste of a slice of really white bread, and a sponge cake of feather-light quality. I normally preferred brown bread, but after years of grey dough found myself yearning for the luxury of a piece on jeely with soft white bread as its base.

The whole of Glasgow seemed to be stuffed up with colds and catarrh, and when I returned to London after New Year it was with a heavy stupefying cold which blotted out all sense of taste and smell. The train sleeper was freezing, and every muscle ached from trying to hold myself in a warm position once I'd found it. When I reached Clapham, I crept upstairs to my top-floor room, filled a hot-water bottle, didn't even trouble to make myself a cup of tea, but quickly undressed and fell into bed. I was awakened by the sound of the landlady's voice, growing stronger from each landing as she panted up the stairs. 'Miss Weir, Miss Weir', she gasped, 'A telegram for you'. I swung my legs over the side of the bed. My head felt about the size of a football and buzzed like a bike of bees. I felt terrible. There was a strange wobbly sensation in my legs, and I thought I might be going to be sick. Suddenly, the thickness in my head cleared, the way it sometimes does when one has a cold, and I heard a curious hissing sound coming from somewhere. What could it be? As I looked feebly round the room, my eye fell on the tap of the gas fire. It was turned full on and it wasn't lit. I had put a shilling in the meter when I came in and boiled the kettle for my bottle, so the gas must have been hissing into the room ever since. Naturally, because of my cold I had neither heard it nor smelt it. I staggered forward and twisted the tap closed, and then threw open the window and gulped in the fresh air to try to clear my head. Mrs. Parker came in and handed me a telegram. It said 'Can you come to the Globe Theatre 10.30 this morning re part in play', and it was signed by H. M. Tennent, one of London's biggest managements.

Although it was now after 9 o'clock, I went back to bed to consider the situation. My stomach swung uneasily between excitement at the telegram's news, and terror that I might have been gassed as I slept if Tennents hadn't been so extravagant as to wire me. For my landlady wouldn't have climbed three flights of stairs for a mere letter. But how had the gas fire tap turned itself on? I knew I hadn't done it, because I never spent precious shillings on the fire when I was in bed. I learned later that my landlady had done a little tidying while I was away and had lit the fire to keep herself warm. When the shilling had run out, she hadn't bothered to put another one in, and when she left the room later she had forgotten to turn off the tap. So of course the tap had still been open when I put in my shilling in the morning. It was a most dangerous practice, and my near escape taught me to check the taps every time I came back to my room.

Having considered the situation from all angles, I could now turn my attention to the staggering news in the telegram. But first I must have a cup of tea. It dawned on me I had had nothing to eat or drink since my supper in Glasgow the night before. Was it only the night before? Already it seemed a lifetime away. I jumped up and put the kettle on, then popped back to bed while it boiled, and savoured the full delight of having been invited to attend H. M. Tennent's pleasure at The Globe. What play could it be for? What stars would be in it? Oh what did it matter who was in it, so long as I was being considered for it too. I'd wear my one and only green suit, and I'd get a bottle of Vick on the way to the theatre, to try to clear my head. The room was now perishing because of the wide-open window, but I had to make sure every trace of gas escaped, so I had breakfast sitting up in bed with my dressing gown on to keep warm.

As my head got a bit clearer, I began to wonder how on earth Tennents had ever heard of me. I hadn't gone to see anyone there. Could it be a mistake? I seized the telegram and examined every word of it again. No, it was addressed to Molly Weir. It was me all right. Oh thank goodness I lived so near the West End. It would only take a little over half-an-hour from door to door, so I had time to give myself a thorough wash, and brush my hair, *and* my suit, to achieve as neat and pleasing an appearance as possible.

They were all rehearsing when I presented myself at the stage door, and a young man handed me a script and told me to study the part of Bertha. I found a corner back-stage and plunged into frantic study of the lines I was to speak for the audition. I took no notice of anything else that was going on, until the same young man beckoned to me to come on stage where the producer was now ready for me. It was the famous Richard Bird, known to all theatreland as 'Dicky Bird'. He explained that they had several people to see so couldn't give an immediate decision about the part, but they'd like to hear me read for it. It was that of an ex-A.T.S. girl who performs all her duties as a maid at the double because of her wartime training, and nearly drives her employer mad because she *will* salute each time she is given an order. 'Will I do it in Scots?', I asked seriously. There was a muffled snort of laughter from the unseen figures in the stalls. 'Nacherally', said Dicky Bird, in mock imitation of my accent, and I blushed with embarrassment. I was so accustomed to using a variety of dialects for the B.B.C. and the amateur productions in Glasgow that the first thing we established was the accent, and it didn't dawn on me that nobody in London would think of me other than as a Scot with the heather growing out of her ears, capable only of speaking with the broadest of Scottish accents.

As soon as I'd said the first line, Dicky Bird's face lost its detached look, and by the end of the scene there were encouraging little chuckles from the darkness out front. I closed the book and handed it back to the young man who hovered in the wings, for I knew they had other people to see. To my surprise, Dicky Bird said 'Don't go. Just sit down there for a moment', and he motioned me to a chair in the wings. I heard a murmured conversation and then, unbelievably, Dicky Bird's voice said, 'Well the part is yours Miss Weir. Go with Bob up to the office and sign your contract and come right back down to resume rehearsals'. I stared at him. What about the other people they had to see? He patted my shoulder and told Bob to take me to the offices, and bring me back as soon as possible for there was a lot to do. As the lift took us upwards, I heard the tinkle of cups and knew the coffee break was over, and that by the next meal-break, I would be one of the company.

Bob ushered me into an outer office, then I was shown into the holy of holies, and found myself facing one of Binkie Beaumont's minions, Beaumont himself being the great white chief who ran Tennents. Even I had heard of him via the press. I wasn't to see him in person until the dress rehearsal as it turned out. They offered me ten pounds per week, which seemed like a small fortune, told me there would be a three months' number one tour (number one again —it must mean something special!), and then the play would open in London. I was to sign where indicated, and could ascertain all other relevant details at my leisure. I signed eagerly, dying to get down to the stage again to see my fellow-actors who, up till now, had been invisible.

Two people were working on a scene on stage, and Dicky Bird faced them from a chair propped securely behind the footlights which were of course not lit. There was just a smallish amount of illumination, it seemed to me, but it all smelt wonderful. The same smell which I knew from the Empire, the Theatre Royal and the Kings in Glasgow. London theatres didn't smell a bit different. I felt quite at home. An elderly chap sat mouthing his lines behind the scenery, clad to the ears in a heavy overcoat, and a young couple nearby were going through their scene in whispers. A beautiful red-haired lady sat with closed eyes, her hand steadily moving from line to line as she went down the page memorising her dialogue. I stared at all of them. My first close contact with real actors and actresses.

We broke for lunch before my scene came up, and when I asked the youngest-looking where they went, she said 'Oh *we* go to so-and-sos, but I expect it would be rather expensive for you.' I bit my lip, and forced a smile, 'Oh it doesn't matter', I said, 'I want to do some shopping anyway', and I flew out of the stage door, determined to let nothing spoil my moment of triumph at having landed a part in a West End play. I danced up Shaftesbury Avenue and I wanted to stop everyone and say 'I'm an actress. I'm rehearsing at the Globe Theatre. I'm going to be in London's West End. And I'm not nearly through my fifty pounds yet.' But instead I found myself in Soho, in front of a mouth-watering window filled with French pâtisserie. I hadn't seen such rich-looking cakes for years. In fact I doubted if I'd ever seen such creamy concoctions. I went in. And to celebrate my first theatre part, in the perishing month of January, I had a cup of coffee, two French cakes, and an ice cream. I blanched when I saw the bill, but recovered immediately. It had been worth it. It had nothing to do with practical everyday eating, and I would remember that lunch all my life.

In the afternoon I was introduced to the rest of the cast. The elderly gentleman was A. E. Matthews, whom I was to know later as beloved Matty, that glorious eccentric recognised by everyone in theatreland as a law unto himself. The others were Marjorie Fielding, a delightful lady who gave me great help, Ronnie Ward whose style afforded me much amusement, Denis Goacher and Barbara White, Charles Cameron (later to be a stalwart of the

Whitehall farces with Brian Rix), Jean St. Clair who understudied me as well as playing the overgrown schoolgirl, and the beautiful red-haired Ambrosine Phillpots.

I found Barbara White enchantingly lovely, and I never understood why she didn't go right to the top with those looks, especially in films. But she was engaged to Kieron Moore, who was quite an eyeful himself, and they made a stunning couple. Kieron was playing in a theatre which had Mondays off, and we were to see much of him on our tour, as he tore all over Britain on Mondays to spend a few hours with his beloved Barbara. When they married, she retired from the bright lights and concentrated on having babies and creating a happy home. I hope Kieron appreciates it was I who taught Barbara to iron during our laundry sessions in the wardrobe between matinée and evening performances. Barbara was astounded by the speed with which I tore through such chores, not realising possibly that the work might have been more professional if I had taken more time, but she was all for learning my method, so I passed on my hit-and-run technique!

The young man who had looked after me at the audition was called Bob, and he was stage manager as well as understudy to Denis Goacher and Ronnie Ward. We even had an Assistant Stage Manager, so that in the event of illness all eventualities were covered. This was a luxury unknown to me in Glasgow. Fancy even the stage manager having an understudy! Later two other understudies were engaged, to 'cover' Marjorie, Barbara and Ambrosine, but they didn't join us until the last week of rehearsals.

It was ages before I discovered how the management had come to hear of my existence. It appeared that the part of Bertha had already been cast, but the comedienne who had been engaged had received a better offer and had accepted it. She had simply walked out and left the company after two or three days' rehearsals. It was quite a tricky part. It wasn't big enough to tempt an established comedienne, which the other girl was, so although they were furious that she had let them down, they couldn't really blame her. Yet it was too important to trust to an unknown inexperienced beginner. Time was pressing, and while they were deliberating as to whether or not they should bring back one of their contract players who was on tour with another play, Dicky Bird met the director who had made that first film with me in Glasgow. That was a lucky meeting for me. When he had asked, half-joking, if she had a good young comedienne up her sleeve, she told him about the film and flatteringly added that although I had finely played a down-trodden little creature for her, it was right against my true type and I had had them all in stitches in the bus coming back each day from location. She obligingly boosted my chances further by telling him that both John Mills and Alastair Sim had liked my work, and that I was an established B.B.C. artist!

So Dicky took her word for it and decided it might be a good idea to have a look at me at least, for at this stage there just wasn't time to hold general auditions all over again. By telling me they had others to see, they had just been paving the way for a polite 'we'll let you know' if I hadn't been any good. If I was any good, I was in. It was a fantastic coincidence that Dicky and Budge should have met while her memory of my work was still fresh, and lucky beyond my wildest hopes that the part should have been one where my accent was not only acceptable but actually enhanced the comedy.

The rehearsals were enthralling, and at the same time they sufficiently resembled the work I'd done in Glasgow to make me feel at home. The main differences were that with stars in the cast, with their own ideas, the finer points were the subject of intense discussion and mutual agreement, and various ways of interpretation were tried before the final style was set. As for me, I just did as I was told which, as I was a Scot with 'foreign' intonation of my own, was surprisingly little. Apart from being shown my 'moves', I was left to get on with it, and luckily everyone seemed to find my peculiar voice rhythms amusing. There wasn't much time for us to get to know one another, for we were all intent on learning lines and in getting the play into shape before the opening night in Edinburgh, which was to take place 2½ weeks after the arrival of that fateful telegram.

We had dress fittings and last minute alterations in Tennent's own wardrobe before the clothes were packed into their big baskets ready for the train to Scotland.

I used to love to visit the wardrobe right at the top of the theatre, and watch the scurry and bustle which took place when they were getting a play ready for the road. A whole team of girls busied themselves pressing beautiful clothes, hanging them up to air and leaving them perfect, ready for the next pair of hands to insulate them with layers and layers of tissue paper and pack them into the yawning mouths of enormous wicker baskets. Hats and gloves and undies stood in neat piles, and handbags by the side, with every item checked to see that it matched the entire outfit.

It was just like being behind the scenes at a top sewing establishment.

When they weren't packing clothes for a tour, they sat busily sewing, altering, repairing, and sometimes re-making dresses which lent themselves to adaptation for another show. And I enjoyed to the hilt the sight of well-known actors and actresses being fitted with their wardrobes for their latest play. And some of them were very well-known stars indeed, for Tennents always had several plays running in the West End at the same time, as well as many on the road, and they used the top talents in all of them.

And when I'd examined all the dresses and the lovely materials, I stood entranced before the rows of new shoes waiting to accompany each outfit.

To my delight, after years of pinching and scraping to acquire respectable shoes and stockings to set off my carefully-hoarded best clothes, I was allowed a split new pair of black lacing shoes, and two pairs of fine black lisle stockings for my part of the maid. The shoes would have to be handed back at the end of the play of course, to go into Tennent's general store, but the stockings were mine for keeps. What a bonus! And I didn't even have to go hunting for my small size three shoe. The wardrobe mistress did this for me, and only took me along at the last minute to check that size and fitting were right. Gosh, it was like having a lady's maid.

Three days before leaving for the north and the opening night, the Post Office, with an unexpected burst of speed, informed me that I could have the telephone installed any time I wished. What luck. I'd be able to ring the landlady if I were to manage home any week-end, and I could rejoice in the knowledge that when the tour finished I'd have no more chasing for pennies and sixpences for I'd have my very own telephone at my command. It was a bit of an expense before I'd even started earning regularly, but I could just about manage the installation charges, and I would have a pay coming in every week for ages and ages. It would be well worth a bit of scrimping now.

Luckily I arrived home early from rehearsal when the engineers were in the house, for to my indignation I found that my landlady was calmly instructing them to instal it in the hall and to make it a coin box. What cheek! When I had been the one to apply for the instrument, and when I would be the one who would be expected to pay for its rental. Worst of all, I would be back to square one, hoarding coins, waiting my turn in the queue, the only advantage being that of merely descending three flights of stairs instead of having to dress and go round the corner to the Post Office. Plus of course the privilege of paying for the installation.

I could feel the sense of outrage rising and threatening to choke me. Injustice always brings on feelings of claustrophobia, I don't know why. But I made myself speak reasonably and calmly. I didn't want to find my things in the street, before I even left for Edinburgh.

'Oh, do you want it in the hall Mrs. Parker?', I asked, all innocent surprise, 'For use of the whole house?' She fluttered her hands and didn't meet my eyes. 'Yes, I thought it would be better here', she said, 'And then we could all use it'.

I swallowed, but managed a reasonable, frowning expression as though I were considering the matter. 'Well', I said, 'You do realise of course that a coin box is a higher rental, and that it will be the house telephone and not mine, but of course I don't mind since you will be paying for it.'

There was complete silence. I gazed dreamily at the ceiling. She rubbed her hands and looked at the engineers. They swung their boxes and said at last impatiently, 'Well, where do you want it missus, we haven't got all day.' They looked at Mrs. Parker and then at me, wondering what on earth it was all about. 'Do you want to take it over Mrs. Parker?', I asked. 'No', she answered, and disappeared into the scullery without another word.

'Follow me', I told the engineers.

My goodness but I was getting devious, I thought. We both knew, the landlady and I, that an attempt at a little bit of sharp practice had been foiled, yet not a harsh word had been spoken which would have been difficult to overlook living under the same roof. And before I left for Edinburgh, I told her that I would leave my door unlocked so that if anyone wished to use the telephone they were most welcome, and they could also give my number to any important personal or business contacts, so that everyone in the house could share my good luck in this way. After all I had the boon of having the telephone right beside my bed and didn't even have to put my clothes on to answer it.

I left a wee saucer for money for outgoing calls, and the other tenants seemed highly delighted with this arrangement.

I knew I was fortunate to be living in a house of such irreproachable honesty that I could leave everything behind an unlocked door. The use of my telephone was a very small thank you to such trustworthy neighbours.

13

WHEN we all met in the morning at Kings Cross Station at the start of the tour, and found our reserved compartments, I felt it was just like Priestley's 'Good Companions'. I was very excited about the whole thing, and considered it was a terrific bonus to have my fares paid to places I'd never seen before, because, apart from London, the rest of England was virtually unknown to me.

I wondered what my Edinburgh digs would be like. I'd never lived in theatrical digs, and was amazed to discover that Equity, the Actors' Trade Union, supplied a booklet of addresses for every single town and city which boasted theatres. There were dozens and dozens of names, far more than the holiday lists in the *Evening Times* which we used to study with such passion when we were looking for a house for our Fair holidays. And this theatrical letting went on all the year round. My goodness, it must be an industry in itself, I thought.

The lower-paid members of the company pored over the addresses, mostly in ignorance of where any of the lodgings were situated in relation to the theatre or whether or not they might be in slum districts. But we were kept on the right track by the troupers who had toured the theatres for years, and warned which ones not to touch with a barge pole, and which ones were truly home from home. Because I had a typewriter, I did most of the writing, and we shared out the favourable replies between us, and before we left London I felt thankful and assured that I would have a place to rest my head in every town or city the play visited. Before the end of the tour though, I was to regret having planned my life quite so far ahead.

The company had been very surprised that I couldn't pass on any recommendations about good Glasgow digs, but because it was my home town I hadn't the faintest idea where 'theatricals' lived. With my own home and other relatives there, I had never had to think of such a thing. However, I could keep them right about the good districts to choose, and the Equity booklet had a list of excellent ones around Hill Street and the Charing Cross area, handy for getting to and from the theatre, and dead centre of the good shopping area. There was some curiosity about where I lived, but the moment they discovered it was half-an-hour's journey by tramcar, they lost interest. Actors, like railwaymen and shipyard workers, like to live on top of the job, especially when touring.

My Edinburgh digs were in a dingy tenement round the corner from the theatre, and the house resounded with the tread of heavy tackety boots as the sons tramped in and out for their meals. She was a nice friendly body though, my landlady, my very first 'pro' landlady, and I was far too excited about the play to bother about cooking smells or the aroma of drying dungarees. I was longing to see the 'set' in position and rushed round to the theatre the moment I'd unpacked. I knew the props and the scenery had gone ahead, and that the men would have been building it all day to have it ready for our first run-through that evening. It was fascinating to find 'my' drawing room, where I made my first entrance, so beautifully realised with walls, doors and windows, and handsome furniture, and when I'd finished admiring the rich effect I tried the window fastenings and the door handles to make sure they worked properly, before going in search of my silver tray and the other props I'd require during the course of the play. It's a good maxim always to check everything you will use in a performance, from doors to teacups, and then you will avoid nightmares during the actual performance.

In contrast to the brilliance of the lighting when audiences are expected, theatres, when occupied only by actors, are dimly lit places with great pools of darkness where single bulbs send little radiance. It's always exciting for the actor, but the magic only begins when the audience arrives.

I had time to walk back to my digs for a welcome pot of tea and some toast, and when I went back to the theatre, the stage was transformed, brilliantly lit, with the electricians going through their paces in readiness for our first rehearsal. We all seemed to have the jittery feeling which comes from knowing time is running out, and that all the weeks of rehearsal will soon be put to the test in front of a critical audience. The real furniture always seems different, and the props unfamiliar, and inexplicable 'dries' become commonplace.

But Dicky Bird was encouragingly happy, and when tiredness threatened to engulf us all in a brittle edginess he said, 'That'll do for tonight. 10 o'clock in the morning, please, for full dress rehearsal'.

As I lay in that unfamiliar bed in that Edinburgh tenement, I was surrounded by the familiar tenement noises I had known since childhood. The footfalls overhead, the bang on the wall, the pulley noises from downstairs, and the sound of front door keys being turned in locks. It was like being back in Springburn again. But oh I was glad it wasn't Springburn, for that would have meant Glasgow, and I didn't feel quite courageous enough to be judged by my very own fellow-Glaswegians on my very first performance with a company of professional actors and actresses. Auld Reekie didn't know I'd gone to London to seek fame and fortune, and I would be of no particular interest to them, thank goodness. They would be watching the stars, not studying me looking for signs of anything special, and I could concentrate on doing my very best to make the most of the author's lines without being too palsied with terror, as I would have been had I been facing a Glasgow audience on opening night.

The dress rehearsal went in fits and starts, as dress rehearsals usually do, until it seemed impossible that we'd ever get through the play in the usual $2\frac{1}{2}$ hours which normally saw the unfolding and solution of all such tales. It went on for *hours*, with unsuspected snags cropping up all the time. Doors opened the wrong way for certain comedy entrances. The sofa was too bulky for swift manoeuvring at a particular point. The tray was too large to get through the French windows. Even the clothes developed a temperament of their own, and buttons mysteriously appeared in the wrong places, or seams twisted, and hems dipped confusingly. The wardrobe mistress pattered back and forth with needle and thread and scissors, and the iron was on the go all day long. Carpenters hammered, and removed screws, and changed fitments round to suit us. We had one clear run-through of the play from start to finish, and it felt quite lifeless. Our hearts were in our boots when we broke for tea.

My dressing room was right at the top of the theatre, and I was sharing with Jean St. Clair, the big Irish girl with the droll looks, and with Caroline, one of the understudies. Jean had a great sense of humour, and as she didn't appear until the very last moments of the play, decided it was far too early for her to be nervous, and so reeled off a non-stop flow of Irish jokes which had me giggling and spluttering with laughter in spite of my own tremors. Once made up and into my maid's uniform, I felt more like Bertha, the ex-A.T.S. tear-away maid, and the neatness and sparkling cleanliness of the outfit appealed to me. Wherever else I fell down, at least I looked right.

By this time, back-stage fairly pulsed with excitement and we all raced around, wishing each other good luck. However strong is the faith of actors in the play, the author, the management and their own hard work, they know they also need a big helping of the final ingredient, luck, to fuse memory, talent and vitality into that special something which spells success. The overture ended. It was curtain up, and on with the show. The laughs came surely and steadily, and I got a roar on one exit line, and a round of applause on another. It was so unexpected, I nearly dried up, and Bob, never taking his eyes from the 'book' where he was on 'cue' duty in the wings, whispered 'Good girl, you're doing fine', as I ran past him for the prop table, to pick up a duster for my next entrance.

In the third act, I had an entrance where it was vital that Matty didn't finish the last sentence of his speech, or it would give the whole plot away. I had to enter carrying my silver tray laden with tea things, and as it felt as though it weighed a ton, and they knew it was very heavy for me, I was ordered not to pick it up from the prop table until the very last moment, so that I could carry it on with sure strong steady arms, without a wobble anywhere. On that first night, long before the plot line was due, I decided to try out the weight of the laden tray once more and I poised myself behind the door to estimate yet again just how much space I'd require to sail smoothly through at the correct moment. This ritual was merely for my own peace of mind, and I was just about to relieve my arms of the dead-weight of the tray when, to my horror, I heard Matty start the vital line *miles* too soon. I hadn't a second to collect my thoughts, much less think of my lines. I wrenched the door open and catapulted on stage, dishes, cakes, bread and milk clattering like castanets. Ronnie Ward gave a snort of laughter, Marjorie Fielding an approving nod, and Matty merely smiled amiably. For a frozen moment my lines vanished, and then as my heart turned over with fright, I found my mouth was opening and shutting and the rehearsed words were coming out.

At the end of the scene, I tottered off the stage like a limp rag. Oh gosh, I hoped I'd never have to go through that nightmare again. But I had. Every single performance! I can say, with my hand on my heart, that I never had a correct cue from Matty in that scene during the entire tour. I used to stand poised outside that door, frantically trying to guess where he'd put the line this time, and indeed how he would phrase it, for he said something quite different at each performance. The cast took bets as to whether or not he would beat me to it! It was agonising, and I ought to have felt like strangling him for making me go through this ordeal eight times a week. But somehow one forgave Matty everything, for the colour, the extravagance and genuine eccentricity of his style in a largely disciplined back-stage world.

The first member of the family to see me as a real actress was my brother-in-law Jimmy. I found him standing in the doorway of my digs one afternoon when I came in for tea. He was home on de-mobilisation leave, had learned that I was acting in Edinburgh and had decided to come through to see the play. I was delighted to see him, for he and my husband shared the same rich vein of wit, and I applauded his good sense in finding my address from the stage door. Come to think of it, anybody who could find his way out of Cherbourg with the enemy at his heels, not to mention other war-time hazards, wasn't going to be stumped merely because he had no address for me in his pocket-book. He would have to stay in Edinburgh for the night, because the last Glasgow train left before our final curtain, and he wondered if there was a spare bed in my digs. My landlady, with all those sons, took his request in her stride. Yes, of course he could stay there, if he didn't mind sharing a bed with one of the boys. This presented no problem to Jimmy, who had had to find his rest where he could during five years of warfare. It was a concealed bed, behind a door in the lobby, but he would find it comfortable, she assured him, and he need only pay for his breakfast. The bed would be her present to a serving soldier, seeing all her boys had been safely at home, some too young to serve, and the others in reserved occupations.

I had had very good notices from the Edinburgh press, but none meant so much as Jimmy's assessment, for I had a great respect for his sense of fun and his lively appreciation of the humour of any situation. I felt as though I had won an Oscar when he told me afterwards that for him the funniest moment in the play was when I tiptoed through the French windows bearing my silver tray (a short cut I had been forbidden to use), caught Matty's warning eye indicating that his wife Marjorie was in the room, and tiptoed cautiously out again without opening my mouth. I had particularly enjoyed working out this little piece of mimed comedy, and I was thrilled to feel it had come over as I intended, to one member of the audience at least. Dear Jimmy, I don't suppose he ever knew how much his compliment meant to me, but at the start of my professional stage career it was of greater encouragement than I could have put into words.

With an all-English company, I was like Ruth among the alien corn, and I really had no one in whom I could confide or with whom I could discuss anything. Jimmy's unexpected visit provided a marvellous opportunity to discuss the whole play, chapter and verse, over supper and it was great to be able to sit up chatting non-stop and know that every word would be understood, with no translation required for English ears.

The play had a fairly cool reception in Glasgow, although again my own performance met with some approval. I was vexed that we hadn't set Glasgow on fire with our drawing-room thriller-comedy, but very thankful that no brickbats had been thrown at me. It would have been too awful to have returned with a London company, looking like a fish out of water. But cool reception or no, all my neighbours had booked for the Saturday night, and were throwing a farewell party for me afterwards. That Saturday performance found me shaking with a horrible sort of terror, which chilled instead of making me fevered, which sent my teeth chattering and a cold perspiration to trickle down my arms.

At least I thought it was fear which produced these nightmarish sensations, but at the party afterwards, held in my neighbour's house next door, everything began to swim before my eyes and I had a sensation of floating. I knew without doubt that this wasn't nerves. It was my old enemy, 'flu. As my temperature rose and sweat began to trickle down my face, one of the husbands said decisively, 'Well, there's one thing certain, you can't go to Newcastle with the company tomorrow. It's bed for you for the next few days'.

I stared at him as though he'd gone out of his mind. 'Not go to Newcastle!', I said, 'I *must*. The understudies don't know their parts yet. And anyway, I couldn't stay here knowing they'd gone without me. They might not have me back.'

Imagine him thinking *anything* short of death would prevent my travelling to my next lot of digs the following morning. I might drop dead on the station platform, but I was going.

On Sunday morning I staggered about emptying the water tank and making sure everything was left neat and tidy and safe, before setting off with chattering teeth for the station.

In Newcastle, three of us had booked in at a guest house recommended by an actor friend, and I will never forget the kindness of that compassionate landlord and his wife. She took one look at my face, packed me off to bed in my room on the third floor and told me to stay there, and tea would be brought up to me. 'It's too far to carry it', I protested feebly, 'I'll get up if you give me a call'. They would have none of it. 'I'll bring it up', said the landlord, 'So you'll stay in bed when you're told.' Oh the bliss of that welcoming mattress. I sank down and down into a deep fevered sleep, only swimming back to a hazy consciousness when a tap on the door told me it was time for afternoon tea. I drained the teapot with greedy thirst, but I had no appetite for the scones or the biscuits which had been left on the tray. Supper (as they called their high-tea-cum-dinner) was at 7.30 on Sundays, and when I crept into the dining room those kind proprietors were dismayed that I'd dressed and come down for it. Why hadn't I stayed in bed? Gosh, I thought, it was bad enough the man having carried up a tea-tray, I wasn't going to have him carting a whole dinner up three flights of stairs. What would my grannie have said? She would have despised such weak behaviour. And anyway, they hadn't mentioned serving dinner in my room and I never dreamt guest-houses would have thought of doing such a thing.

I stayed in bed most of Monday, only visiting the theatre after breakfast to see if there was any mail and checking where my dressing room was, and how the scenery fitted the new stage. It was to become a great thrill looking for mail on the green baize board behind each stage door, or sometimes in little pigeon holes in the stage-door-keeper's office. I really felt the complete actress when I'd enquire with studied casualness, 'Any mail for me George?' (they all seemed to be called George), and if a letter was handed over addressed to me c/o whatever theatre we were appearing in that week, I felt part of the very fabric of show business.

On this Monday morning there was nothing and I crawled thankfully back to the guest house and bed, very relieved that I was having full board this week and there would be no need to do battle with the local shops for my groceries. During the tour I was to find that we never arrived at any town at the right time for anything. Eggs had been delivered last week and their allocation had gone so none for strolling players. Tinned fruit wasn't expected till next week, so our coupons couldn't be used for that covetable item to add zest to our diet. When we demanded onions, because we'd read in the papers that this area were having their quota this very day, they smiled and said that alas they'd had theirs much earlier in the month, and couldn't expect any more supplies till the following allocation. We'd be half-way to London by then, of course.

I remember in one town I took a great notion for parsnips. My landlady had incautiously told me she thought there might still be one or two around, as she'd managed to buy some at the weekend. Any fresh vegetables were as manna from heaven and I wouldn't rest until I'd found some for myself. I went into every single greengrocers in the neighbourhood, and in the end victory was mine. The last one in a row of grimy little shops yielded up almost a pound.

I rushed back with them, gave the landlady instructions to cook only one with my stew, and drooled all afternoon at the thought of having this delicious vegetable stretched over at least three meals to add savour to my dinners. When I sat down to dinner later that night, I was astounded to find that my fellow-actor, Charles Cameron, was sitting before a plate containing a liberal helping of parsnips. 'Oh did you manage to get some too, Charles?', I said innocently, for I knew he hated shopping and I was quite interested to know how he had tracked them down. I never even began to suspect the truth. 'Oh no Molly', he said, seizing a forkful as he spoke, 'They're yours. I just told the landlady to cook them all. I knew you wouldn't mind, and I can always get some more for you tomorrow.'

When I could find my voice, I nearly shattered the dishes with my roar. 'You *can't* get me more tomorrow Charles Cameron', I yelled, 'For there *aren't* any more to be got. How *dare* you take food without knowing whether or not you could repay it'. He was staring at me, open-mouthed, obviously baffled by my rage. I then turned on the hapless landlady, 'And *you* had *no right* to give that man my parsnips'. And I turned and walked out of the room, my food uneaten. Charles was tall and handsome and I could imagine how persuasive he had been, but I was unforgiving. I had to come back and eat my dinner of course, for I was hungry, but I waited until he had finished. I couldn't have swallowed a mouthful with him in the room—it would have choked me.

Food, after years of scarcity and rationing, assumed an almost unbelievable importance to us at that time, so much so that I have to confess that I don't remember a thing about Charles's performance in the play. I only remember that he stole my parsnips. When I met him years later and recalled his name the instant I saw him, he was flattered and suprised at my being able to put a name to him so quickly (actors are notoriously forgetful of each other's real names). I had the grace not to tell him that his name and face were riveted in my memory for ever, and meant only one thing to me, that his soft words to the landlady had buttered MY parsnips!

I managed to get through the week at Newcastle by staying in bed most days and just getting up to go to the theatre at night. Although there was one terrible day when I decided a breath of sea air might just be the thing to get some energy into my aching bones, and I nearly didn't have strength to get back to the guest house, much less to the Theatre Royal. Somebody had told me we were only a bus ride from Whitley Bay, and as I've always been mad about the seaside and convinced salt air would cure anything from ingrowing toenails to galloping dandruff, nothing would do but that I'd make for the miles of sands as soon as I'd swallowed my lunch. It was the first time I'd had any real exercise since I'd caught the 'flu virus, and I had no idea of the bracing strength of those wintry winds, or of how weak I was. I set off at a fine pace across the sands, gulping down great draughts of sea air, but, to my dismay, instead of bounding along with greater and greater vitality after all this beautiful ozone, my head spun with dizziness, my legs wobbled like a jelly and, worst of all, I couldn't draw a breath. What was the matter with me? There wasn't a soul within miles—nothing but sea birds and me. Thankfully my eye caught a little beach hut and I struggled towards it, collapsed on to the bench, and fought to get my breath back. I sounded like grannie in one of her bad doses of bronchitis. I wheezed like an old gramophone. I had gone too far to go back the way I'd come, and there was a staggeringly long way to go yet before I could catch any sort of transport. I grew so scared, I wouldn't allow myself to rest as long as I felt I ought, but set off in a zig-zag motion towards the end of the beach and, I hoped, the route to the buses. I kept turning my back to avoid being choked by the wind, and it seemed to take hours before I reached the path which eventually led me to a bus, and home. When I got to my room. I threw myself down on the bed, and I felt so weak that I didn't know how I was ever going to summon enough energy to walk downstairs for tea, much less do a show that night. I felt that this was what it must feel like to be drunk. And in a sense I suppose I was. Drunk with far too strong air gulped into 'flu-weakened blood and lungs.

Eventually I made myself swing my legs to the floor to see if I, could stand upright. I could. I determined to say nothing to anybody, so that if they behaved normally towards me, expecting nothing unusual in my performance or manner, then I might just get through the evening. Luckily Jean St. Clair was in sparkling form throughout tea, so my quietness went unnoticed, particularly as she and one of the understudies started arguing as to which of them had left the bathroom in a mess, with towels on the floor. They made such a row that I could rise from the table with a casual 'See you later. I've my apron to check with wardrobe', and make my way to the theatre without them. I needed all my precious energy for the performance. At a chemists I picked up some glucose, which the man behind the counter recommended as a first-class energy-giver after too much exertion. Thanks to its help, and to keeping my own counsel, the final curtain saw me still in one piece, with nobody suspecting how near I had come to missing the performance. That afternoon taught me one valuable lesson—that you can have too much of a good thing, especially if that good thing is strong pure sea air when the body is weak.

I learned too, the truth behind Lady Churchill's precept, 'Never enlarge upon your difficulties except to tried and trusted friends'. For if people don't know you are in difficulties, they won't undermine your struggle by too much sympathy which can sap the will.

After Newcastle, we were to visit Sheffield, Manchester, Northampton, Nottingham, Blackpool, Liverpool, Cardiff, Swansea, Leeds, Birmingham, Cambridge, Bournemouth and Brighton. These were all Number One dates. I was delighted by the prospect of seeing so many new places, for with my husband overseas and no home responsibilities while I was chasing a career, I was footloose and fancy free. But those who had left comfortable homes, and in some cases husbands, wives or families, weren't so pleased to be touring. I soon saw why. It was too soon after the war for travel to be anything but a penance. There was no new rolling stock on the railways, the trains had little or no heating, and Sunday travel took hours over the normal time tables. 'Actors and fish always travel on Sundays', Reggie Gosse our manager would say with his genial smile. The other manager, Ossie Wilson, always made me laugh because of his firm determination *not* to share his train beer. There were no buffet cars and hardly any food or drink of any kind to be had on station platforms. When we'd assemble on Sunday mornings he would call out in ringing tones, 'I hope anyone who wants beer has made proper provision, for I do *not* share my train beer with anyone. Is that clear? Good'. Nobody could now expect misplaced charity from him, or have any hope of softening his heart by pleading sudden thirst.

I was most impressed by Ossie's courage in warning off moochers like this, and I applauded his attitude. I remembered only too well my own irritation with those foolish Virgins who came on our Guide outings without a bit of food to cook, well content to take advantage of the wise provisioning of more obedient girls. Now if only I had had Ossie's courage and strength of character, I might just have taught such improvident girls a lesson which would have served them in good stead all their lives.

Although practically everyone bought Sunday papers to while away the hours spent on freezing journeys on those terrible trains, once we'd read each other's horoscopes, Matty wouldn't let us read a word. He'd fling his arms wide and knock the papers away from us as we attempted to digest the news. 'You don't want to bother with that rubbish', he would roar, 'It's been the same for the last 60 years and it won't be any better in the next 60—let's talk and keep ourselves warm.' (When I first saw him I thought Matty was about 60 years old, and I was absolutely amazed to learn that he was actually 76.) On those train journeys he would keep us so enthralled that we almost forgot our numb toes and fingers as we listened to tales of Sir Gerald du Maurier, and of the horse which Sir Gerald had taught to stop outside Harrods while he went in to do his shopping. One one occasion he had lent it to a distinguished Parliamentarian whose own horse had gone lame, and when the Hon. gent had finished his ride in the park and reached Harrods on his way to the stables, the animal had stopped dead in its tracks and absolutely refused to budge. It was deaf to command or prod, and by the time the beast decided shopping time was over, a small crowd had gathered round the scarlet-faced rider wondering what the famous man was doing sitting outside Harrods as though on traffic duty.

But the tale of du Maurier which shook me to the core, new recruit that I was, was of the night he and Matty stood in the wings waiting for their entrance in a new play, and, to while away the time, started discussing a play they had both been in some years earlier. When they eventually walked on to the stage, they did a whole scene from the *first* play. 'But Matty', I said aghast, 'Weren't the audience all mixed up?' 'Not they', he roared. 'Never noticed a damn thing'. Then he added as an afterthought, 'It was a far better play anyway!'

He told me that Gladys Cooper at 17 was the prettiest thing he had ever seen in his life. 'With the possible exception of Ellaline Terris', he added. 'There was another beauty'. In this first play of Gladys Cooper, in which he was starring of course, he told me that for her first appearance on stage she was seated on a sort of cushion, like little Miss Muffet, and when the curtain rose she was discovered there. 'The curtain rose'. Matty told me, 'There was one long intake of breath, and then the whole audience broke into spontaneous applause.' He added that it was the only time in all his long career that he knew of such an instinctive tribute to sheer beauty.

'Och Matty'. I said to him during one of those journeys (this was before he wrote his biography). 'You should get it all written down, for you have so many memories that nobody else shares'. 'Tried it once, young Molly', he said. 'They sent a damn girl with a notebook who sat and gazed at me waiting for me to talk—couldn't think of a damn thing, so *that* was no good'. I believed him. He needed the stimulus of fellow actors before he could let himself go.

These cold journeys took their toll of the company's health, and there always seemed to be somebody who was coughing or sneezing, and terrified of losing his voice. Matty was hit like the rest of us lesser mortals and his went into very bad bronchitis.

We always had a theatre doctor allocated to us in each town for, like cricketers, actors are notoriously accident prone, and, like the Chinese, when it's a case of 'no work no pay' the show must go on! The theatre doctor prescribed one dessertspoonful of a strong chlorodyne mixture for Matty, three times a day after meals. He loathed the stuff and one day, whether by accident or design, he forgot to take the medicine as prescribed. He may even have decided to get the whole nastiness over at one fell swoop, for he took all three dessertspoonfuls after his light pre-theatre meal. This concentration of chlorodyne was far too much for him in what was almost a lethal dose, and as he returned to his dressing room at the end of act two, he collapsed in the corridor outside my dressing room. Everybody thought he had died, for the sound of his crashing down brought us all into the corridor. To my amazement, the others retreated in fright, but I hadn't been a Girl Guide for nothing. I flew to his dressing room, found towels and soaked them in water, grabbed a cushion to put under his feet, and loosened his collar. The understudy meantime was dressing with frantic speed, to be ready for the third act, which was due to start within a few minutes.

As I dabbed his forehead and wrists with the wet towels, Matty gradually recovered consciousness. The manager appeared and told him not to worry, everything was under control, the understudy was ready to take over. 'What' roared the now recovered Matty, whom I was helping to his room, 'Understudy be damned! I've never missed a performance in sixty years, and I'm not going to start now!' And go on he did, in spite of lips as blue as Stephen's ink, and sublimely ignoring the fact that the rest of us were nervous wrecks wondering if he was going to die on stage. He was so groggy that he had to sit down for the entire third act, all the rehearsed moves thrown out of the window, and we had all to adjust our moves by instinct to accommodate this new position. We ducked round him behind the sofa, said a line and then drifted towards him, pussy-footed round one another until we nearly had hysterics, but we ended the play as written, and the audience wasn't a bit the wiser.

Next morning, because I felt that an old man like him needed it far more than I did, I took my solitary egg, my ration for the month, round to his digs. 'Now eat it all', I commanded him, 'You need the nourishment an egg can give after that carry-on last night. We don't want to go through all *that* again.' He seemed very amused, and promised to eat everything but the shell. The following forenoon he appeared at the door of my digs with a slice of ham between two slices of dry bread. There wasn't even a paper round the 'piece', and I may say his hands were none too clean. 'Here y'are, my girl', he said, thrusting his offering into my hand 'A slice of good Belfast ham in exchange for your egg.' Then hè looked round the tiny hallway with a conspiratiorial air and whispered in my ear, 'How much do you pay for these digs?' '£2 12s. 6d. a week with attendance. Why?' 'Ha!', he snorted, 'I *thought* that old devil next door was overcharging me, I'm paying £2 15s.'. I shouted with laughter. It was the most unlikely conversation between the star of the show, on top salary, and the youngest member of the company earning rock-bottom wages.

They tried to persuade him to go to an hotel after his collapse. 'Not me', he told me on our way home in the tramcar to our digs alongside each other, 'Can't stand the damn places. Vacuum cleaners roaring away at six in the morning and pipes rattling and wheezing all night with all those damn fools having baths.' He was right too. In hotels, actors have to fit in with the rules of the establishment, and must eat and sleep according to the staff's convenience. In theatrical digs, the household revolves round the time-tables of the actors, and the good pro. digs are a home from home.

During one of our tram journeys together, Matty startled a conductor of whom he had asked the time. As the chap started to undo his muffler and fumble about inside an inner pocket to find his old-style watch, Matty fumed impatiently. 'Oh don't strip to the bone, young fella—the nearest hour will do.' He was without doubt a coughdrop, and every outing with him ended up in the rout of those more accustomed to douce obedient citizens. In one town a delivery of melons coincided with our arrival, and Matty decided his wife and sons in London must share this good fortune. He made up an enormous parcel which we both took along to the Post Office, as I wanted some stamps there anyway. When it was weighed, the parcel was too heavy for the permitted maximum. Matty opened the whole thing up and instead of extracting a whole melon, proceeded to reduce the weight slice by slice, which he ate, standing there at the counter! The parcel went on and off the scale as each slice was consumed, and by the time the correct weight was achieved, the Post Office was in an uproar. If they remembered that scene, I'm sure none of those present that day would have been a whit surprised when, in later years, Matty took on the whole Town Council, and posted himself outside in the street, on guard, to prevent their removing the gas lamp which stood outside his house and which he loved. He was a law unto himself, and lovely with it. He posed a terrible threat to those who expected utter conformity to orthodox behaviour, but he was an inspiration to all eccentrics, and embryo eccentrics like me.

He gave me a great demonstration of how an audience can imagine they are seeing something which is not there at all.

Because he lived at Bushey, and wanted to get the earliest possible train home after the show, he started preparing for the homeward journey at the end of the first act of any play in which he was appearing. I saw him do it with ours, and his theories were proved to work. 'Once the audience has accepted the picture of you at the start, young Molly', he said, 'They retain that impression throughout the play, so long as any changes you make are steady and gradual and normal'. So after act one, he used to begin the gentle removal of his stage make-up. Any shading was wiped off first. After his next exit, the eyebrow line was thinned. Then a little greasepaint. And so on. Until by act three his face was cleaned, ready for the street, and nobody had noticed a scrap of difference. They had indeed retained the impression he had created in act one, and this had sustained belief throughout all the gradual removal of the make-up which had created the original picture.

He had a pair of 'going-home' trousers, which he wore for the last scene of every play, whatever the period, and quite irrespective of the type of jacket, robe or waistcoat which appeared above. They were a brownish tweed, and again because of the roguish confidence with which he did everything on stage nobody noticed when this trouser-swopping took place, I proved this for myself when, years later, my husband and I went to see a play starring Matty and Mary Jerrold. I didn't say a word about Matty's strategy, and just waited to see if my husband would notice anything. Up till the final scene, Matty had been in evening trousers, with a short dressing gown on top. The moment he came in for that scene, sure enough, there were the 'going-home' trousers under the silk dressing gown. When I whispered the secret to my husband during the curtain calls, he could hardly believe he hadn't spotted the change. Especially from evening trousers to tweeds. But he hadn't. *Nor* had he noticed that when the hypnotic Matty took his final curtain, his face was naked of the make-up he had worn when the curtain rose. A magic personality, without a doubt, who knew every trick of the trade.

He was a great character. I felt greatly privileged to work with him. Everybody loved him. Even British Rail responded to his eccentric reasoning. He had read somewhere that so long as the wheels of a train are turning, it is technically in motion, so on homeward journeys he actually persuaded drivers to slow down almost to a halt as they reached Watford, the wheels barely turning, so that he could throw his luggage on to the platform and leap out after it. This saved the nuisance of having to go all the way to London, and back again to Bushey. Of all Matty's tricks, I think this was the one which impressed me most. I've never been able myself to persuade train drivers to this point of view, and every time my train roars through Watford without stopping, I think of Matty.

14

EACH town we visited offered fresh surprises, and I was enchanted to discover that although Sheffield gave me the most uncomfortable digs of the tour, the countryside outside the grimy centre was well worth exploring. The weather was crisp and sparkling, and I found two soul-mates in Marjorie Fielding's understudy, and the Welsh Assistant Stage Manager, Eirig. We roamed the hills and dales during the day, and one red-letter afternoon we found a welcoming hillside Inn which offered fresh country eggs for tea, without asking for a single food coupon in exchange. Manna from Heaven indeed, which left a lasting impression on my mind, and erased everything else I may have felt about the industrial north.

But the landlady resembled a character from Dickens. She was so short-sighted that she never even noticed the sooty oily smuts which drifted on to the food she brought in to us, and worse, the scattered hairs from her brindled coiffure, which I daren't pick out from the stews or spaghettis, for she stood and toasted herself at the gas fire while we ate our suppers. Imagination of what her kitchen must be like threatened to choke me even more than the hairy food, but I had to make a show of getting it down because she thought she was being so good to us.

Her taste in pictures was macabre, to say the least. My bedroom walls were adorned with paintings of rats, peeping round the corners of barns, squaring up to one another like boxers, rolling eggs with their feet. Before I went to sleep, I had to turn the pictures to the wall, shuddering as my eyes came so close to the horrid painted vermin, or I'd have had even worse nightmares than I suffered during that awful week in such unsavoury digs.

Bob, one of the stage managers, also stayed at those digs and although he laughed at my fussiness over the hairs and the smuts in the food, he was scared enough of her not to knock her up when he arrived home after midnight, preferring to throw stones at my window to bring me down to open the door for him. We were each allowed a key, but the door was bolted at midnight and no excuses were accepted.

Actually the reason why Bob was so late that night was because he had gone to see a late performance of 'Lost Week-End', that marvellous film about a dipsomaniac which was supposed to serve as an unforgettable lesson to all heavy drinkers. Bob, in the words of the true Glaswegian, liked a good bucket, and when I said primly that I hoped the film had taught him the error of his ways—(I was mad at being wakened out of my hard-won sleep under the picture of the rats)—he said he had been so shattered he had had to find a club, and calm his fears with a few whiskeys!

It was at Blackpool that I started my love affair with seaside resorts out of season. The miles of wide bare sands, the clean-washed look of the town devoid of trippers and candy floss, the friendliness of shops which had time for me. All this made a strong appeal and taught me there is much charm to be found in a resort when it is not wearing its holiday face. So much so, that I have deliberately sought such conditions ever since. Never again for me high season holidays and crammed beaches.

During one of the Sunday train calls, Reggie Gosse told us we might have to extend the tour for a week or so because London was enjoying a theatre boom. The entertainment-starved demobbed soldiers were packing the theatres, and managements couldn't be expected to take off plays which were playing to full houses. There were one or two grumbles, but in the end everybody accepted the logic of the situation, for it was felt we had a good play on our hands which could easily run for a year in London. I, in my ignorance of the vast passing population which went through London, couldn't imagine how there could be enough people to attend a theatre eight times a week for twelve whole months, but the others said a year and I took their word for it.

During the tour, a steady flow of air letters from my husband in the Middle East followed me from theatre to theatre. We both longed for the day of his release from the Air Force, but hadn't the least idea when his class would be sent home. And then, in Liverpool, there on the green baize board was the letter I had been waiting for. He would be home any day. His section were due to arrive in England some time during the week beginning 19th March. That was this week! As soon as his papers had been cleared, he would join me.

My heart turned a dozen somersaults of delight. It had been over two years since I had seen him. And here I was, meeting him as an actress. It was going to be *marvellous*. And then I had a sudden thought. What about my digs, so carefully and prudently booked for a lone female? Would my landladies be able to change my booking to a double room? Would they even believe he was my husband? Or would they, as the more ribald members of the company suggested, imagine I had found myself one of the 'Brylcreem boys', (the nickname for Air Force lads), and was taking him under my wing for the rest of the tour? I wished they hadn't sown that seed in my mind, for now I was in an agony of embarrassment as I wrote to the landladies, and I tried to sound honest and respectable so that there couldn't be the slightest doubt that I was speaking the truth and sought space for a newly-returned husband.

Each day I looked for the telegram which would tell me he was in England. But none came. And then on the Friday night, as I came off stage after my first entrance in the second act, there he was standing in the wings. My Sandy. In uniform. He looked tanned and splendid. He held me at arm's length. 'My, you're awfu' wee', were his first romantic words. 'You're no' very big yourself', I retorted, and, on shaking legs, went on to make my next entrance. So his first sight of me after all that time apart was in full stage make-up, dressed in cap and apron as Bertha.

The cast were thrilled to the marrow that the romance of our reunion had taken place before their very eyes, and the ladies all insisted on contributing their most glamorous nighties and undies to form my borrowed trousseaux. They guessed, quite rightly, that my own were nothing to write home about after years as a low earner, with little cash and fewer coupons to spend on fripperies. I didn't really want to take their things, but they seemed so hurt by my attempts at refusal that I weakly accepted everything. I was terrified at the mere thought of washing such delicate and expensive finery before handing it back, for I knew full well that if I spoilt anything it was quite irreplaceable. They were pre-war silks and crêpe-de-chines, their treasures, which they were lending, and nothing like that could be bought anywhere in England just then. As it turned out, only one ghastly nightie refused to be tamed and remained creased and sad however much I ironed it, but nobody seemed to mind. I'd have been mad at getting my best goonie back in such a poorly-ironed state. No wonder they say 'toffs are careless'.

Temporarily free of all responsibility, my husband was able to enjoy the hilarious turn his life had taken. He sometimes shook his head, with a bemused air, and said he couldn't imagine anything which provided a greater contrast to conditions in the Middle East with the R.A.F., than finding himself touring with a company of 'theatricals'. He too found the whole set-up very reminiscent of Priestley's 'Good Companions', just as I had. Especially the theatrical digs. When we'd arrive at a new address, we'd pretend we were a double act. We would stand on the door-mat side by side, strike a pose, throw our arms towards the heavens and announce to the closed door, 'We are the Flying Scots'. We'd then dissolve in laughter at our own clowning. Sometimes, to our confusion and dismay, a soft-footed landlady would throw the door open as we were going through this pantomime, and we'd swiftly transform ourselves into meek, well-behaved quiet tenants in case she'd think she was dealing with a couple of lunatics and shut the door in our face.

Spring came very early that year, and after the bitter winter, and years of war, this first peace-time awakening melted the heart. Sandy revelled in the soft beauty of the Welsh and English country-side after the harsh light and parching heat of the Middle East, and the tour turned into a long glorious holiday. During long enchanted days we wandered along the sea-shores, or climbed the hills, and we remembered a hundred things we had to say about the time we had been apart. Letters cannot say it all. It was all quite, quite perfect. Even the landladies managed to greet us with smiling faces, in spite of having had to re-arrange accommodation to suit us, and with our Scottish voices had no doubt at all that we were legitimately Mister and Missus!

The weather grew balmier, and Cambridge in May was a dream. No wonder so many romantic tales had been woven around the River Cam, and the punts, and the lush meadows. After the industrial north, this was fairyland. There was blossom on the bough, and the trees unfolded delicate foliage to delight our senses. The little chintz and mahogany furnished parlour put at our disposal by a charming landlady couldn't fit into the category of 'digs' by the wildest stretch of imagination. It was a picture-book setting, and we loved every minute of that week in Cambridge. And if we loved Cambridge, Cambridge loved us. The undergraduates roared their approval of the play and we came off flushed with success after each performance. We had had every last roughness polished during the tour, and we all felt we were ready for London.

Cambridge was to be a week of decision for all of us. It was in the little chintz parlour that my husband picked up the book which made him decide he would study for the qualification of shipbroker when he returned to Scotland. He had always been in shipping, but knew that after the break caused by the war he would take a little time to pick up the threads of his job. This then would be the right moment to expand his knowledge and help his prospects.

It was in the theatre, after Friday pay-call, that we actors faced our moment of decision. We had been asked to remain for a few moments as the manager had something to say. We were within a week of the London opening, and nobody wanted to voice the foreboding we all felt, that we were going to be asked to continue the tour. But instinct was right. It was put to us that the situation continued of too many good plays chasing too few theatres. Try as it might, the management simply hadn't been able to spot a single play which looked like tottering to a close. We were asked to consider extending the tour by another month, by which time conditions might be more favourable for us coming into London.

I would gladly have agreed to go on with the tour. Sandy was still on demobilisation leave, and we were thoroughly enjoying ourselves, for we felt this was as good a way of spending it as any other. In fact it was such an original way of spending his leave that we couldn't quite get over it. Once the play opened in London, there was no knowing when we would have any length of time together, for I would be there for the duration of the run and he would be returning to an empty house without me. So an extended tour suited us very well.

Alas, the stars were growing impatient. Other offers were coming in, and above all they were anxious to go home to rejoin their families. Even more so than today, it was star names which sold plays and drew audiences, so when they said they preferred to finish the engagement at the end of the following week in Brighton, it was the final curtain for all of us. It hadn't occurred to me that their refusal to tour would mean the end of the play. But it did.

Before we said goodbye, Marjorie Fielding sent for me. 'It's such a pity for your sake, we're not having a London opening', she said. 'This would have established you in London as a real comedienne. That part is yours and no-one else's'. At the time I took this with a pinch of salt, although I thought it was very nice of her to bother telling me such a thing, but in the light of later experience I've come to believe she may have been right. Theatregoers and managements would have seen me in my own style of comedy, in a strong part, playing my own age, and yet a part not taxing in a way which would have brought out the hatchets if I'd fallen short of expectations. I believe I could have made steady progress from there. I've often thought that if 'A Play for Ronnie' had opened in London as planned, my future would have been found in the theatre and not in the other media.

But it was not to be.

Our fates are hinged on many contingencies and my footsteps were turned in quite different directions for the strangest of reasons, simply because the theatre was doing too well. The post-war boom brought my short stage career to a sudden halt when continuity was essential.

Marjorie Fielding said something else to me which I have never forgotten. 'If you stay in this profession Molly', she said, 'And I believe that you will, you'll surely find that you either have no work at all, or you'll get three offers all at once, all clashing. You will only be able to do one. So sit down, look at them from all angles, and decide in the light of your knowledge *at that time* what is best for you to do. Having made your decision, forget the other two. If you don't, you'll become embittered by the memory of bad decisions, which only seem bad because of *later* knowledge. And you'll become an old woman before your time. Never waste time looking back regretting jobs you didn't accept.'

I didn't realise then how hard it was going to be to follow this excellent advice, but time has proved how right this wise lady was. Because she foresaw so clearly how things would be, I've tried to profit from her kind words of wisdom, although not always with conspicuous success. The hardest thing in show business is to refrain from saying, 'Och if only I'd taken the other one'. Whenever I'm tempted into this profitless folly, Marjorie's words appear before me in letters of fire, and I bless the thoughtfulness which prompted a leading lady of the theatre to pass on the fruits of her experience to a raw recruit.

The tour ended at Brighton and we were all brought back to London, where we disbanded, and although we had all lived so closely together for 14 weeks, there were some of that company whom I never met again. I found that very sad. Sandy and I spent a few days in London, sight-seeing in the day time and squashing uncomfortably into the lumpy single bed at Clapham at night. We couldn't make up our minds whether our future was to be in London or Glasgow. I had had excellent notices in every town we had played, and Sandy felt it would be only fair to let me try to consolidate this success while he was busy studying and settling into civilian life in Glasgow. To allow me to do this, I should keep on the London flat for another six months at least and see what would follow 'A Play for Ronnie'. I wouldn't stay in London all the time, of course, but pop back and forth as events dictated, and Sandy preferred the idea of my having a settled base in Clapham rather than seeking odd digs from time to time.

With that decision taken, the rent was paid, and we headed for home, back to Scotland, together.

Oh it was lovely to see all the husbands back home again, and the look of strain fade from the faces of the young wives now that they could pass the reins of responsibility to a stronger pair of hands. The children were so proud of their returned daddies, and the whole avenue radiated pure happiness. Everybody was in demand, as baby-sitters were at a premium, for all wanted to go on the town to celebrate their release.

I hardly dared breathe a word to anybody that I wasn't home for good, for it seemed the basest ingratitude to welcome a safely returned husband, only to abandon him to an empty house. My mother and my ma-in-law both thought I was out of my mind, and that Sandy was worse for letting me go. 'Whit in the name o' Goad dae ye want to go away doon there again for?', my mother demanded, 'Ah thought ye'd be gled tae get hame tae yer ain hoose, and look efter Sandy.'

But we knew what we were doing, and Sandy thought he would quite enjoy coming to London when I didn't come north. I left him my easiest recipes, with all the instructions written in shorthand, so it was a splendid opportunity for him to refresh his memory of his shorthand studies at the same time. Nothing like hunger for sharpening the brain, and he'd have to transcribe those outlines before he could unravel the cooking secrets. I may say that many a dish was left at a vital moment while he dashed to the telephone and checked with me the meaning of a forgotten outline!

Some weekends he came down to see me, and at others I went up to join him, and we didn't realise we were setting a pattern we were to follow for many a long day. I can never understand why the Railways run at a loss, for I am confident that the money we have spent in fares over the years, merely to be together, would have been enough to make any dubious line solvent.

In London I made the usual appointments to see agents, and producers, and this time I extended my range beyond theatre and films to T.V. but nothing much was happening. If I thought I had created a tiny ripple among the critics in the provinces, not a whisper of my performance had reached the ears of anyone in London.

As always when things reach stalemate, I turned my thoughts to studying again. I would take singing and dancing lessons. Where could I find better coaching than in the capital? I found my mentors in the most casual way. A girl met in the canteen gave me the name of her singing teacher, while another met in an agent's waiting room passed on the name of her dancing coach. I didn't check whether or not they were first-class. It was enough to have a name or a telephone number I could contact.

The dancing teacher was a charlatan of the first order. It was Mr. Torrance of the piano lessons all over again*, that rascal who had used my piano-time to retreat behind a newspaper and who taught me nothing, while taking my mother's hard-earned cash.

This 'dancing master' asked me to show him what I knew of dance routines, seemed delighted with my execution of the 'time step' which my mother always referred to as the 'clog wallop', directed me to the barre, showed me how to do a few exercises, and vanished into the back premises, never to reappear until the hour was up, when he collected his fee and shut the door behind me.

I went once a week, continually waiting for the moment to arrive when I would be shown some exciting new dance routines. The London weather grew hotter and hotter, and perspiration poured from me as I exercised like a dervish at the barre, while my dancing master remained serene and cool, having moved not a muscle during the entire lesson.

I don't know how long I would have tolerated this behaviour, but one day when I ventured to put my head round the door leading to the back premises, nerving myself to ask when I was going to learn some routines, I heard him 'phoning in a bet to his bookmaker. The ingrate was taking my money, doing nothing to assist me to become another Vera Ellen, and putting my fee on horses! That was the end. I handed him my fee at the end of the lesson—and it was every penny of half a guinea—shook hands with him, and told him I was off home for a holiday. I never saw him again. Nor did I ever see the girl who had given me his name. Perhaps they were in league to rob the innocent!

The singing teacher, however, was a great find. I went to his office in a music publisher's building off Charing Cross Road, where all the musicians hung about, and we practised scales, and ran through the many excellent numbers he found for me from the current revues and musical shows. This was the great age of the revue,

* BEST FOOT FORWARD

and the numbers were both witty and tuneful and great fun to interpret. I went to this splendid coach off and on for years afterwards, and we became good friends. It was typical of the London scene though, that we had no idea where each other lived, and after I'd been going into London for several weeks for my lessons, I asked him one night if I might have his home telephone number as it might be necessary for me to cancel my next lesson and I'd only know the evening before. When he gave this to me, I looked up in great surprise. 'Macaulay?', I said, 'That's my exchange. Where do you live?' 'In Clapham', he answered. Not only in Clapham, would you believe it, but two doors away from my room! And I'd been spending money on fares all that time when all I needed to do was walk ten yards! After that I always went to his rooms and we rehearsed there, at no travelling expense for me, and a great convenience for both of us.

Everybody seemed to be going on holiday. London was a steaming cauldron. I'd never known such heat. The grass in the parks was scorched brown, something I didn't know was possible. I'd certainly never seen it happen in Scotland. It grew airless and humid as day followed day, and my room at the top of the house caught and held the heat, and it was like the blast from an oven when I opened the door. Miss Chree seemed never to be there, and Lois was with her friends. Even the landlady had gone to ground, and the rent book was pushed under my door without benefit of a friendly word. Everyone seemed to have her own fish to fry.

Suddenly it seemed the height of folly to be wandering around London on my own when nobody showed the slightest interest in employing me. Neither in films, theatre, or TV was anything promised for the immediate future. I'd done everything I could. I'd go home for a while, and try again after the holidays.

But before I went, I'd just see what radio had to offer. I hadn't really tried very hard for radio work, feeling that I could always get such engagements in Glasgow. I wasn't in London for B.B.C. work. I saw London as the mecca of theatre, films and television, not radio. But there was one radio show which could only be done from London. And it was the best show of all. There could be no harm in having a crack at it before I went home. I would try for I.T.M.A.

I was quite ignorant of the mainsprings of this immortal show, which had sustained and gladdened the hearts and minds of all Britain during the war, and which had also been listened to by partisans on many illegally-used sets in enemy controlled territory.

I only knew that it starred Tommy Handley, and that it was written by Ted Kavanagh. Beyond this, I knew nothing. I hadn't the faintest idea as to the whereabouts of Kavanagh's office, and indeed I only knew he was the writer because I had met him with Tommy one day in Aeolian Hall when they were having lunch. The first time I had seen them there, I had gazed long and intently at Tommy's famous face, but had been far too shy to dream of going over and speaking to him. When I told my landlady, with great excitement, that I had actually been in the same canteen with 'that man' and a big red-haired chap, she was contemptuous of my lack of gumption in not seizing my opportunity to have a word with him. 'Next time', she said, 'That is, if you're lucky enough to *have* a next time, go over and speak. You can't expect them to know who you are. But everybody knows who Handley and Kavanagh are. It's up to you to introduce yourself'.

Sure enough, my luck was in, for on my next visit to Aeolian Hall where I had an appointment with Ronnie Waldman, there they were again sitting at lunch, Tommy Handley and the same plump red-haired man. The B.B.C. canteen in those days was a very democratic place, where the famous and the unknown queued up together for meals.

I waited until they were sipping their coffee, then, with beating heart, approached them. I think I really only found the courage to do so because I couldn't have faced my landlady if I had had to confess that I had seen them again and hadn't spoken. I hadn't the least idea what I was going to say, and when they looked up to see who had stopped by their table, I found myself murmuring something about how wonderful it was to see Tommy in person, having listened to him all during the war. I told them how much the people in Scotland enjoyed the programme, and how we marvelled at the topicality of the scripts. Tommy laughed and said, 'Well, this is Ted Kavanagh. He writes the words. I just say them'. As I shook hands with Ted, I said, 'I'm Molly Weir', remembering my landlady's advice to introduce myself. He at once asked, 'Do you know what a tattie bogle is?'. 'Yes', I answered, a bit surprised by the question, 'It's a scarecrow'. They both laughed, I said cheerio, and that was that.

So I was able to tell my landlady that I'd had the spunk to talk to them, and that Ted Kavanagh had revealed as I walked away that he had heard me in Down at the Mains. That was almost as hard for me to take in as it was to realise that I'd had the cheek to speak to them at all.

So, I thought, before I go back to Glasgow I'll try to see this Ted Kavanagh again, just in case there might some time be something in the show for a Scot. You never knew your luck.

As I stood at Piccadilly Circus, wondering if I could be bothered in all this heat to go back to Aeolian Hall to try to find out the address of the Kavanagh office, I saw coming towards me one of my Glasgow radio friends, Ian Sadler. 'Ian', I called, 'Have you any idea where Ted Kavanagh's office is?' 'Down there', he said, and turned me round to face the street running down the Circus to the Mall. And he gave me the number. Ian smiled and said that I must be the only aspiring actress in London who didn't know that address. I was almost within spitting distance of it, without being aware that I was.

When I asked the girl at the desk if I could see Mr. Kavanagh, she threw me a glance in which she blended scorn for my nerve and pity for my ignorance. 'Mr. Kavanagh', she said, as if I had enquired for God Himself, which in a way I suppose I had, 'You can't see Mr. Kavanagh without an appointment, and in any case he is at a meeting and cannot be disturbed'.

At that psychological moment, the door to an inner office opened and Ted Kavanagh came out carrying a sheaf of papers. He had heard my voice apparently, for he stopped. 'Are you in London nowadays, Molly?', he asked. My goodness, I thought, he must have a phenomenal memory for faces and names. He'd only met me once. 'More or less', I answered cautiously. I didn't want to tell a lie. I had a room in London, but I was on my way home after all, so 'more or less' seemed reasonably accurate.

'Wait a minute', he said, and disappeared into his office. What was I having to wait for, I wondered? The girl looked at me with dawning respect. Clearly I wasn't so insignificant as I looked.

A few minutes later he appeared again, handed me some scripts and said, 'Ring Francis Worsley at Aeolian Hall and make an appointment to go to see him tomorrow. We're holding auditions for new voices for ITMA all day'.

My mouth fell open. I clutched the scripts he'd given me to my beating heart. It was unbelievable. It was one of those show business coincidences which sound too fantastic to be true. Without so much as a whisper from the grape-vine, of which I wasn't a part anyway, and in complete ignorance of any future plans they had for the show, I had innocently gone into Kavanagh's office at the precise moment when a complete re-shuffle of the cast was to take place. Plans had been made to introduce a post-war freshness to ITMA by the introduction of anything up to four new voices, and thanks to my shot in the dark, I now had a chance to try for one of those voices.

If I hadn't been at Piccadilly Circus on that day and at that time, and if I hadn't met Ian Sadler, or had decided to postpone action till a later date, or indeed if Ted Kavanagh hadn't come into the outer office when he did, I would have missed my opportunity, for there was only the next day for the final auditions. Tommy was off on holiday immediately afterwards.

One day later would have been too late.

Five minutes either way could even have been too late.

When I rang Aeolian Hall, I asked for Miss Frances Worsley and I heard a suppressed giggle at the other end of the telephone. I seemed fated to bestow the wrong sex on everything connected with the Bond Street premises of the B.B.C. What with Miss Oley Anne Hall, and now Frances for Mr. Francis Worsley who, I now learned, was only the producer of the whole show! He was the third of the great triumvirate, the creators of ITMA. Tommy Handley, Ted Kavanagh and Francis Worsley. Kavanagh had rung him confirming that I had been given scripts. Now I was told to be at the studios at 11 a.m. next morning. I was to have a look at the scripts, and also bring along any other material I had which would demonstrate any comedy talent which might be useful.

I flew home and rushed immediately into the landlady's cubbyhole, to tell her my exciting news. She was quite sure it was because she had encouraged me to speak to them that they had given me this chance. I didn't want to rob her of her triumph by mentioning that Kavanagh hadn't exactly been out combing the streets looking for me, and had probably forgotten all about that brief encounter over the coffee cups until he saw me in his office.

I decided I must be fully rested for the auditions next day, so after tea I undressed, threw open the window to make the room as cool as possible, and studied the scripts I'd been given until I could have said them backwards. I tried out every accent, with every permutation of tone and vocal range I knew. I sounded flat as a pancake. I wasn't within miles of the sparkling attack I'd enjoyed listening to in past ITMAs. Och I hadn't a hope. I leaped from the bed and rummaged through my songs and old scripts. Maybe if they had time to listen to me doing 'Please Captain I've swallowed my Whistle', and my imitations of Dietrich and Francis Day, I'd make a better impression. I'd take them with me, just in case.

I tossed and turned all night, and felt as limp as a rag next morning. It was a morning of shimmering heat again, and when I presented myself at Aeolian Hall and was shown into the studio, I was astounded to find Tommy Handley himself at the microphone. 'Oh', I said, my voice squeaking with surprise, 'Have I to read with you?' Somehow I had never imagined Tommy would read with everyone. I thought he would be saved to read with the winners. 'Who else did you think you'd be reading with?', he said with a chuckle, and I blushed for my ignorance. Of course, when I thought about it, they'd have to hear each voice with Tommy's, for how else could they judge how it would sound against that inimitable style?

Somebody called from the control room and told me to start with script number three.

We went through them all, Tommy and I, and he was kindness itself. He made me feel I was giving a good performance, calmed the worst of my fears by laughing in all the right places, and turned the whole thing into as happy an occasion as it could be, considering my heart was beating like a drum at a military tattoo. I realised that not only was I getting a great chance, but I was also being given every assistance to make the most of it. I knew that whether I succeeded or whether I failed, 'that man' was going to be right up there in my personal gallery of the 'greats' of show business, not just because he was the brightest star in radio, but because he was a kind, gentle, man, with time to be generous to an unknown performer who was consumed with nerves.

While I went through my own comedy material, Tommy left the studio to join the others in the control room, and I turned my back to the glass panel because I couldn't bear to watch their reactions to my comedy numbers. When I had finished, the pianist gave me an encouraging wink. Then there was a silence.

'Thank you, Miss Weir. We'll be in touch if we want you'.

As I walked through the corridor, Ted Kavanagh barred my way. 'Where can we contact you when we've made our decision', he asked. I gave him my Clapham number. When I ventured to ask if it would be all right if I went on holiday, he patted my shoulder. 'Of course', he said, 'So long as we have your London number. We won't come to any decision for at least six weeks'.

And then I was in the street.

This time my stomach told me nothing. I had no inner advance warning to prepare me for success or failure.

I would just have to wait and see.

15

IF Sandy found theatrical touring was a bewildering contrast to his life in the R.A.F., my life as a Glasgow housewife was almost equally strange compared with my existence in my bed-sitter in London. I felt as though I were two different people. In Clapham I was perfectly capable of staying in bed till 10 o'clock in the morning, then dressing to the nines and sallying forth to involve myself with interviews and engagements all day, not returning to my room till around 8 o'clock in the evening. The idea of housework scarcely entered my head, and my personal shopping and laundry were taken care of almost on the wing, as it were.

In London, all entertaining was done in tearooms. Nobody ever invited you to their house. You met in canteens or in Joe Lyons, and you sat for hours over a cup of coffee and, if you were lucky, a sandwich. I was one of the few actresses who did any cooking, and even I had now reduced my culinary adventures to eggs and cheese and the odd pot of soup. This wasn't because I had gone off cooking or eating, but because of the ghastly shock I had in the tube one day when I became very conscious of a very strong smell of fat nearby. I gave surreptitious little sniffs to right and left of me, wondering if anybody was carrying cooked food in their brief-cases. No, they were all very correct business types. It clearly wasn't any of them. And then a horrible suspicion dawned. Could it be my own clothes which were sending off the fatty fumes? It could, and was.

All those chops and joints of meat I'd cooked in my little tin oven had wafted their greasy vapours into the soft wool of my suit, and of course the moment one went into a warm humid atmosphere the vapours were released. I hadn't realised that when clothes are merely concealed behind a curtain they're not protected from cooking smells, for I had never before, not even in Springburn, had my best clothes hanging where the food was cooked.

Everything had to go to the cleaners.

And that was the end of the frying sessions in Clapham.

Now that I was back in Glasgow with a man to feed, a house to look after, and droves of visitors and relatives coming out and in, the bachelor girl existence I'd led in London seemed like a dream.

As soon as I heard the children's voices in the morning from neighbouring gardens, I was out of bed, and busy from then till bedtime. I hadn't remembered how dirty a house became when people were living fully in it every day, or how many clothes two people soiled. I was forever washing and polishing, taking down curtains and putting them up again, dusting, making beds and lighting fires.

All the family were delighted to think I'd shaken the dust of London from my feet so soon. They knew nothing of the ITMA audition. I had been sworn to utter secrecy by the B.B.C. because they wanted no hint of their plans to leak out to the press until they were ready. Sandy was the only one I was permitted to tell. We had talked round and round the difficulties of our situation if I actually did get this part, for as the show went out live each week it meant I'd have to be in London. Sandy had now started with his old shipping company again in Glasgow. How on earth would it all turn out?

Then we decided we were mad planning so far ahead. It was most unlikely anyway that I'd be offered ITMA for I didn't think I had impressed them very much. We agreed to put it right out of our minds and enjoy ourselves and make the most of this glorious summer weather.

I plunged into the Glasgow life-style with zest. Nobody here entertained in tearooms. Visitors were entertained at home and the whole place had to be gone over again, from top to bottom, to make it all quite perfect. Not that anybody would have criticised, but that was the custom and I conformed like everyone else. I baked cakes and shortbread for our visitors and the relatives, scones and pancakes, fruit bread and pies, and revelled in the luxury of two ration books. It was the double coupons for the tinned food which were the nicest bonus, and one could indulge in all sorts of little luxuries not possible with one lot of coupons.

Nothing was any trouble. Once I even made doughnuts for eight people, going like a dervish over the boiling fat, and serving them sizzling hot from the pan. If I'd been on piecework in a bakery,

I couldn't have worked faster, or looked greasier than I did at the end of this session. But nobody in Glasgow pretended there was a cook hidden in the kitchen, and nobody minded my scorched shining face, least of all me. Only London agents paid attention to looks. Glasgow visitors were much more interested in what was provided for their stomachs, and I was delighted to please them.

I did go over the score on one terrible occasion, though, when the local shop had a delivery of ground almonds, a luxury item nobody had seen for years. I decided a little touch of Cordon Bleu artistry wouldn't come amiss, and attempted to make chocolate-almond petits-fours of pâtisserie-like richness. I ignored the expense, as I concentrated on getting the squashy mess into my forcing bag, determined to turn out professionally shaped squiggles and crescents. 'Squeeze steadily but firmly' the instructions said. I did so, and the whole chocolate mixture exploded like buckshot from the other end of the bag, and hit the cooker, the tiled walls behind it, shot up my arms and into my face, and as I ducked, sent the last lot over the kitchen door. Tears pouring down my cheeks at the thought of all those expensive ingredients wasted, I choked at the sight of the chaos all round. But even as I sniffled and gulped, my brain was recovering from the shock and a solution was emerging. The house was practically new. The place as clean as a whistle. I shut my mind to the full implications of what I was doing, and scraped the lot off, and salavaged a respectably sized bowlful from the cooker and walls and a small cupful from my arms and face. I was thankful I worked with clean hands and didn't use make-up on my face in the kitchen! I shaped the chocolate mess into little circles with my fingers, and put them into the oven and prayed for a miracle.

I didn't say a word of this to anyone. Not even to Sandy. At least not until afterwards. He'd commented on them before the visitors arrived, mark you, and said he'd never seen such oddly shaped things before. 'All hand-made pâtisserie is irregularly shaped', I said firmly, 'That's the authentic touch'.

The visitors drooled over them. They were crisp on the outside and gooey in the centre, and they tasted delicious. I watched cautiously before I ventured to try one myself. I realised the visitors weren't just being polite. My chocolate disasters *were* really scrumptious. If there was anything in them which shouldn't have been there, it was either killed in the cooking or disguised in the richness of the mixture. Anyway, nobody was poisoned. But I never made them again. Not even to this day.

I loved the long light evenings, for in London it grows dark so much earlier than in Scotland, and many a stroll we took at midnight round quiet streets, when fingers of light still caressed the sky.

There was a great happiness in just being together without fear. No air-raids. No black-out. No dangerous separation. The simplest pleasures were a matter for rejoicing. Coming into the house and being able to switch on a light without having to think of enemy bombers. Street lamps which could lawfully illuminate our path when it grew dark. Two eggs in one week when there had only been one the previous week. A delivery of skins which inspired our butcher to make mouth-watering sausages, with real meat, and more than a hint of pre-war goodness. An extra half-pint of milk. Enough coupons to buy a pair of summer shoes. Life was very good.

Such was my euphoria that it was fairly easy to forget the world of show business, and that somewhere away at the back of my mind there was a question waiting to be answered. Would I be hearing from Aeolian Hall one of these days, or had it all been settled, and would the nearest I would ever get to ITMA's history be as one of those who had been asked to attend an audition? Oh well, if that were all it was to be, it was more than a lot of people could say.

We hadn't thought Sandy would get another holiday, since he hadn't rejoined his firm until late spring, but they were very fair and said returning servicemen couldn't be penalised because of the timing of their demobilisation, and they put his name on the holiday list with the others.

This was a marvellous and unexpected bonus and we decided we'd go mad and go to a really classy resort, and book in at an hotel instead of our usual modest guest house or digs. We've always loved islands, and this time we chose the Isle of Man, a resort which holds great glamour for Glaswegians. From our youth we'd heard colourful tales of wild goings-on at Douglas, but we ourselves preferred the quieter elegant appeal of Port Erin and we managed to book in at a tasteful looking hotel for a fortnight.

It was a glorious holiday from start to finish.

We found the island enchantingly beautiful; when young people describe holiday resorts, they seldom dwell on scenic beauty, and so the sheer loveliness of the Isle of Man came as a great surprise. We would race down the close-cropped turf and gaze on the Calf of Man, letting our eyes search the wide horizon, and rejoicing in the emptiness of sea and sky. We watched fishermen handle huge crabs, and wondered wistfully why the people in our hotel kitchen had no thought of purchasing such beauties for the guests. For it was an undeniable fact that although it was an hotel, and not one of your drab guest houses, the food was decidedly on the skimpy side. So much so, that I couldn't help thinking we should have fared much better if we had just taken a wee house and had spent our money on all the plentiful food which we could see in local shops, but which never seemed to find its way on to our plates. Baskets of eggs filled the windows of the local dairies, and all we had for breakfast was one tiny kipper apiece. It was such a shame, and we were so hungry with all that sea air. I wanted to buy eggs and ask the kitchen to cook them for us, but my husband was aghast at the mere idea.

But if we were critical of the food, we had no such reservations about the company. They were a great crowd, with quite as many English as Scots among them, and we had no difficulty in identifying with all of them. We went bathing, a dozen or more of us, laughing and gasping in sparkling seas, and we became children again as we scampered across miles of golden sands and tossed a huge painted ball to one another. The sun shone from cloudless skies, and we grew tanned, and so filled with energy we felt we could have run right round the island on our own two feet. All the weariness and tensions of war-time finally vanished like morning mists in these blissfully sunlit, health-giving days.

There was a heady excitement for us in savouring all the pleasures of this first post-war holiday together, and everything combined to invest our stay in Port Erin with an unforgettable magic. And we weren't the only ones who felt like this. For of course it was the first post-war holiday for all of us. I was astounded when we all went in to say goodbye one evening to a young couple who would be leaving very early next morning. They were one of our bathing crowd, and as we chorussed our 'Cheerios', the young wife dissolved in floods of tears. I had never thought an adult could cry for something so slight as the end of a holiday. But perhaps she knew it wasn't just the end of an ordinary holiday. It was the end of the world's honeymoon, when it was enough just to be alive and safe and together. We asked for little more just then. I never forgot that young wife, and I truly hoped that she would find nothing worse in the future to make her cry more sorrowful tears.

For us, something else was to make this holiday even more memorable.

One night, in the middle of dinner, a waitress beckoned me to the door. 'You're wanted on the telephone', she said. 'It's a call from London'.

Sandy and I looked at one another, and I found that my legs were shaking as I crossed the room. I stared at the telephone and couldn't find the courage to pick up the receiver. Thoughts flew through my head like the buzzing of bees, and my mouth went dry. Was it the ITMA office? Would they ring me up just to tell me they didn't want me? How had they found my holiday number? Maybe it wasn't Aeolian Hall at all. Maybe it was only my landlady speaking from my own telephone in Clapham. She, after all, had my Port Erin number. No. It *must* be ITMA. They would have obtained the number from my landlady if they were anxious to find me. But if they were as anxious as all that, then it *must* be to tell me they wanted me. But hadn't they said they would let me know one way or the other? I found I couldn't remember whether or not that was what they had said. I felt sick. I hadn't realised I could find the possibility of disappointing news so calamitous. Had I then secretly expected success? I didn't know I had. But if indeed this call was to put an end to any hopes I had cherished, then I must just nerve myself to face rejection and never let them see how much I cared. I remembered with sudden vividness grannie's scorn for showing my disappointment too openly when I hadn't been included in the back-court concert, and it was like a bracing dash of cold water.

I picked up the receiver.

'Francis Worsley here', the voice said, 'Is that you Molly? Good. We want you for ITMA.' I let my breath go in a long half-crying gasp. 'The show comes back on the air in September, but we'll give you all the details later about actual dates and rehearsals. I just thought you'd like to know you're to be with us'. I gave a shout of delight, which I stifled at once, for I thought it was all still to be a secret and I was afraid somebody might overhear. The telephone was out in the open hallway, not even in a booth. I forced myself to reduce my excited responses to a whisper until Francis said, 'This is a very bad line, I can hardly hear you'. When I told him why I was whispering, he laughed, 'Oh that's all right Molly', he said, 'You can tell anyone you wish now. The papers have been informed, and the news will break tomorrow morning with the early editions'.

I laid down the receiver. A thousand emotions exploded inside me like fire-crackers.

When I went back to the dining room and looked at the clock, I could hardly believe that iess than five minutes had elapsed since I had left it. Five minutes which changed my whole future. My husband took one look at my face and laid down his knife and fork. 'What was it', he asked, taking my hand. 'I'm in ITMA', I said, 'They want me for ITMA'.

And all at once the whole dining room knew, and, unbelievably, everybody was standing up and cheering. If they had heard I was to be crowned by Royalty, they couldn't have been more thrilled and excited. ITMA had always been more of an English taste than a Scots one, but I had had no idea of the strength of English feeling about this show until I saw the reaction of the quite considerable English crowd at that hotel. For a Scottish crowd to have shown such enthusiasm, I think I'd have to have scored the winning goal for Rangers!

Everybody was speaking at once. They were all congratulating one another that they had *actually* been right *there*, in the room, when the news had broken. This would be something to tell their folks when they went home. Fancy, they had actually heard about it before it had even got into the newspapers.

Sandy and I were quite stunned by their enthusiasm. We'd never expected anything like this. We knew it was important for us, but we hadn't thought it would be of such riveting importance to an entire holiday hotel. It was a slight foretaste of what was to come much later in London.

Even the Management went mad. A party was arranged there and then, and for once they forgot their frugal attitude and we had a buffet which they couldn't have bettered if they had had a week to prepare for it. Nothing was held back for later hunger. The fatted calf was well and truly killed.

We danced and we sang, and I recited and did all my impersonations. The children were allowed to stay up just this once, and we played games and roared through 'The Grand Old Duke of York' and Musical Chairs and other party games for their benefit.

When at last we crept away to bed in the wee sma' hours I had no voice. Excitement and all that yelling had robbed my vocal chords of all sound.

But it didn't matter.

Nothing mattered.

It was less than twelve months since I had left Glasgow with fifty pounds in my Post Office book to seek fame and fortune in London.

My gamble had paid off.

I had been in a play put on by one of London's top West End managements. I had broadcast from London.

Now I was the newest recruit in the greatest radio show anyone had known, a show which would take its place in the history of the second world war as surely as the air battles over London. And although the war was over, I would become part of that history.

One toe was now placed securely on the ladder.